Sicuanga Runa

SICUANGA RUNA

The Other Side of Development
in Amazonian Ecuador

NORMAN E. WHITTEN, JR.

UNIVERSITY OF ILLINOIS PRESS

Urbana and Chicago

This book is printed on acid-free paper.

Library of Congress Cataloging in Publication Data

Whitten, Norman E., Jr.
  Sicuanga Runa: the other side of development in
Amazonian Ecuador.

  Bibliography: p.
  Includes index.
  1. Canelos Indians. 2. Indians of South America—
Ecuador—Ethnic identity. 3. Power (Social sciences).
4. Ecuador—Ethnic relations. 5. Amazon River Region—
Ethnic relations. I. Title.
F3722.1.C23W48 1984   986.6′400498   84-155
ISBN 0-252-01117-1 (alk. paper)

Contents

Acknowledgments

The Research Board of the University of Illinois at Urbana-Champaign provided the assistantship that allowed Gary Apfelstadt to draw the diagrams, maps, and especially the ceramic representations presented in this work. The drawings of the ceramics were necessary because we could not capture the various facets of indigenous skill and creativity by simply photographing the pottery. Except for bending some pieces artistically so as to portray more of them than a photograph could, and for flattening the insides and outsides of drinking bowls to demonstrate the complete design, each of the representations of ceramic art is wholly accurate. I could not have completed this book without the integrated artwork provided by Gary and discussions with him about the intricacies involved. I only regret that the reader does not have access to the originals, in color, for they are stunning renditions. Some complex insights into women's psyches were gained when the woman, looking at the recreation of her own pottery—and seeing for the first time the interior and exterior of the piece simultaneously—offered a re-exegesis of what she was thinking when she first decorated it. Without the assistance of the Research Board and without the intellectual and artistic insight of Gary Apfelstadt, this book would not have been written as it is.

The Committee on Latin America of the Social Science Research Council/American Council of Learned Societies granted the funds leading to the completion of research upon which this book is based. Originally, Sibby (Dorothea) Whitten and I had planned to write an immediate sequel to *Sacha Runa* and to complete it some years ago. As we worked, however, some materials turned out to be too dense and were published in technical journals; others moved as we wished, but became watered down for more popular circulation.

As we explored facets of the dynamic lifeways of the Canelos Quichua peoples, especially working in three diverse communities, many other anthropologists undertook substantial work in Ecuador, and Ecuador itself accelerated its processes of ecological alteration, political-economic revision, cultural transformation, and social upheaval.

Work on *Sicuanga Runa* was set aside in 1978 and 1979 while I edited, with the assistance of Kathleen Fine, the volume *Cultural Transformations and Ethnicity in Modern Ecuador*, completing that task in 1979 and returning, with Sibby, for two intensive phases of SSRC/ACLS-sponsored fieldwork. This manuscript was prepared between fall, 1981, and late fall, 1982. Twice during its preparation I returned to our principal field settings, to work through some of its facets with the people who have been merged into the characters developed herein.

The SSRC/ACLS fellowship could not have been as productive as it turned out to be had it not been for preceding research sponsored by a John Simon Guggenheim Fellowship (1976-77), a grant from the Wenner-Gren Foundation for Anthropological Research (1978), and various facilitating and interstitial small grants made by the University of Illinois at Urbana-Champaign through the Center for Latin American and Caribbean Studies (Paul Drake, director), the Office of International Programs and Studies, the Scholar's Travel Fund, and (jointly with Marcelo F. Naranjo) the Center for International Comparative Studies. In 1979 and 1980 funds were provided for applied activities (jointly with Sibby Whitten) attendant upon a health-care delivery program by Survival International-England and Cultural Survival. I am grateful for the confidence in these programs expressed by Stephen Corry of Survival International and Theodore Macdonald, Jr., and David Maybury-Lewis of Cultural Survival. The applied work presented us with many of the dimensions of power that later came to the fore in more basic ways. A monograph discussing these activities was recently published by Cultural Survival. Acknowledgment of these sources of funding cannot begin to express my appreciation to agencies willing to take a chance on seemingly diverse projects that straddle scientific and humanistic interest without any pretense at hard-core social scientism.

The Research Board of the University of Illinois and the university's "Study in a Second Discipline" program also contributed to my thinking and to techniques utilized in the field research upon which this book draws. Thanks to funds provided by the Research Board I have been privileged to work intensively with several scholars, all of whom have helped to shape my thinking. Work with Mary-Elizabeth B. M. Reeve on a project of ecology, economy, and ideology of select areas of Ecuador undergoing developmental pressure was extremely helpful, and it is gratifying to note that her doctoral thesis on comparable processes in Curaray will soon be available. Kathleen Fine and I worked through many dimensions of urbanism and urbanization, cultural transformations, ethnicity, power, and social relations in Ecuador, during and

after the editing of *Cultural Transformations*. Her dissertation on a sector
of urbanizing Quito will also soon be available. William Belzner and
I have worked together on concepts of cultural patterning, cosmology,
epistemology, and ideation among various peoples of Amazonian Ecuador, especially focusing on music. His thesis on Shuar and Achuar
musical structure and mythology is in preparation. I am indebted to
each of these committed anthropologists for insights and reflections
more numerous than I could possibly list, as well as for direct commentary on drafts of sections of this book.

Without the collegial support of James Karr (ecologist and ornithol-
ogist), my mentor for a semester in the Department of Ecology, Ethology,
and Evolution, I might have shied away from some areas that are
sketched herein, and which will become more salient in future publication on ecology and economy. I am especially grateful to him for
demonstrating to me broad divergences in the use of terms and concepts
by ethnologists and ecologists, and in setting forth clearly the as-
sumptions, techniques, and directions of modern perspectives on ecosystem analysis both from the standpoint of evolutionary biology and
from that of energy conversion.

An equal debt is owed to another University of Illinois colleague,
Carmen Chuquín, who, with Sibby and me, shared a major effort to
"debundle" allusive messages contained in songs gathered in the territory of Nayapi Llacta during times of incredible upheaval. The col-
legiality through the years of Elizabeth G. Dulany led me to submit
Sicuanga Runa to the University of Illinois Press. Her sensitive and
humane handling of the manuscript and her expert editing are greatly
appreciated. Theresa Sears, long-time editorial associate of the *American
Ethnologist*, took over the difficult task of page make-up in the final
phase of book production. In this work, as in many other collaborative
activities, she has my heartfelt thanks.

My debt to Ecuadorian hosts in many walks of life is enormous.
Acknowledgment has been given elsewhere to the people whose assistance has proven invaluable over the past twenty-two years. Here
I wish to single out only those without whose assistance *Sicuanga Runa*
might never have been written, even though, perhaps paradoxically,
most of them do not constitute the primary characters in this book:
the late Virgilio Santi and the late Gonzalo Vargas, Luis Vargas Canelos,
Celia Santi, Marcelo Santi Simbaña, Faviola Vargas Aranda, Abraham
Chango, Clara Santi Simbaña, Alfonso Chango, Luzmila Salazar, Ve-
nancio Vargas, Elsa Vargas, Pastora Huatatuca, Segundo Vargas, Balvina
Santi, Camilo Santi Simbaña, Soledad Vargas, Julian Santi Vargas, María
Aguinda Mamallacta, Ruben Santi, Delicia Dahua, Gaspar Dahua, Blanca
Santi, Lola Santi, Vicente Aguinda, María Grefa, Venancio Arturo Var-

gas, Blanca Vargas Dahua, Baltazar Vargas, Teresa Dahua, Juan Machoa, Matilde Collahuaso, Bolívar Santi, Clemencia Santi, Rafael Santi, Lucilla Dahua, Leonardo Santi, Gladys Salazar, Gregorio Chango, Apacha Vargas, Dario Vargas, Reinaldo Chango, and Ursula Vargas.

The research would not have been completed without the indefatigable intellectual and practical support of María del Carmen Molestina, of the Instituto Nacional de Patrimonio Cultural del Ecuador. Her interest, help, and total scholarly integrity are deeply appreciated, as is her critical and painstaking commentary on the penultimate draft. Other people who have helped in various ways, at various times, include Joe Brenner in Puyo and Quito; Juan Bottasso in Sucúa, Quito, and Cayambe; Absalom Guevara, Antonio Salazar, Ignacio Ulloa, Roberto Salazar, Abraham Escobar, and Gonzalo Ballesteros in Puyo. Each of these men, in very different ways, has contributed significantly to a wide spectrum of activities and thoughts attendant on our various research projects.

It should be clear from this text that it owes much to the insights and unflagging fieldwork—basic and applied—of my wife, Sibby Whitten, with whom not only tangible experiences but also intersubjective impression retrieval of the questing self have been deeply shared. She came up with many of the analyses of thought constructions reported in this work, and demonstrated to me in several places and on many occasions how my own ideas could be improved measurably by judicious re-examination of materials that either she or I or the two of us together had elicited. I nonetheless assume all responsibility for the finished product. If the reader comes upon errors of omission or commission, or finds that some analysis lacks credibility, the fault is mine.

Notes on the Setting and Characters

Surnames have been omitted or altered as in *Sacha Runa* so as to prevent identification of individuals by a conjunction of name, community, and territory. Only in the case of public figures have I retained actual names. In addition, each of the main characters—Sicuanga, María, Challua, Marta, Taruga, Elena, Jaime, Lluhui, Shiny Shoes—is a composite of real people, each of whom lives far from the specific sites with which the book's characters are associated. Only Javier Vargas (Nayapi), Acevedo Vargas (both deceased), and Camilo Santi are actual persons.

Precise geography is also deliberately blurred in the narrative: Nayapi Llacta/Nueva Esperanza is a composite of three hamlets/*llacta*s. The events themselves are real, but scenes within events have been drawn from people and places in such a way as to render impossible any attempt to pinpoint exactly where something took place, or who said what to whom.

As is always the case in such endeavors, there is a thin line between real history and scrambling data so as to disguise actual names or identities of people caught up in dynamic and sometimes compromising situations. The materials on Nayapi are presented as oral history begins, but the development quickly reflects the merging of people and places as Nayapi's expanding family and kindred are described. Nayapi's specific qualities, and those of the other characters set in the fictional hamlet/*llacta*, are drawn from analogous actors and events occurring widely in space. Everything described, however, actually happened; there *is* real history behind the story.

To disguise actual people still more, the illustrative photographs and drawings of ceramics are from various areas. In Chapter 5 I have not presented an entire array of pottery actually produced, say, by Marta, or by any of the three women whose work Marta represents. Instead, an eclectic array of ceramics is shown to demonstrate how pervasive the ordering of concepts is. In agreement with many of the *huarmiguna*, however, I do give the name of the artist whose creation is reproduced in this work. The reader is once again cautioned that the degree of scrambling is such that acts or thoughts cannot be attributed to the artists whose work gives vivid illustration to the text.

Sicuanga Runa

"[Anthropology] must . . . descend into detail, past the misleading tags, past the metaphysical types, past the empty similarities, to grasp firmly the essential character of not only the various cultures but the various sorts of individuals within each culture, if we wish to encounter humanity face to face."—Clifford Geertz, *The Interpretation of Cultures* (1973), p. 53.

Nueva Esperanza, 1968

On June 13, 1968, Sicuanga's brother Jaime looked out the door of the house he was building on the south side of the recently cleared and very muddy plaza of the new hamlet called Nueva Esperanza (New Hope). Dawn was just beginning to break, but his sharp eyes, attuned to every nuance of the cleared space beyond his home, instantly saw what he then took to be a horrible anomaly. He saw four big frogs, a foot long and a foot wide, sitting on a split-bamboo mat. They were sort of like *juing* (Dendrobatis sp.), but they were way too big. Although they had no teeth he was afraid they were there to devour him. He wasn't asleep, he wasn't dreaming, but he "saw" something that he knew didn't exist. He turned away and went inside, then turned back and looked out, and they were still there. Now there seemed to be lots of them, all unknown, and they went *waugh, waugh*. He killed two with his machete and again went into the house; then he came back and they were all still there. Again he went inside the house, returning to look when the sun was up, and there were no frogs.

Really shaken now, Jaime crossed the plaza to visit Lluhui, the aging shaman and founder of the new community. Lluhui listened carefully to Jaime's tale, focusing attention on the fear of being eaten. "Prepare a soul-vine brew," he told Jaime, "and we will 'see' tomorrow night what these things are that so terrify you,

The view from Jaime's door.

Juing. Teresa Dahua, *caserío* Nueva Vida, Comuna San Jacinto del Pindo.

and that you believe could devour you." Jaime did as he was told, and the next night he and Lluhui drank *ayahuasca* together an hour after sunset. As the spirit world unveiled its other realities, and after conversing with *yacu mama* as black anaconda, Lluhui "saw" just what the frogs were. They were *maquinaria*: big, heavy-duty machinery. Such machinery had not yet arrived in urban Puyo, and there was no road to Nueva Esperanza in the Upper Amazonian rain forest. Nonetheless, Lluhui could "see" the future transformation of the frogs into a large Komatsu bulldozer, a road scraper, and seven dump trucks working one behind the other, first coming up a hill, then turning and backing to the area in front of Jaime's house before dumping their loads of heavy stones taken from the Pastaza and Pindo rivers. There was also a heavy roller there making everything flat, squeezing the water out of the plaza and making a giant Andean-type *cancha*, cleared space, that would become sun-parched hardpan eventually, with lagoons in the low spots, unless modern trenches were dug and maintained. This is what Lluhui "saw" in his Banisteriopsis-induced trip to the spirit world, and this is what would exist in the Runa's everyday waking world before many more years passed. Jaime, explained Lluhui, had glimpsed a reality lying between the other world of the spirits and the world of people; both exist, but the plane of existence is different. Sometimes, though, just before

4

dawn, these planes come together in strange but interpretable ways.

Lluhui told Jaime of the machinery going *roooom, vrrroooom, aaarrrgggh*. "This is why we have made our plaza," Lluhui explained patiently; "what you saw yesterday morning is what is coming soon." Now Jaime was not frightened. The next day he resumed work on his house, completed it, and lived without fear, wondering when the great *maquinaria* that no one in urban Puyo had ever seen would arrive in front of his house.

As Sicuanga listened to Jaime tell of Lluhui's insight a few days later, he thought deeply about the past, present, and future of linear time, and shook his head. Looking at his wife, María, he said, "Many, many outsiders will come soon and Jaime will want whatever their machinery will make. Then he'll need lots of money, and get himself all 'wrapped up,' and change our lives along with his."

1

Introduction

"There is a moral holocaust at work in the soul of a society undergoing the transition from a precapitalist to a capitalist order. And in this transition both the moral code and the way of seeing the world have to be recast. As the new form of society struggles to emerge from the old, as the ruling classes attempt to work the ruling principles into a new tradition, the pre-existing cosmogony of the workers becomes a critical front of resistance, or mediation, or both." —Michael T. Taussig, *The Devil and Commodity Fetishism in South America* (1980), p. 101.

Nayapi's Christian name was Javier Vargas. He was born in Canelos sometime in the mid-nineteenth century, and he died near the Pazyacu River where it empties into the Pastaza in the late 1930s. He was one of the founders of the trade site of Puyo, having arrived there as part of a delegation from the Dominican administrative center at Canelos in 1899. National legend, as reiterated annually at the Twelfth of May celebration of the founding of Puyo, has it that Friar Alvarado Valladares is the true originator of civilized Puyo. For, it is publicly and redundantly recited, this Spanish evangelizing man of the cloth brought "half-civilized Indians" from Canelos with him to create a new order at the previously savage site in the rainy, forested valley at the base of the Andes. Today Puyo has a growing population of 12,000 people; it is by far the largest, most dynamic, most urban, cosmopolitan town in Amazonian Ecuador—itself the focal point of national development. In many ways Puyo's growth may be taken as a microcosm of nationalist-sponsored change in Upper Amazonia and elsewhere.

Nayapi was given his indigenous name by Yu, his father. In today's Nature, Nayapi is a swallow-tailed Kite (*Elanoides forficatus*). In *unai*, mythic time-space which existed long ago—beyond linear time—and continues to exist today, far away and right here, Nayapi is a great fisherman, predator of riparian life. In the long and complicated myth of Nayapi there are many events as the great man travels from house to house. Two women, Manduru huarmi (red woman) and Huiduj huarmi (black woman) also trek from house to house in the Nayapi myth, sometimes with him, sometimes not.

As the myth proceeds, Manduru and Huiduj come to the house of a foreign person, Machin Runa. While they are asleep in the center of his oval house, Machin ties them up with *chambira* palm fiber, and when they awaken at dawn, they find that the fiber has grown into spiny bamboo. They are trapped in a cage of spines that could impale them if they were to struggle against it. They cry out—"Who can help us?" Hearing their cries, the birds of the forest arrive one by one. First comes Paushi (curassow) and he can't help; he doesn't have the capacity to cut the bonds, and he dulls his beak trying. Then comes Pahua (guan) and the same thing happens. Munditi (hoatzin) tries, then Yami (trumpeter), then Carunzi (chachalaca)—still failure, still inability to accomplish the task of freeing the women. All of these birds were warriors, according to the ancient, enduring knowledge of the Puyo Runa and of their Canelos Quichua cultural congeners.

Sicuanga Runa arrives with his great machete, and he cuts and slashes and takes the spines out of the bamboo and frees the two women.

Sicuanga.

They then blow their magical breath on Sicuanga Runa—"*Suuuuu* Sicuanga Runa,*" they say, "stay this way." Huiduj paints him black with genipa; then Manduru paints his beak, collar, and the area between his tail and his body red and yellow. Together they give him white, fluffy cotton for his breast. He becomes, and he stays, Sicuanga. He flies, he is the toucan bird. The two women then change other birds into their present, diverse avian forms, and they make game animals for humans to eat. They also blow on Machin and make him a monkey person, almost human, and he, too, stays that way. Then the two women say, "What will we be?" One says, "I'll be *manduru*" (*Bixa orellana*), and the other says, "I'll be *huiduj*" (*Genipa americana*), and they become the two trees whose seeds provide red and black dyes to the Runa.

This little bit of mythology can be told in the present tense, as I've told it here, or it can be told in the past. It doesn't matter, for *unai* existed and exists, both here and elsewhere. In Spanish a myth is called a *cuento*, a tale. The Runa have no word for "myth," though one could get them to name the basis for myth-telling "our cultural knowledge" or "early ancestors' talk." They see *unai* and its encompassing time-space in terms of an integration of vision and knowledge, thought and reflection. An important component of this dynamic integration is the synthesis of beauty and power. The synthesis is fluid in its symbolic properties and it allows one to gain insight into and distance from changing events, yet at the same time to perceive the immediate precisely by relating the new or unknown to the known.

Sicuanga Runa does not have a myth of his own, so far as I know. What he represents, though, is crucial. Outsiders—foreigners—today correspond to the mythical Machin Runa. Machin Runa is human, but the nature of his humanity is not known, nor is it clear whether he has a Runa-like soul, or whether spirit substances exist in his inner "will," which defines much of the good and evil of the self. He is, however, part of the Runa universe and he will remain so. Machin Runa, this foreign person, tied up two women; Sicuanga Runa freed the women, who continued their adventures from house to house, turning beings into their present forms by blowing upon them with their magical breath. Manduru and Huiduj made animals for humans to eat. They created the colors red and black to provide beauty to the world. Sicuanga Runa freed them so they could continue doing all this.

Sicuanga is a warrior among warriors. People who are feisty, who do not accept without argument the authority of the state, the church, or of their fellow men and women may be called Sicuanga Runa. When one feels hemmed in, the person who provides release from the bonds may be nicknamed Sicuanga Runa. To me, Sicuanga Runa expresses an individualist alternative to inevitable social bonds by a capacity to "cut," to release, to allow one's life to proceed, to allow things to become what they will.

Nayapi, in whose myth Sicuanga Runa appears, was a real person in the Puyo area. He was *sinchi curaga*, a strong leader, a person who derived authority from his close relationship with the Dominican priests of Puyo. From these *curas* he acquired and redistributed trade goods such as machetes, pots and pans, ax heads, powder and shot. He was also known as *curaga* because he could, when necessary, rally the dispersed, dissenting native people in the Puyo area against the threat of unacceptable encroachment. But just as he rallied people against the church from time to time, he also drew them together for the church, and for the state. Nayapi was a legendary power broker between church-state centralized authority and dispersed indigenous dissidence. Sicuanga is a mythical source of power that cuts across or through such brokerage, and a contemporary source of beauty and power that endures in the face of ordered adversity.

Although Nayapi, his wife, and their many children had a *chagra*, a swidden garden, near Puyo, they also maintained distant *chagra*s a few hours' trek south in a rugged forest territory known by national and international explorers as a no-man's land. Nayapi acquired access to about 2,000 hectares of land when, it is said, he confronted a Jurijuri spirit in a great but hidden opening in a formidable jungle hill near a rocky feeder stream of the Pazyacu River. There, at midday, alone, near the Jurijuri's secret cave, Nayapi drank the powerful hallucinogen Datura and traveled in the spirit world with the forest spirit Amasanga. Together, spirit and *curaga* drove the Jurijuri—overseer of jungle animals and other peoples—from his lair, and as the worlds of spirit and human again separated from one another three days later, Nayapi controlled the land while Amasanga controlled the forest and environing weather, upon which the fertility of the land depends. In conquering this territory and making it his *llacta*, Nayapi created a bond between nature and supernature which developed and consolidated into his binding social space. This space was to be contrasted to *Machin Runa allpa*—foreigner's turf: it was to be Nayapi Llacta, his territory, and that of his consanguineal and affinal heirs.

Mamach, Nayapi's daughter, first expanded her *chagra* in Nayapi Llacta. Her husband, Lluhui, cleared the trees for her, and she brought hundreds of stems of manioc to plant. But before she planted she put one manioc stem in front and one on each flank of the pile; then she painted these manioc *curaga* sticks with *manduru* and painted her face

Mamach's *chagra* is cleared by Nayapi.

Mamach's *chagra* matures and develops in Nayapi Llacta.

with the same *Bixa orellana* paint. This way, it is said, Mamach and manioc knew one another. If Mamach failed to make friends with the manioc in this way, to let the manioc know her through the mediation of *manduru*, the manioc would suck her blood. Then Mamach hid her special black garden stone in the *chagra*, and at night, with two of her young daughters, she sang and danced to the garden spirit Nunghui. The next day she and her daughters began to plant. She, with Nunghui, made their *chagra* her territory.

Mamach's husband, Lluhui, was a strong shaman, *sinchi yachaj*. Many people came to him when they were ill, some trekking there from the high Andes or deeper Amazonia. Together, patient and shaman would drink another hallucinogenic brew, called *ayahuasca* (soul vine). While the visionary world of darkness flickeringly interacted with the Runa world of the night fire, shaman and client would discuss the illness and its possible sources. Then, while sitting on a *bancu*, a wooden stool carved in the form of an Amazonian river turtle, Lluhui would fly to distant lands, warding off incoming darts, lances, and other missiles, and then he would return, with greater shamanic capacity than before. He would then use the various sources of an expanding universe to suck out magical darts sent by evildoers envious of his growing strength and of the good fortune of his growing number of patients; if the evil were intentional, he would retaliate by sending killing missiles of his own back at the odious, living source. Lluhui's power to heal and to inflict illness was drawn from the spirit domain of the encompassing water system, from Sungui, an ever-present spirit force that encompasses forest spirit and *chagra* spirit just as the hydrosphere encloses the biosphere and noösphere. Lluhui, many people said, would one day become a *bancu*, a seat of power for the spirits, and then he would "see" beyond time.

Royal Dutch Shell Exploration Company, a British tea company named Cotts, and other such international concerns had moved into the Puyo area in the 1930s, and World War II brought an armed Peruvian invasion up the various rivers just east of Puyo in 1941. In 1945 a son of Javier Vargas, Acevedo Vargas, and his brother-in-law Camilo Santi, together with many other brothers and brothers-in-law—each the founder of a *llacta* or close relative of a founder—asked the president of the Republic of Ecuador, Dr. José María Velasco Ibarra, for the land they collectively now controlled. This request was granted and the Comuna San Jacinto del Pindo was created in 1947.

Javier Vargas had earlier sold his land in Puyo to a refugee German and moved permanently to Nayapi Llacta. He and his growing family took care to fan out to the fringes of their *llacta*, where they encountered other former indigenous residents of Puyo, and other people, too, similarly engaged in territorial occupation and boundary marking. At first Nayapi Llacta became tied by kinship to a settlement of San Jacinto located on the Pindo River. This area was nucleating just south of Puyo in the 1930s. But in the 1950s, after the formation of the *comuna*, some of the children and grandchildren, and their spouses and children,

The Pastaza River at Mera, entrêpot for Royal Dutch Shell and Andean colonists.

firmly broke bonds of ensnarement in hamlet San Jacinto proper and
moved as a group to the territory, settling near the site where Mamach
first made her *chagra*, and where her now-aged husband, Lluhui, continued to demonstrate his shamanic curing powers. A decade later, in
the 1960s, this expanding group declared itself to be a separate, "proper,"
quiquin llacta, with ancient roots apart from San Jacinto, and demonstrated this separation by clearing a rectangular plaza, building their
houses around the plaza, and naming their brand-new settlement Nueva
Esperanza. As a new hamlet of the Comuna San Jacinto del Pindo,
they validated their ancient *llacta* status by reintegration as a *caserío*
into the *comuna*. The first thing they did as a *caserío* was to ask the
municipal authorities of Puyo to build a road to their rain forest site.

Nayapi's father, Yu, had come to Canelos long ago. Whether or not
he brought Nayapi with him, or whether Nayapi was really born there,
is not clear. But Nayapi and his father were baptized in Canelos,
receiving their Christian, "civilized," Vargas name from one of the
evangelizing friars. Yu himself was a monolingual Achuar speaker from
the Capahuari River area. The priests called him a "Jívaro." *Jívaro*, in
Ecuador, is the opposite of *Cristiano*. Yu and his brothers had waged
incessant war against the Chirapas (whom the priests also called *Jívaro*)
on the right bank of the Pastaza River. Once Nayapi went with his
father and others, after a kin festival in Canelos, to attack the Chirapas.
There, it is said, the warriors, called *sicuanga runa*, took a head and
held another hidden festival with the head as the festive base somewhere in the Sigüín Mountains, ancient territory of the Caninche, not
far from the entry point of the Puyo River, where it empties into the
Pastaza. Yu gained tremendous prestige from this ceremony, and Nayapi
inherited some of the aura of participation. But he also inherited the
yet-to-be-reciprocated killing debts that could one day follow. The aura
and those debts continued to descend through children, through his
ayllu, and to become attached to territory.

As the years passed the people of Nayapi Llacta married not only
others from adjacent *llactas* but from the Capahuari area as well. Since
Achuar from that area were related to people from other areas, and
since people like to know whom they are marrying in a social sense,
Achuar from different areas related by kinship to those in Capahuari
territory also came to be regarded as potential spouses. The Achuar
rule of marriage residence is that the man move to his father-in-law's
site, so Nayapi Llacta saw the in-movement of some Achuar men, one
of them nicknamed Challua, and the out-movement of some Puyo
Runa men. Some men and women married northward too, into the
territory of Nayapi's first wife (he remarried after her death), who had

Upper Copataza, ancient territory of the Caninche.

come from the hinterland of Archidona. Nayapi Llacta grew and developed as a bilingual (Achuar-Quichua) community with two dialects of Quichua being spoken (Napo and Canelos). Nayapi himself knew Spanish well, having learned it in Puyo, and some of the Achuar knew more Spanish—having learned it in Peru, or in trade with Peruvians—than did those born and reared in Nayapi Llacta itself.

The multilingual community of Nueva Esperanza flourished; it became progressive by national standards, though it retained a reputation for pugnacity among the Runa inhabiting the *comuna*. There were many fights there, shamanic activity continued until the death of Lluhui, and many people, including Sicuanga and his large family, left the plaza area to live on the *llacta*'s territorial fringes, near other growing hamlets.

I first visited Nueva Esperanza in 1970, walking there on a partially palisaded jungle trail to attend a general assembly of the entire Comuna San Jacinto. I returned there in 1971, with my wife, Sibby, to begin a set of associations described elsewhere (N. Whitten 1976). In 1972 Sibby and I moved into Puma Llacta, near Nueva Esperanza; we lived there for one year, alternating that residence in the Comuna San Jacinto with another residence in Puyo. During that period the jungle trail remained and the system of forest, river, and *chagra* exploitation could be described as a variant of traditional Upper Amazonian cultural ecology. In 1979 a road was constructed near Nueva Esperanza and we moved to the edge of the *caserío* there; by 1981 the road was an all-weather one, with a foundation of about six feet or more of five- to forty-pound stones. These were dredged from the Pastaza and Pindo rivers, hauled in large trucks, dumped, and then rolled, overlaid with a couple of feet of smaller stones and gravel, and rolled again. Sugarcane and cattle—both cash crops—were being purchased roadside out of Nueva Esperanza by 1980, and some of the Runa were caught in economic nets of debilitating bank loans, debts and obligations to competing religious orders, and contrasting obligations and debts to rival indigenous political movements. On May 23, 1982, I attended the inauguration of a new bridge over the Chingosimi River, as well as the encompassing celebration accompanying the completion of the road right up to the cement school on the south side of the plaza of Río Chico, a hamlet analogous to Nueva Esperanza. On the afternoon before the inaugural celebration, I was told the story that opens this chapter.

In the early 1970s the people of Nayapi Llacta were struggling to make their presence known to a military dictatorship bent upon obliterating what it took to be the remnants of semi-civilized indigenous existence. In the early 1980s these same people were caught up in movements of indigenous federation and confederation. In 1981 the people of Nueva Esperanza participated in the armed takeover of land, driving colonists off the western sector of their communal territory and creating a political stir in Puyo that ramified nationally to all indigenous formations. In that same year a confederation of indigenous people formed, linking indigenous movements in each of the nation's Amazonian provinces, Napo, Pastaza, Morona-Santiago, and Zamora-Chinchipe, and an international conference on technical aspects of indigenous affairs in Amazonia was held in Puyo. All of these events affected Nueva Esperanza, and through it some of them affected Nayapi Llacta as well. But paradoxically, because Nayapi Llacta continued to maintain its inner integrity and continued, on its own terms, to articulate with national formations as manifest in Puyo, it also became known for its *resistance to* indigenous movements (in spite of the fact that some of the movements' leaders came from Nueva Esperanza).

The 200 people of Nueva Esperanza represent a microcosm of developmental capitalism in its effects upon small communities; the same 200 people of Nayapi Llacta represent a microcosm of Upper Amazonian cultural ecology. The people in this developing community are, at one and the same time, participants in an enduring Upper Amazonian cultural ecology and in a stratified, developing, nation-state that is itself discovering by conscious effort a heretofore unknown set of ecological, social, and ideological principles.

The people of Nayapi Llacta are culture bearers of an indigenous Upper Amazonian cultural complex that includes congeners around the rim of Amazonia. They also participate in a pan-Andean-Amazonian sociocultural complex that ranges through the highland areas of Ecuador, Peru, and Bolivia. If ever there was a full-blown confluence of Andean and Amazonian social and cosmological currents it would seem to be here, at the foothills of the Andes, in the rugged, verdure-canopied mountains of Ecuador's Oriente. As participants in Andean and Amazonian indigenous cultural systems these people contrast vividly with colonial, republican, and modern emphases on national culture. But they are as much a part of national culture as are members of any other small community in this rural, OPEC, developing nation. They participate in the formation of genuine Ecuadorian culture in ways that are still totally misunderstood by developers of Ecuador, not to mention scholars who make "developing nations" their academic specialty.

Given these statements, it behooves us to focus directly on the concept of *contradiction*. According to Webster, it is "a condition in which things tend to be contrary to each other." *Antinomy* is a contradiction raised, so to speak, to a higher level—"a contradiction or inconsistency between two apparently reasonable principles or laws." This book is about a couple of hundred people whose lifeways reflect remarkable consistency in a situation characterized by radical change. It is about people who participate in a subsistence economy and in a market economy, who live in both dispersed and nucleated residential patterns, who speak two (and sometimes three) languages, who may be seen as assimilating to modern Ecuadorian ways, and who are developing into a militant ethnic bloc. It is about a people who, like other people, become ensnared in binding sociopolitical networks generated by negotiation, transaction, and various forms of attachment, and about a people who act so as to cut the very bonds that imprison them. This book is, above all else, about a people who maintain a capacity to respond—a *power*—based on internal integrity (or structure) and on adaptability. It is about cultural continuity: it explores the nature of contradiction and antinomy in social life and seeks to contribute to a theory of power—to understand the ability to carry out one's will, despite resistance.

This book is the sequel to *Sacha Runa*, a prominent theme of which is the duality of ethnic patterning. That work took as its subject the entire culture area of the Canelos Quichua in historical and contemporary dimensions. As a sequel, *Sicuanga Runa* focuses on the site of Nayapi Llacta/Nueva Esperanza to explore the theme of the duality of power patterning.

GROWTH AND DEVELOPMENT

This introductory chapter cannot close without a discussion of the
concepts of "growth" and "development." These concepts are central
to much of the social sciences and have come to stand as magical
embodiments for practical activities in most, if not all, contemporary
nations. Most of the concepts in the social sciences upon which theories
are constructed are metaphors. They are built around terms taken from
realms of science and technology such as physics, biology, or engi-
neering and are applied to domains of social relations, culture, personality, politics, or religion to help us think mechanistically or systemically about the very nature of our common humanity. The trouble
is that, having applied terms or tropes to domains to which they do
not belong, we treat the metaphors as natural features of the domains
that we are trying to understand. That is to say, we reify—when what
we should be doing is using a concept to gain new insight into the
nature of society itself.

Take "development" and "growth" for example. The verb *develop*,
Webster tells us, derives from Latin by way of French with an etymology
meaning "to wrap up." Its current meanings, as given by Webster and
Random House, include "to cause to grow gradually in some way;
cause to become gradually fuller, larger, better . . . to bring into activity,
as an idea . . . to unfold gradually, as a bud . . . to make more available
or extensive, as electric power. . . ." *Development* takes on the additional
meanings of "a step or stage in growth, advancement, etc." To understand more of this vital concept, taken as a theory-constitutive
metaphor by those who seek salvation through it, let us turn to "growth,"
using once again the verb *grow*. Here Webster offers "to come into
being or be produced naturally; sprout; spring up . . . to exist as living
vegetation; thrive . . . to increase in size and *develop toward maturity,
as a plant or animal does by assimilating food* . . . to increase in size,
quantity, or degree, or in some specified manner . . . to become." It is
with the simile italicized above that we learn how strange the figures
of speech that feature "development" and "growth" really are when
applied to human society. Here—and I think that this is the crux of
social science thinking with regard to development and evolution—
we find *growth* defined as *development toward maturity*. "Development,"
as in "the developed societies," "the undeveloped societies," "the developing societies," expresses an epistemology that is fundamentally
teleological—it presupposes a concept of social maturity by metaphoric
extension and then reifies the extension by metonymy. Maturity, of
course, is a state of being full grown, ripe; maturity occurs when an

organism or ecosystem reaches its maximum development or accentuation of form.

A virgin forest is mature when its layers of vegetation reach climax state—they won't develop any more—and when relationships among nutrient cycles in the ecosystem are as predictable as a model of energy equilibrium can make them, from one viewpoint, or when the various species come as close to predictable relationships in co-evolutionary terms, from another viewpoint or perspective. A swidden garden is mature when the caloric intake to the Runa is maximum in proportion to labor expended. No matter how one views it, maturity must be measured with some instrument.

Unfortunately, we usually forget the need for an instrument, for something to give us a sense of proportion in discussing what is, and what is not, "mature." Use of powerful metaphors like "development" or "growth" can lead to unending rhetoric by choosing only some of the properties of a symbol in a given domain. In the domain health/illness, for example, a cancer is said to be mature when it has grown to the point of development where it is about to kill the host. This analogy takes us back to the simile italicized above: *growth*: "develop toward maturity, *as a plant or animal does by assimilating food."* By definition nothing grows—nothing develops toward maturity—without devouring something else. By use of this simile one can easily contrast a perspective that sees social development as a movement

"Development": a sector of Ecuador's Macas-Puyo road, on the Sigüín range, 1981.

toward social maturity ("the good life") with another that sees social development as a devouring malignancy. The contrast has developed into senescence in the social sciences, especially when "evolution" versus "dependency" arguments are elaborated; but the rhetoric that the contrast generates will undoubtedly be with us for a long time to come.

"Development" (*desarrollo*) is a prominent facet of contemporary nationalist ideology in Ecuador, and the people of Nueva Esperanza are caught up in consequent policies and practices just as they are bound to the various developmental cycles and growth sequences of their ecosystem, their economy, and their society. But just as the metaphors of development may wrap up or package the new ideology, binding the Runa to the nation in myriad ways and hemming them in within "their own" system, the metaphor presented by Sicuanga Runa's participation in Nayapi's myth provides the symbolic stuff from which a cutting and release is born. This releasing mechanism allows us to construct a dynamic, generative perspective on the other side of development.

2

Amazonia and the Ecuadorian Nation

"The Oriente is a Myth."—Galo Plaza Lasso, onetime president of Ecuador, onetime representative of Ecuador to the United Nations, onetime ambassador of Ecuador to the United States of America.

"Ecuador has been, is, and will be an Amazonian nation."—Popular political motto often emblazoned on official stationery and publications within the Republic of Ecuador.

"The Amazonian forest lives *on* the soil more than *out of* the soil; the role of the soil is that of a mechanical substrate rather than a provider of nutrients."—Harald Sioli, "Zur Ökologie des Amazonas-Gebietes" (1968), p. 167.

". . . the tropical rainforest may well be nature's chief library of experience from which humanity can learn, not only how to do things but also what vast variety of things may be possible. . . . Norman Myers was moved to say that doing away with it would be like burning the ancient library of Alexandria—that if present patterns of converting tropical rainforest persist, it may be the worst biological debacle 'since life's first emergence on the planet 3.6 billion years ago.' "—Peter T. White, "Nature's Dwindling Treasures: Rain Forests" (1983), p. 24.

". . . if current trends continue most of the undisturbed Amazon forest 'may vanish' by the end of the current century. . . . The western nations are 'marching' to the east, and Brazil is 'marching' to the north and west. Plans exist or are being made to move hundreds of thousands of families into the Amazonian fringes and interior, to convert tropical forest to pasture, to develop commercial agriculture, logging, and mining. At great cost, roads are being built and the infrastructure for colonists and settlements is being established."—William M. Denevan, "Development and the Imminent Demise of the Amazon Rain Forest" (1973), pp. 130, 137.

On May 24, 1981, less than two weeks after Puyo celebrated its seventy-second year since the legendary "civilized founding" by Friar Valladares and his faithful semi-Christian Indians, the Republic of Ecuador was stunned when the soccer game being televised nationally between Chile and Ecuador was interrupted with the news that President Jaime Roldós Aguilera, his wife, Martha Bucarám de Roldós, and members of his cabinet and aides had lost their lives in a plane crash in Loja, near the Peruvian border. The twenty-fourth of May is Ecuador's Independence Day and Roldós had delivered a stirring speech in Quito just before boarding the recently purchased U.S.-built Beechcraft airplane, outfitted with sophisticated equipment for mountain flying, for his ill-fated journey. His last words, recorded by all the media, were these: "*Ecuador amazónica desde siempre y hasta siempre . . . ¡Viva la Patria!*" What is the Amazonian world that Ecuador has been for ever and ever?

AMAZONIA: ITS CENTER AND RIM

River Sea and Floodplain

To picture the Amazon itself, think of a sea or great flowing lake. The Amazon as a river sea flows for 4,000 miles from its source in the Peruvian Andes, descends at an average of 26.5 feet per mile for 600 miles, and then, for 85 percent of its length, drops only a quarter-inch per mile. One-fifth of all the fresh water in the world pours from the 200-mile-wide mouth, east of Belem, Brazil, at a rate of 175,000 cubic meters per second. Ocean liners navigate up this great water system 2,300 miles to Iquitos, Peru. Rainfall in the Amazon basin is seasonal and averages 100 to 150 inches per year. In the western Upper Amazonian territory rainfall is seasonal in some areas but more constant in others, where it reaches 200 inches or more per year.

The "river land" (of flooded banks and flooded forest) of Central Amazonas may be under twenty-five or forty feet of water during the regular wet season, when tributaries meander between the natural levees, forming oxbow lakes. As the river recedes with the onset of the dry season, banks become progressively available for planting crops in rich, newly deposited alluvium. This is the *várzea*, floodplain of the Amazon; it and its tributaries can extend for fifty miles inland.

The water world of the Amazon proper is also sea-like in its denizens, which include 2,000 species of fish, river and lagoon mammals such as porpoises and the now nearly extinct manatee, and abundant reptilian life. Reptiles are most dramatically represented by the great an-

25

aconda, which grows to forty feet in length, the huge cayman or South American alligator, and the super-abundance of river turtles about the size of a manhole cover. Aboriginal cultures of the Amazonian *várzea* apparently exploited the agricultural resources effectively, together with various aquatic and upland protein sources.

The floodplain system of indigenous culture was utterly destroyed after 100 to 150 years of European contact. At least a million or more people—perhaps two million—who practiced a poorly known but effectively creative production system were obliterated by diseases such as malaria and smallpox and by warfare.

We are not completely ignorant, however, of Amazonian floodplain technology and production within the ecosystem, for ethnohistory and archaeology come to our aid. With a simple material culture, without draft animals or steel tools, peoples of the *várzea* were organized into permanent villages and towns ranging in population from a few hundred to up to 5,000 or maybe 10,000, perhaps more. These population concentrations were, in turn, organized into kingdoms or states, which waged war with long-distance campaigns, traded widely, and enjoyed a rich variety of maize, manioc, and many other crops, high-grade aquatic proteins and fats such as turtles and their eggs, caymans and their eggs, manatee meat and oil, and some upland game. Some of these states are reported to have been able to field an army of 60,000 or more men. Peoples of the *várzea* system brewed huge quantities of beer made of manioc, other root crops, palm fruits, and maize, stored it in large and beautifully decorated jars, and served food and drink in fine ceramic ware which was roundly praised, appreciated, and collected by Europeans. Reptilian symbolism itself, associated with both fish and cultivation, is represented centrally in monumental works in the eastern zone of the Peruvian Andes, near the Amazonian headwaters (Lathrap 1977). And Andean festivals routinely celebrate visits of Amazonian peoples and objectify Amazonian-Andean oppositions through display of animal skins and bird-feather headdresses.

Indigenous technology of the *várzea* included the corralling of thousands of 150-pound river turtles, and hunting strategies were so organized, it would seem, as to preserve manatee and cayman populations. Western productive processes, by contrast, drove the manatee to near extinction and sharply reduced the turtle and cayman populations. In the case of the latter, national developers in Brazil saw little reason to maintain these populations. After all, it was reasoned, caymans eat fish and humans eat fish. Caymans, then, must compete with humans over fish resources. Brazil needed an increased fish supply in the 1940s and 1950s, and the market for cayman skins was also most lucrative. The strategy became one of extensive cayman destruction under the ideological aegis of "development." The results are well known to many ecologists: as the cayman declined in numbers, so too did the fish decline. Eventually research was done which revealed that the cayman was, indeed, a key ecological feature in the maintenance and expansion of fish populations. Caymans eat fish as they swim up the Amazon to spawn. They then slowly excrete their nutrients back into the nutrient-poor mouth lakes or lagoons of the Amazon's affluents, thereby maintaining the nutrients necessary for fish there. The decimation of fish predators, in this case the cayman, reduced fish populations and limited the protein supplies for local communities. In short, the cayman's predatory feeding activity and consequent processing of nutrients was and is necessary in maintaining the electrolyte content of nutrient-poor waters, which in turn is essential in the maintenance of, or increase in, fish production.

Reconstruction by linguistic and archaeological evidence, and by ethnohistoric sources, documents expansive migration out of Central Amazonia in northward, westward, and southward directions. Such a migration of Tupi-speaking peoples penetrated the area under discussion in Amazonian Ecuador, probably bringing with it, in one wave or another, the focal patterning of the richly decorated ceramic tradition. The antiquity of ceramics and horticulture themselves in this area, however, vis-à-vis Andean and Amazonian cultural currents, must await further empirical study.

Before leaving the Amazonian floodplain area mention must again be made of the catastrophe sponsored by world demand for tropical products. Native peoples of Amazonia tapped their wild rubber trees, making such items as boots, bottles, bowls, and syringes (which may have been used to administer both medicines and hallucinogens), and to waterproof ceramic bowls. Some attempts to export manufactured rubber goods were made by Brazilians with varying success. When Goodyear invented vulcanization in 1839, however, the stage was set for a colossal extractive industry which led to the annihilation of many Amazonian peoples and the dispersal of many others to northern, western, and southern hinterlands (right into the areas of present concern). By the turn of the twentieth century rubber plantations in Asia were producing (having been established much earlier by the smuggling of seeds out of Brazil), and the burgeoning economy of Central Amazonia collapsed.

Forest and Swidden

There is no forest in existence comparable to that of the Amazonian uplands (the contrast is with the *várzea*—one should not think of English uplands, or North American uplands), where the rain forest extends for over two million square miles and is cut by over a thousand tributaries to the Amazon. In this forest are found over 40,000 species of flora, of which only 10,000 or so have been classified. Insect life is extraordinarily diverse, and some of it provides a steady, if backup, protein and fat supply for humans. Diversity is a central feature of the forest, where well over 200 separate species of trees may be found on an acre, and where some trees may serve as environment for fifty or more other plants. Different species of plants have evolved different sets of chemical inhibitors to protect them from predators. But predators such as insects, fungi, and bacteria have also developed specialized mechanisms for exploiting given species. Diversity is not only the forest's central feature, it is the key mechanism by which predation and normal degeneration produce and reincorporate decay while at the same time protecting the various species from decimation by pest or plague.

With a rich realm of Central Amazonian indigenous culture essentially destroyed (Sweet 1974; Hemming 1978), it is necessary to turn to the Amazonian periphery for some direct information about the majority of today's native peoples. Taking the middle of the Amazon proper as a point of departure and drawing an arc north, circling west, and coming around to the south, most of the more intact native cultures remaining in this vast land are encountered.

Groups such as the Akawaio of Guyana, the Yanomamö, Makiritare, Pemon, Panare, Piaroa, and Kariña of Venezuela, the Desana, Cubeo, Bara, and Barasana of Colombia, the Cofán, Siona-Secoya, Canelos, Shuar, and Achuar of Ecuador, the Aguaruna, Lamista, Shipibo-Conibo, Campa, and Amhuesha of Peru, the Sirionó and Chiquitano of Bolivia, and the Mundurucú, Kawahib, and Nambikwara of Brazil all provide us with rich evidence of *contemporary* native wisdom with regard to this tropical forest (or savannah-gallery forest) land. Most such people today live on the periphery of the Amazonian heartland *and* on the periphery of their respective nations, usually in extremely rugged country where refuge from earlier destruction could be found. Today, however, the refuge zones are becoming rapidly incorporated into the "developing" infrastructure of industrializing and "modernizing" nations which seek to transform the zone from one of low energy resource utilization to high energy utilization.

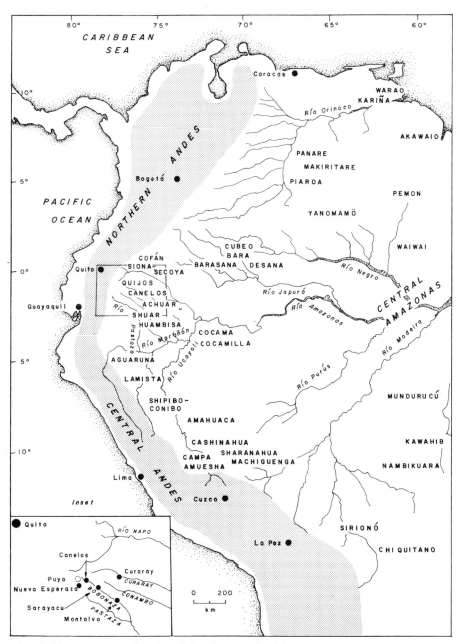

Map 1. Contemporary Peoples of the Amazonian Rim

To understand this forest land in terms of a culture complex, some features of agriculture quite alien to recognized methods of food production in temperate zones must be examined. Here at the University of Illinois the inscription over the main door of Davenport Hall (where the departments of Geography, Anthropology, and Soy Bean Experimentation are housed) proclaims, "The Wealth of Illinois is in her Soil, and her Strength lies in its Intelligent Development." Whereas my colleagues in development agriculture think of the integrity and richness of soil per se, and strive to protect it and enhance its vital nutrients, indigenous Amazonian people think of the integrity and richness of the *forest*. It is the combination of forest and hydrosphere—rainfall and river activity—that provides the basic features of the soil itself in Amazonia. Amazonian soils away from the floodplain are generally low in nutrients. The vegetation provided by the rain forest itself captures and stores the nutrients, and protects the soil from excessive solar radiation and erosion. Leaf litter constantly drops from the trees to build up a mat. Tiny hair roots grow quickly in the leaves of this mat, sharing with the diverse leaves common mycorrhizal fungi. Without this mat, which is part of the forest lying on top of the soil, there would be no exchangeable nutrient base for abundant plant life.

Within the leaf mat and under the soil the complex of fungi also exhibits a striking degree of mycorrhizae with the tree roots. Fungi, root-leaf mat, and tree roots are all in a special complex chemical association that facilitates the uptake of minerals by the roots. Without the mycorrhizal association the trees would not absorb the nutrients, no matter how much manufactured fertilizers were poured onto them. Indeed, when such fertilizers are poured onto the root-leaf mat itself, 100 percent absorption quickly occurs (Jordon 1982). Nutrient capture in the foliage itself is also critical, and recycling of nutrients is facilitated by a much faster fall of litter than we are used to thinking about. Ten times the amount of nitrogen, for example, is returned to the Amazonian soil through litter than is returned in eastern U.S. climax woodlands. Moreover, it has been estimated that 75 percent of the potassium, 40 percent of the magnesium, and 25 percent of the phosphorus available to growing plants are returned to the ground by rainwater dripping from the leaves. In fact, 50 percent of the tropical forest rainfall itself may come *from* the forest. Unlike temperate-zone soils, where nutrients can be stored until needed (unless severe erosion occurs), Amazonian soils are much more vulnerable to leaching and permanent nutrient loss. When such loss occurs, restoration, including reforestation, is extremely difficult if not utterly impossible. In other words, the cycle of nutrients, minerals, and even water coming from forest and going to forest must be *continuous*. Obviously, to fit the moist tropics of Amazonia, Davenport Hall's inscription would have to read, "The Wealth of Amazonia is in her Forest, and her Strength lies in its Intelligent Development."

There are three vital features of indigenous agriculture in tropical forest ecosystems. These include the ideas and practices of swidden cultivation, as opposed to permanent, fixed-field agriculture, polycultural crop production, as opposed to monocultural crop production, and vegetative reproduction of root crops, as opposed to seed-reproduced crop plants. This combination of factors may have a time depth of 6,000 or more years in lowland South America, so it is logical to assume that they have developed to a reasonably mature relationship with the ecosystem.

Swidden horticulture is shifting horticulture, where long-term fallow allows for the regeneration and maintenance of the forest itself. Forest maintenance is an effective, efficient form of environmental maintenance for agriculture. Polycultural crop production refers to the planting of many different species of plants side by side in the same garden; diversity is characteristic. Vegetative reproduction, or vegeculture, refers primarily to the root crops—starch-rich cultivars with enlarged tubers, roots, or rhizomes—characteristic of the tropical New World, of which manioc (also called *yuca* and cassava) is probably the best known in lowland areas, and the potato in the high Andes. (Plantains and palms can also be propagated exactly as root crops; the former are always so propagated, the latter often so.)

Manioc, which many of us in temperate climates know primarily in the form of tapioca, a by-product of a flour produced by Amazonian Tupian peoples, has some interesting properties. Many varieties of manioc can be peeled, boiled, and eaten. But the one- to eight-pound elongated root itself does not store well in the moist tropics when it is taken from the ground and left unprocessed. It stores beautifully for a year or two, though, when just left in the ground. Contemporary native peoples of Amazonia have perfected two methods for processing manioc, and other crops, for storage. One of these is to cook it, pound it into a pulp, squeeze it, and toast it into farinha flour, which can be used to bake an unleavened bread (like a huge, flat griddle cake). Another is to introduce the proper enzyme-yeast starter into the cooked pulp and ferment it, sometimes with fungal or other additives. The various fungi in the fermented mash enhance the vegetable-protein content of the brew. The mash is mixed with water to make a basic gruel-like food staple, normally very low in alcoholic content. At the time of conquest the brew was called *chicha* (as was a much headier

Andean-Caribbean brew made of maize) in several languages and became part of New World Spanish (and now English) meaning home-brewed beer. Drinking large amounts of manioc chicha during the day is characteristic of many Amazonian cultures, a refreshing technological innovation adapted for strenuous work in hot, humid settings.

Food-processing and native agronomy of Amazonia present the Western world with some lessons in environmental management. Swidden horticulture, together with polycultural crops and vegetative repro-duction, replicates (at least in part) the tropical forest ecosystem. In its mature stage, a swidden has about three vertical layers of crops, with interspersed species providing partial protection against pests. The roots of all plants of the swidden utilize the mycorrhizal fungi associated with leaf mat and with forest trees. Within three to six months the maturing swidden develops a continuous canopy above to break and diffuse rainfall and filter sunlight, and also develops an undersoil root lattice to retard leaching and recycle vital nutrients. Eventually the forest itself is allowed to return, as fallow, and another section of the forest (primary or secondary, depending on a complex set of factors) is cut down. This debris is then used as mulch or burned fertilizer for newly planted polycultural root crops or seed crops. As monocropping develops, selection should be for manioc with more potent chemical inhibitors to prevent insect predation and with lower glucose content to prolong storage. The result of such selection can also lead to a headier beer as conversion into cyanotropic glucosides is enhanced.

David Harris, an ecologist, argues emphatically that swidden culti-vation is an extremely productive agricultural system in terms of yields per unit of labor expended in its productivity (as opposed to a measure of productivity in terms of per-unit area of land cultivated): "Its pro-ductivity can equal or even exceed that of some types of permanent fix-field agriculture. Provided that no land shortage threatens the main-tenance of any optimum cycle of cultivation and fallowing, swidden plots can yield as much or more than comparable fields under contin-uous cultivation" (Harris 1972).

The swidden garden, usually only a half to three hectares but ranging up to seven or more, is a common site of natural vivariums. People cut palm trees and deliberately leave them to rot slowly in their pulpy interiors. After large edible weevils (some specific to specific palms) deposit their eggs in or on the logs, their big larvae and pupae thrive on the pulpy centers. All of these palm-weevil larvae and pupae are rich sources of protein and fat, and many are harvested by people to supplement their animal-, fish-, and vegetable-protein diets. Hunting and collecting, too, are especially good on the edges of gardens, par-ticularly when a swidden is being allowed to return to forest.

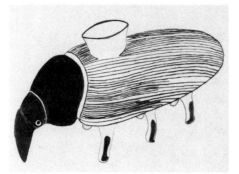 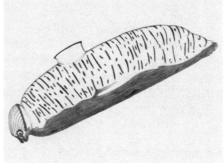

Tucu and *tucu curu,* palm weevil and its larva. Apacha Vargas, *caserío* Nuevo Mundo, Comuna San Jacinto del Pindo.

The knowledge of this general system exists in specific cosmological structures of master symbols that allow native peoples with requisite vision and knowledge to communicate widely and freely about ecosystem dynamics by reference to focal spirit beings. One example of the integration of master symbols comes from the Canelos Quichua people of Ecuador. They conceptualize the hydrosphere—that all-encompassing system of water which includes rain and rivers—as an ultimate source of power. The expression of this power is usually given in forms that evoke imagery of great rivers and their effects on the planet and on life itself. In describing the life-giving dimension of this power source, which they call Sungui, the Canelos are careful to explain that forest spirit master Amasanga must *control* this power of the hydrosphere if destruction is not to occur. This is not spiritual mumbo jumbo but good environmental management—good technology (see Bugliarello and Doner 1979)—for without the buffering influence of the forest soil fertility would indeed be destroyed, irreversibly so, by the alternation of direct rainfall and baking sun. *Control of power* is a vital and central imagery of Canelos Quichua religion, cosmology, and agronomy, as it is with other peoples of Amazonia (and of the Andes). Nunghui, the master spirit of garden soil and of pottery clay, is credited by the Canelos Quichua with continuous human control of the agricultural system, alteration of the forest, and domestication of natural life. But never would Nunghui set the system of ultimate power out of control. The cosmological paradigm of Sungui, Amasanga, and Nunghui expresses the dynamics of water, forest, and tenuous domestication of nature in Amazonia. By one transformation or another we should have comparable paradigms specific to widely divergent Amazonian native peoples, or Andean native peoples.

Amazonian "Development"

The Amazonian peripheries occupied by native peoples are today caught up in modernization plans and practices which stress the transformation of these territories from wastelands to "productive, developed regions" of their respective nation-states. All too often the forest regions are regarded as uninhabited and thereby open to colonization. Native people may be dislocated or killed, and when they are left in their reserves or territories, they are frequently pressured to adopt new forms of monocultural, permanent-field, chemical-fertilizer, high-energy-utilization agriculture aimed at the production of commercial crops—sugarcane, bananas, tea, African palm, coffee, cacao—or to change overnight into cattle ranchers. Moreover, their means of processing food for storage by fermentation are widely deplored by national developers and foreign evangelical missionaries. Native peoples are often forced to provide mere physical labor for new plantations or timber, mining, or petroleum companies. Mining of minerals, petroleum extraction, and commercial farming require rapidly expanding infrastructural supports of roads and airstrips, and these in turn greatly accelerate attempts to impose a system of production inappropriate to the rain-forest ecosystems.

The emphasis of developers in much of the area under discussion is in converting the forest into something else, and effects of this conversion are predictable from direct, indigenous information on ecosystem maintenance or from allusive, indigenous cosmology. As the forest is cleared extensively (rather than sectioned out by swiddens), and all tree trunks, roots, and vegetation are removed, monocrops are planted and cattle are introduced. Soil and water integrity can then degenerate rapidly in nonrenewable ways. More commercial fertilizers are often used, costs soar, labor requirements increase, wages do not keep pace, yields decline rapidly. More forest is cut and cleared, rainfall decreases, the land is baked, and the spiral of destruction rises rapidly to new levels of expanding barrenness. Starchy foods are imported and protein becomes scarce. As pests attack more and more monocrops, pesticides are used increasingly, killing off backup protein and fat supply for humans. Without any root-leaf mat above the soil the mycorrhizal associations of fungi-roots-nutrients are destroyed, so that when developers begin to introduce reforestation, nothing much happens. A wasteland is created.

Direct protests by indigenous people are undercut by a profession of faith in Western technology by many scientists and developers. After all, developers may argue, if dependence on Western goods is to be lessened, or averted, then the economic structure of modernizing nations must conform increasingly to that of the industrial, high-energy-utilizing nations. The problem with this developmental reasoning (beyond the fact that the analogy of growth to maturity is absurd, to begin with, when applied to society) is that the Amazonian ecosystem will not allow the sorts of productive strategies which are apparently effective in areas such as Illinois and Iowa, or in the Ukraine. Indigenous peoples' indirect protests are also undercut when they endeavor to reach the minds of developers and others by recourse to their own religious convictions, for the very concepts of spirit force, of sentience through soul substance, which provide anchoring reference points for ecosystem and social-system maintenance, are normally viewed as devils and demons by Christian missions.

The pulsating cultural forces of a tenuous arc of indigenous societies around the rim of Central Amazonia must be understood in their own terms, from the standpoint of their varied and shifting articulations to modern nation-states, and from the contradictory relationships and antinomies that the articulations feature.

ECUADOR, 1961-81

All of mainland Ecuador is divided into three parts: Coast, Sierra, and Oriente. In addition, there are the Galápagos Islands lying 600 miles out to sea. The first two parts feature a bi-urban schism between Andean Quito and coastal Guayaquil. Today the former (the capital of the nation) burgeons with political-economic strength drawn from petroleum revenues, while the latter continues its commercial leverage, which grew out of a base of commercial agriculture, shipping, and banking. National attention, within this two-city dialectic of economy, social relations, and ideology, has increasingly turned eastward toward its small segment of Amazonia, endeavoring once again to validate the claim that "Ecuador has been, is, and will be an Amazonian nation."

In 1961 Quiteño developmental design included the "opening of access" to products from its two rain forests—the Northwest Coast and the Oriente—and the development of its own coastal port of San Lorenzo (N. Whitten 1965, 1974). Land in both areas was called baldía (unutilized and therefore public), although such land was in fact inhabited and under swidden-management technology. Guayaquil at that time drew strength from its own elite, from the southern Andean oligarchy located in Cuenca, as well as from an expanding in-migrating labor force out of the central and southern Andes. Political divisions then could be mapped as a north-south division as well as in terms of the three regions. Conservative-liberal oscillations cut through the

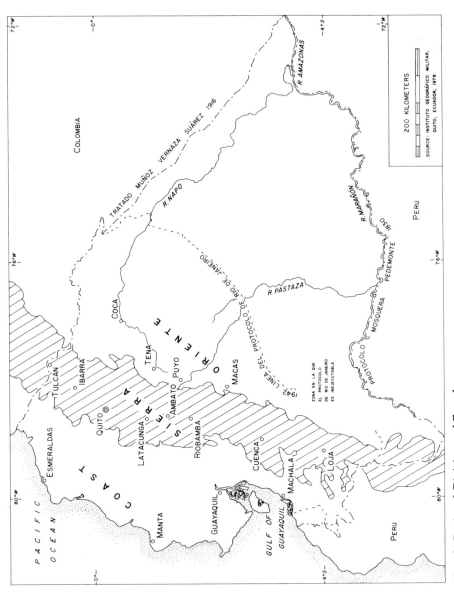

Map 2. Regional Divisions of Ecuador

north-south and regional splits. By 1981 political forces accentuated the more stereotypical regional divisions, as Guayaquil interests and Quiteño bureaucracy both focused upon the Amazonian territories. And while national politics ranged along a spectrum of coalitions from left to right, ethnic-based to class-based, all parties promoted accelerating developmentalism to solve problems of poverty, inflation, and increasing class and ethnic conflict that seemed to have occurred as a result of the developmentalism of the 1960s and 1970s (Hurtado 1980).

In 1961 the nation was governed by a rapid succession of *caudillos*, politicians that drew factions from rival parties (often during a crisis) while trying to keep their own parties from fissioning. From 1970 through 1979 Ecuador was governed by military rule, during which period increasingly nationalist centralization gave more and more concessions to foreign—especially Euro-American—petroleum companies and consortiums and to imported industry. In 1979 Ecuador returned to civilian rule under the *caudillo*-like and charismatic leadership of Jaime Roldós Aguilera, who initiated a period of intensified nationalist, pluralist, ethnic consciousness. Roldós was a free-thinking president, a man who condemned suppression, torture, and dictatorship in Central American and Southern Cone nations, who looked at socialist and capitalist rhetoric in terms of the praxis of each, and who turned to competing governments for technical help and sought to maintain, above all else, a program of human rights to allow Ecuador to "shine as the light of the Americas." Another such president, though in military garb, was President Torrijos of Panama. Within a month of one another each of these presidents, traveling in highly sophisticated military planes, crashed straight into the side of a mountain, though their pilots were skilled fliers and thoroughly familiar with the topography of their respective nations.

Between 1961 and 1981 Ecuador changed from one of the poorest nations in Latin America to a near-marginal OPEC country. As it developed from poverty into wealth (as measured by the Gross National Product), land redistribution in the Sierra caused the breakup of many enormous haciendas. But members of the *oligarquía*—as those constituting perpetual power groups are called—retained their centralized control by diversifying holdings among family members. One-lane roads that twisted through the mountains and valleys of the Sierra and between Sierra and Coast became two-lane and even four-lane asphalt roads; air transportation went from a few flights a day to hundreds; great, modern buildings grew up throughout the Sierra and the Coast; schools proliferated and universities as well as institutes began large-scale programs of technical, developmental, economic, and social applied research.

In 1961, when Guayaquil was (and still is) known for its central position in the maintenance of freedom, and the Coast generally for its liberal presence, and when Quito was (and still is) known for its dignity, culture, and urbane Christianity—and the site where heroes bled for Bolívar's liberating movement—the Oriente was known primarily as a mostly uninhabited, flat, Amazonian jungle morass, sparsely populated by a few groups of "savages." One group, the "Jívaro," were known worldwide for their shrunken heads. Another, the "Auca," were famous for spearing some North American missionaries. During the 1970s the sudden discovery of many indigenous peoples inhabiting the strategic refuge zones, flood banks, and hill country of the Oriente led to a florescence of the ideology of regrettable ethnocide, which proclaimed that just as the richness of the native cultures was being discovered, the people themselves were being forced into accelerated assimilation, or simply obliterated, by the forces of modernization. Roldós, in his inaugural presidential address, sought to overcome this ideology. He spoke of the dynamic peoples of the Amazonian area and pledged his support to them. Two years later, the Oriente bore witness not only to consolidated *comunas, colonias,* parishes, and other settlements of jurally and/or politically recognized indigenous peoples, but also to an armed takeover by indigenous peoples of previously "rented" or "sold" land. Many (though by no means all) of the indigenous lands became more secure, by Ecuadorian standards, in 1980 and 1981 as indigenous federations, confederations, councils, and even a tenuous international confederation of national confederations (especially between Peru and Ecuador) formed. Some of these are currently becoming legally and/or formally recognized through appropriate national and international agencies. As native peoples gained ground nationally, the ideology of *indomestizaje*—which excludes native knowledge systems from developmental and social planning—also expanded, even permeating the rhetoric of native movements.

Nayapi Llacta/Nueva Esperanza

In 1961 the northern and western edges of the dispersed settlement of Nayapi Llacta were about an hour and a half's walk through the forest southeast from the colonist settlement of Tarqui. Tarqui, in turn, was a two-hour walk or half-hour truck ride from Puyo. Today one can come within two kilometers of Nueva Esperanza from Puyo in about thirty minutes by truck or car. Although Nayapi Llacta existed in 1961, Nueva Esperanza did not. It formed as a named entity and was nucleated into a plaza in 1968. The techno-ecological, social, and cosmological bases of Nayapi Llacta conform to the criteria of the Upper

Amazonian area described in the previous sections. Its national form, as Nueva Esperanza — which taps developmental resources upon which it is coming to depend—derives from a social structure which is sketched below.

Social and Ethnic Structure of Ecuador

An oligarchy constitutes the pinnacle of Ecuadorian social structure. These people are, by all sandards, an international elite who generally have large landholdings, banking interests, and commercial ties. They are often educated overseas and think of themselves as a "society" in Guayaquil and Quito (and also Cuenca). They regard one another as *muy culto* (very cultured, enlightened, civilized, educated), and seem to stand above the class structure in many ways. Basically, their family ties (landholdings, and control over industry and banking) allow them to ride out reform movements for, one way or another, their access to corporate holdings and invested capital gives them the economic where-withal to maintain their privileged social status as a small, intertwined, and intermarried society of civilized people. Below the oligarchy there exists a system of people stratified by access to resources. They are known by their life-style, by their political impact, by their cars, house size, servants, by their ability to take trips to international resorts, or by their ability to educate their children abroad. Most of the military officers of Ecuador have moved up the class hierarchy thanks to the extensive military educational system that began in 1899 and expanded greatly between the 1940s and 1970s (Hurtado 1980: 260-65, 355-60).

Members of the oligarchy often speak of the Ecuadorian nation, in the abstract and from historical perspective, as *mestizo* (mixed), and freely and affectionately call one another *cholo* or *cholito* (undefinable at this point but think of a stable, "mixed"-brokerage racial category), *negro* or *negrito* (black, dear black), or *viejo* or *viejito* (old one, dear old decrepit one—implying loss of power). That is to say, they address *equals* in such terms (there are no people remotely classifiable as *negro* or *cholo* in the elite groupings, and people who *are* old are not addressed as *viejo*); but they regard themselves as *blanco* (white), and refer to one another in terms that are non-ethnic or non-racial. *Blanco* is inextricably tied to the concept *culto*, and the casual, affectionate-address use of ethnic contrast terms while using the familiar *tú* form of the second-person pronoun sets the elite, as civilized carriers of Ecuador's culture, apart from those in the economically defined classes.

Within what many social scientists (e.g. Leeds 1964; Germani 1962) call the "classes," personal, self-identification is clearly *blanco*, though the reference terminology varies considerably, reflecting a collective emphasis on phenotypic variability. Aspiring intellectuals like school-teachers and university students often assert, in the plural, that they are *mestizos*. But care is taken in the deployment of address terms to maintain respect terminology (the *usted* form of the second-person pronoun), and an avoidance of words like *cholo* or *negro* directed to those in the same socioeconomic category who manifest phenotypic traits suggesting indigenous or black "blood." People in the classes, however, use terminology freely in a referential manner as they speak of the *longos* (Carvalho-Neto 1964) or *indios* (both Quichua-speaking peoples of the Sierra), or of the coastal *negros* (blacks) of Esmeraldas Province, *montubios* ("unrulies") of Manabí, *monos* (monkeys) of Guayas, of the *indios* or *salvajes* (Indians or savages) of the Oriente, or of the *yumbos* (half-civilized, dependent, poor Indians) there.

While characteristics of the oligarchy's address pattern typify those near the top of the economic class hierarchy, such terms disappear completely as address words from the middle to the bottom of the hierarchy. At or near the bottom one finds little, if any, use of the *tú* address form, little use of cognate familiar constructions, but increased deployment of a third form, *vos*. *Vos* is an archaic address term for "you," used by elites and upper-class people for their servants. Low-class people address one another by this term to express respect for one another, but it is also used by low- to middle-class people as a demeaning, status-differentiating marker of address for people classed as, or classifiable as, one of the two antitheses of *blanco*: *negro* and *indio*. Use of *vos* and even *tú* is complex in Ecuador as class-defined status and ethnic-defined status intertwine in specific regional contexts, and as access to economic wherewithal and ethnic affiliation influence one's position in society. Polysemy—using a term to mean different things—is an ever-present possibility as one descends the class hierarchy because, basically, the less economic clout one has, the more he or she may be regarded, stereotypically, as manifesting ethnic characteristics that contrast in an undesirable way with those associated with the elite. The easiest way to describe the structure within which these polysemic uses of address and referential terminology for "you," "us," and "them" unfold is by a diagram.

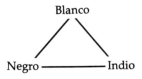

Blanco

Negro ——————— Indio

This tripartite paradigm pervades every structure at every level in Ecuador. No one of the three points of contrast can be dropped without missing a fundamental significance in interpersonal stereotyping and classification. Basically, Ecuador's historical dynamic is established by the insistence on the fusion of three *peoples*, denoted by the Spanish term *raza*. The *raza*, that for which the "day of the *raza*" is established and celebrated nationally and internationally, is that of Spain specifically, Iberia more generally, and Europe in still more general terms. This is the source of "culture" and of "society." The *raza* is *blanco*: it is "we" who are "true Ecuadorians." The phenotypic variation from Iberia was tremendous, ranging from blond and blue-eyed through dark, swarthy, *ladino* (Afro-Iberian mixture). Because of the phenotypic variation within the *raza*, *blanco*ness is defined in terms of adherence to "culture," to "civilization." This process of acquisition of desirable culture and civilization, as an entranceway to "society," is often called *blanqueamiento* (whitening). But the majority of Ecuador's people, it will be remembered, are regarded as "mixed." So *blanqueamiento*, through a history of regaining Iberian civilization in the New World generally and in Ecuador specifically, has led to *mestizaje*, to phenotypical and genotypical intermingling. The fundamental Latin American modification to the diagram is indicated below.

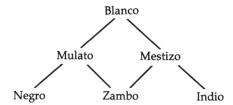

Here the genetic intermingling of *blanco* with *negro* produced *mulato*, a mixed category; the mixing of *blanco* with *indio* produced *mestizo*, a mixed category.

Consider the concept of *civilización*. "Civilize" derives nationally today, through the republican era and back through the colonial era, from being *blanco*. Past indigenous civilizations are acknowledged as existing, and (with some notably and overtly racist exceptions) the concept of past indigenous civilizations syncretizing with Iberiana is acknowledged. In this way *mestizaje* (or *indomestizaje* as it is sometimes called) becomes more than a *blanco-indio* admixture of phenotype and customs; it becomes an all-encompassing *raza*, or people, or nation. But again, since the mixture signals past contributions rather than present peoples, the act of "becoming national" is seen as a process of ethnic lightening, of movement toward Iberian culture, of *blanqueamiento*. White remains in a superordinate position of desirability over *mestizo* for those who are not *indio* or *negro*.

To complete the paradigm, then, *negro* mixed with *indio* to produce *zambo*. In addition to being the third "mixed" category of the triangular paradigm, *zambo*ness may also be regarded as intrusive into the concept of *mestizaje*, and more so vis-à-vis *indomestizaje*. Although no concept today of past civilization attaches to this category, in Ecuador (or Colombia or Peru, for that matter), the idea of inner strength does come through. *Mestizaje* as a doctrine is also polysemic. On one side it expresses a concept of miscegenation, of genetic mingling. It may subsume the concepts of *mulato, mestizo,* and *zambo* as "mixed." As such it contrasts with *blanco, negro,* and *indio,* differentiating each as "nonmixed" (and by extension "non-national") and places *blanco* in a superior position to *mestizo* as "being civilized" is superior to "becoming civilized."

Let us turn to the two paradigms that emerge from segmenting the *blanco-negro-indio* one into two sets of three mixed categories, *mulato, negro, zambo,* and *mestizo, zambo, indio:*

Here we have two models of social structure that are "below the classes" in contemporary Ecuador. Each triangle replicates national ethnic/class structure. In short, the concept of *mestizaje* can be manipulated so as to relegate the lightest of the mixed categories (*mulato, mestizo*) to the top of a pyramid of prestige, while keeping *negro* and *indio* at the far extremes. *Zambo,* as the least *negro* and most *indio* of the *blanco-mulato-negro* descent model and as the most *negro,* least *indio* of the *blanco-mestizo-indio* descent model, assumes the role of anomaly in some contexts, or disguised "paradigm filler" in other contexts.

In Ecuador today peoples who maintain a subsistence existence, who manifest lifeways at odds with cultural features associated with *mestizaje* and *blanqueamiento* are, if "black" by phenotype, regarded as marginals or cultists. If they are indigenous by phenotype or stereotype, they are regarded as either peasants or primitives. People classed as *cholos* or *cholas* are often seen as brokers to such marginals, peasants, or primitives. The concept of *chola* is attached to marketing women, and concepts of shamanic power are sometimes attached to *cholos*. *Cholo* may be synonymous with *mestizo*, and the process of *choloficación*, from the standpoint of lower classes or subsistence-oriented peoples, is often regarded as the acquisition of an ability to interact in urban contexts as urban dwellers without recourse to symbols of ethnic patronage or ethnic asymmetry. Hence, *choloficación* may be taken as part and parcel of an ideology of *mestizaje* that, in the process of *blanqueamiento*, runs right up against the *blanco-mestizo* ethnic/economic barrier that separates the oligarchy of Ecuador from the class-mobility system, which is itself oriented to the social values of the oligarchy. This is illustrated in Figure 1.

This pyramidal template reflects the cognitive ordering of Ecuadorian developmentalism. Upward mobility into and through the classes involves *blanqueamiento*, but the *mestizo* contrast with *blanco* closes the class-mobility system by restrictive criteria. Polysemy in the *mestizo*

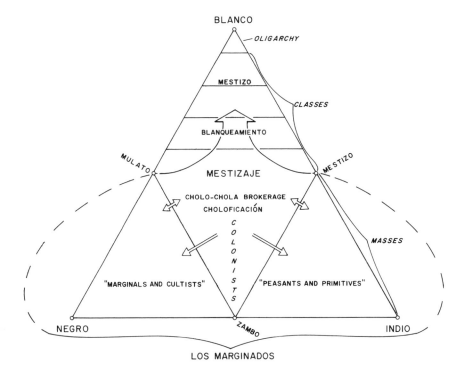

Figure 1. Developmentalist Ordering of Ecuadorian Social and Ethnic Structure

ethnic marker is manifest by dual positioning on our pyramid. For those classed *negro* and *indio* to be of the nation but different, ideologues come up with the concept of *marginado* (margined), and stereotypes reflecting differentiation of black from native serve to constitute contrast sets which vary from area to area.

Over the past two decades, between 1961 and 1981, the weight of this class/ethnic pyramid and the myriad of assorted concepts put into practice by a burgeoning, developmental-capitalist-oriented central bureaucracy came to encompass sectors of the techno-economic, social, and cosmological system of Ecuadorian Amazonia (see N. Whitten 1981a). As the tangible infrastructure within the city of Puyo grew and radiated to the hinterland, the Amazonian fringe-land sketched in the first section of this chapter became tenuously incorporated into a pyramid that has its apex in the office of the president of the republic.

From near invisibility in 1961, an indigenous movement gained national status in 1981 to move the *indio* point of the paradigm directly into the realm of the oligarchy, bypassing the route of *blanqueamiento* and resonating with the emergent ideology of *indomestizaje*. Chapter 6 deals with some features of this movement, together with its pragmatic and symbolic underpinnings.

While the movement gained in national and international status, members of Nueva Esperanza/Nayapi Llacta vigorously explored not only the dimensions of their own ensnaring microcosm of the national social order, but dimensions belonging to Upper Amazonian cultural ecology as well. In many ways the Puyo Runa became "wrapped up" in development policies and practices. But in just as many ways they cut through such ensnaring bonds, to move on to other events and episodes.

A FRAMEWORK FOR ANTHROPOLOGICAL ANALYSIS

One of the many vexing problems in the social sciences relates to the issues arising from the study of consistency in radical change. In a modern OPEC nation such as Ecuador, the problem is compounded when concepts are drawn uncritically from domains where the concepts of growth and development have analytical strength. If we take a simple anthropological definition (Carneiro 1967) that states that growth refers to the expansion of like units and that development refers to the introduction of new units, we have analytical clarity. For example, a hamlet south of Puyo has a normal size of from 50 to 200 people, and this size grouping can exploit tropical forest and urban resources reasonably and comfortably. If, then, such a hamlet divides when factions of its some 150 people start squabbling over resources and 50 or so hive off to form another site in the larger territory, we have an example of social "growth." But if, in the face of social fission, instead of hiving off to a spatial-social replication, an office of the national government is implanted in Nueva Esperanza/Nayapi Llacta, with authority to impose sanctions on those who squabble too vigorously with one another, with the right to impose taxes and to redistribute the concentrated funds not only of the taxed community but also funds drawn from other communities, then we could say that Nueva Esperanza/Nayapi Llacta has experienced "social development." The problem, of course, with such "technical" language is that the metaphor of growth toward maturity, toward something "better," is, by analogy, implied. In fact, the etymology of development may be more apt: Nayapi Llacta is, indeed, becoming wrapped up in the process of Nueva Esperanza's "development," and its reactions to increased developmental packaging may—indeed probably will—be surprising. Thousands of years of cultural-ecological experience and consequent knowledge systems do have their effects, the principal one of which is a symbolic structure by which experience can be related to knowledge and by which rational interpretation leading to social praxis is enhanced.

Analysis of such situations must take place at several levels. One level involves us in understanding activities in Nueva Esperanza/Nayapi Llacta in terms of the political economy of the nation-state as it impinges on the techno-environmental efficiency of Upper Amazonia. Another level of analysis takes us to the structure and praxis of power and processes of social reproduction that have evolved out of the Upper Amazonian tropical forest-riparian-swidden techno-environmental efficiencies and pan-ecological, cosmological underpinnings of Andes-Amazonia. When we apply the structure and praxis of power vis-à-vis a changing political economy we can come to grips with consistency in radical change.

Political Economy and the Frontier

Settings in which issues of consistency in radical change crop up are frequently those that we call "frontier" ones. A frontier is, at one and the same time, a region unto itself and a region defined by a distant centrality. That distant centrality today generally has two dimensions, that of its nationality and that of its statehood. Both nationalism and state bureaucracy extend and permeate inevitable geographic, ecological, economic, social, ethnic, and cultural limits, and by so doing create boundaries conceived of from the center's perspective as the frontier—

that which is both a limit to and a threshold of further expansion or contraction. One consistency at the boundary is that of acquiescence in the face of overwhelming official control of capital resources; another consistency is that of threshold transcendence through the manipulation of extant paradigms in novel ways. The consistencies, as the loci for patterned oppositions, must be understood as part of a common formation in many plural cultural and ethnic systems.

Two unusual ethnographies of the early 1950s—*Caravan: The Story of the Middle East* and *Tristes Tropiques*—different though they are, provide ethnographic markers with theoretical implications for understanding the lifeways of people bound up in increasing nation-state control. The first of these is the product of the somewhat romantic writings of Carleton S. Coon. *Caravan* takes us on a sojourn that begins with the order of a cultural mosaic from which we eventually arrive at the end of order, in the land of insolence. Although no structuralist, Coon did hammer away at a most salient contrast, which exists "between the *tame and the insolent*, the domestic and the independent, which makes provision for the supply of rebels who, since the beginning of the Bronze Age, have kept urban civilization of the Middle East refreshed and in motion" (Coon 1951: 295; see also Gulick 1976: 30-47; Geertz 1973: 297). Coon emphasizes that the concept "land of insolence" (*bled al-makhzan* also means disorder or dissidence) contrasts systemically with the land of government—the loci of nation-states of the Middle East. He goes on to argue that the "insolent" are either organized or potentially organized into a series of "institutions" ranging from extended families and clans, through "tribes," and on into "federations and confederations" (Coon 1951: 319), and that the series itself articulates with its urban antithesis: civilized society. Coon also stresses that segmentary opposition is the driving mechanism for both increasing levels of complexity through alliance and the processes of fission and realliance.

Out of analyses such as Coon's, and of course those of Evans-Pritchard (1940, 1948), Bohannan and Bohannan (1953), E. Peters (1963, 1970), Gluckman (1965), Barth (1959), Gulick (1955), and others, anthropology made breakthroughs in the analysis of organizations lying outside of effective nation-state bureaucratic control. But in the process of making its contributions, cultural anthropology's very rigor of ethnographic precision implied that such systems of segmentary opposition could be understood in their own right, without recourse to the distant centralities to which they were, at least tenuously, attached, and by which the very nature of their segmentation was to some extent influenced (Fried—e.g. 1967, 1975—is a notable exception, as are Gulick 1955, 1976, and Geertz 1973).

We must consider, with Coon, the so-called tribal people of the Middle East and elsewhere to be both within and beyond effective control, and (following Adams 1975) must separate *control* from a concept of *power*. The frontier, in short, must be considered to be a region characterized by the dynamics of nation-state expansion and contraction, as well as by its own simultaneous autonomy, resistance, acquiescence, change, and persistence.

Let us consider the concept of political economy, keeping culture in mind in the process. Clark Wissler, a scholar concerned with cultural ecology and well grounded in diversity and consistency of cultural traits among North American native peoples, argued that there is a universal patterning to culture. Following many scholars—all of whom established the basis for a modern, humanist science of anthropology in the nineteenth century—he listed many basic features of all societies, including material traits, property, society, government, knowledge, and art, as universals. Within any given culture all such universals are related to one another systemically. As such, culture—as a template of correspondences—articulates human thought to the environment, the cosmos to ecology, and, of course, the tangible and the intangible to the nature of human relations—to society—itself (see, e.g., Kroeber 1963 [1939]: 5-6). Recently, Harris (1968, 1979) recast the notion of universal pattern to make it correspond, in his opinion, to the material dimensions of a general theory of society offered by Karl Marx. By so doing Harris sought to bring a macro-materialist, Marxian perspective to the understanding of culture, and thereby to eschew critical analysis of human relations that at another level allows us to utilize native concepts and their analogs to gain insight for further interpretation. Harris takes ecology as his base, social structure as a system of resource allocation, and regards ideology as a device for organizing ideas so as to justify the system of resource allocation while mystifying that very system to its participants. Harris places a universal patterning of culture on a vertical axis, thereby giving primacy to the base.

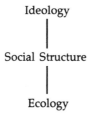

Ideology

Social Structure

Ecology

I am sympathetic to the ideas that lie behind this ordering of cultural patterns and agree that it helps us understand some key facets of state

systems and perhaps even some important features of chiefdoms and
"big man" systems. But premature vertical presentation is simplistic;
it reduces cosmology to ideology and confines it to a realm of mystification and obfuscation, thereby severely restricting the utility of seeing
social structure in its various pragmatic and symbolic dimensions.

Let us begin less precipitously with a horizontal ordering of cultural
universals. By ecology we refer to environmental parameters and the
interaction of humans through their technologies with the habitat.
Social structure includes human activities and interactions, their strategies and networks, the social formations that they consciously and
unconsciously construct—those that they tell us about, those that we
induce from observation, and those that we infer from analysis. Cosmology refers to thoughts about the cosmos, including environment
and social relations, the seen and the unseen, the tangible and the
imagined, that render the whole or its segments into a system of
conceptualized order embracing disorder.

Ecology —————— Social Structure —————— Cosmology

Human activities themselves are constituted into a series of pattern
generalizations that in turn seem to correspond to levels which range
from repeated behavioral interactions to rules and regularities. For this
reason many scholars see a hierarchical relationship between human
behavior (interaction), social organization, and social structure (e.g. Firth
1951; see also Leach 1960, Murdock 1960, and discussants such as
Sahlins 1976).

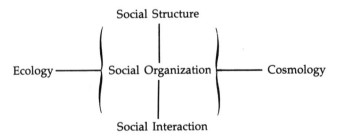

The materialist strategy of Harris (and the cultural-ecological meth-
odology of predecessors such as Julian H. Steward, Robert Murphy,
and Eric R. Wolf) teaches that the articulation between ecology and
social structure occurs systemically as social relations themselves serve
to *allocate resources*. Resource allocation as a social system of wealth

distribution is what we refer to as *economy*. Social structure also corresponds to sets of ideas which we call *ideology*, and economy and ideology both have pragmatic and symbolic dimensions.

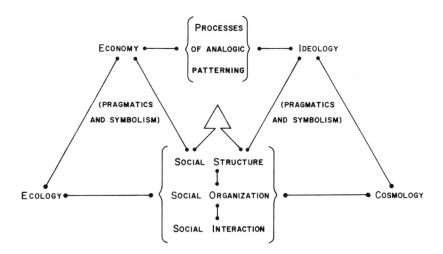

In such a view, economy and ideology are systemically related to one another by the constitutive cultural processes of analogic patterning.

To complete this picture we need only place the notion of *political economy* at the apex of our hierarchy of concepts. Political economy conjoins public policy of the state with the organization of wealth to constitute a unified system of control of resources, including such dimensions of human thought as can be projected through various institutions. We now have ecology–social structure–cosmology as a horizontally ordered universal human baseline subject to continuous cultural patterning (including transformation and change), and political economy as a specific system of wealth distribution and resource control. Political-economic forces emanate from the formal and informal apparatus of the expanding nation-state. State economy and its transformations mediate policy and ecosystem parameters, on one hand, and state ideology (in interaction with its competitors) mediates state civic religions and cosmological formations of a given people, on the other hand. The interactions of economic-social structural-ideological factors lead to processes of analogic patterning which in turn generate replicating consistency in such institutions as law, politics, and religion.

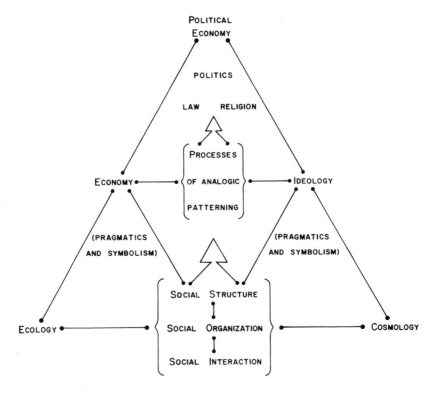

Carleton Coon's contribution to this otherwise static picture of a political economy–driven system is that each centralization of a political economy has its frontiers and that the frontier itself provides oppositional processing of every system of control. Coon's striking statement that the Middle East's land of insolence or dissidence, which "makes provision for the supply of rebels who, since the beginning of the Bronze Age, have kept urban civilization . . . refreshed and in motion" must be projected into our current world and built into every model of society.

Power, Cultural Consistency, and Social Reproduction

The perspective above helps the anthropologist to keep sight of the omnipresence of the expansionist state—the "structure of domination," as many Marxists call it. But it can also cause us to lose sight of the generative powers of ongoing cultural systems. Such systems are not only caught up in the webs of bureaucratic expansion attendant on state control, they also contain the capacities to cut and to re-spin, as it were, the strands that constitute networks of internal relations, and to some degree to overcome the barriers of emergent, sporadic, and omnipresent control systems. We must, then, also deploy a set of concepts that allows us to understand how people produce what they need, reproduce their webs of relationship in a meaningful way, and gain the power necessary to respond to contingencies, constraints, inducements, benefits, and costs.

At about the same time that Carleton Coon was publishing his material on the Middle Eastern cultural mosaic, Claude Lévi-Strauss was casting his deep, structuralist gaze upon an ethnographic journey across Central and Amazonian Brazil. Coming early to the issue of power within the antipodes of the civilized and the savage worlds, and his own trip to the farthest point in the universe (the Tupí-Kawahib village deep in the rain forest north of the Tapajós River), Lévi-Strauss offers an insightful foreword to his own sojourn by invoking his conceptualization of a North American Indian power quest:

> The man who wishes to wrest something from Destiny must venture into that perilous margin-country where the norms of society count for nothing and the demands and guarantees of the group are no longer valid. . . . Once in this unpredictable borderland a man may vanish, never to return; or he may acquire for himself, from among the immense repertory of unexploited forces which surrounds any well-regulated society, some personal provision of power and when this happens an otherwise inflexible social order may be cancelled in favor of the man who has risked everything (Lévi-Strauss 1964 [1955]: 41).

Both Coon and Lévi-Strauss felt that the delicate balance achieved by the non-urban could not survive modern, quasi-industrial society and the attendant expansion of the nation-state. But both of them picked out qualities of peoples who indeed were surviving, and who valued greatly the rich quality of survival's cultural processes. This is what places these scholars in "forebear" position with regard to theory development. Both of these influential anthropologists, however, saw disaster ahead for the "insolent" and the "savage." In his own way, each of these eminent scholars abandoned his subject matter at the end of his journey, and in so doing brought his story to a premature close.

In this book we deal with data drawn from a setting characterized by both pervasive nationalism (often regionally defined) and ethnic surgency (often with nationalist rhetoric). Here both nationalism and ethnicity are characterized by what Geertz (1973) calls "epochalism" (the position of a nation or ethnic bloc in world society at a given time) and "essentialism" (the publicly espoused ethnic-cultural underpinnings of a surgent unit) to contribute to the understanding of ethnic plurality. Rather than take a journey, though, we anchor this discourse in one place, and rather than close the story, we leave the plot, with its proclivities for repatterning, open.

To begin, let us return to the horizontal system of ecology-social structure-cosmology. Our task now is to understand a given culture in terms of replicating patterns of thought and action. These are the phenomena normally studied by anthropologists. The trick of seeing consistency within different realms of culture revolves around the ability of an ethnographer to understand and translate into scholarly discourse the ways by which the people with whom we live, work, and study see things. Most of us think that such an ethnographic enterprise is enlightening and clarifying; a few of our colleagues, notably today Marvin Harris and some of his students, feel that we are "mystified" by such thought systems.

We seek, first, an understanding of the production of goods, services, resource allocations, etc., in some consistent manner. This, in turn, demands a system of reproduction of form. In the late nineteenth and early twentieth centuries great thinkers such as Karl Marx in the *Grundrisse* and Marcel Mauss in *The Gift* came up with a simple if difficult-to-grasp transformation that pervades all cultures: People tend to see the order of their social relations as a set and flow of goods, and they tend to view their goods and the relations by which they are produced as natural. The rules for social reproduction—by means of which both cultural continuity and cultural transformation take place—correspond to the rules for material production. Rules are recognized by patterned consistency, which permeates all realms of socioculture, including what we call legend, myth, history, religion, folklore, and magic. The anthropologist comes to understand such consistency by examining correspondences from one domain to another. This emphasis on "reading" the various means by which people communicate unites the disparate modes of anthropological analysis from neo-Marxists such as Michael Taussig, to structuralists such as Marshall Sahlins, to post-structural semioticians such as Clifford Geertz, to dramaturgical symbolists such as Victor Turner. What separates "us" from more orthodox Marxists, from cultural materialists, and from Lévi-Straussian structuralists is our insistence that the peoples with whom we live and work—our "informants" or "consultants"—can and do read with us (e.g. see Geertz 1983). *Reflexivity* and the spinning of yarns (now called "webs of signification" in more technical parlance) for the native exegete, in other words, may be as analytical as mystical. The job of the anthropologist is *intersubjective*; as such, it is interpretive (Geertz 1973, 1983; Dolgin, Kemnitzer, and Schneider 1977; Whitten and Ohnuki-Tierney 1981).

We seek in this work a clearer perspective of a double set of consistencies—one emanating from the political economy of the nation-state, the other from the generative base of native cultural ecology. This brings us back to the duality of power patterning, where paradigm manipulation of bureaucratic efficiency and commercial activity contrasts with paradigm manipulation of ecological imagery and the replication of Upper Amazonian socioculture. The contrast is based upon the confluence or forced coincidence of the two systems, not upon the imposition of logical oppositions. Duality of power patterning probably exists in all systems, but it becomes especially salient in situations such as the one we are examining. On the left side of the next diagram is what is often called "infrastructure." Here we have the control of resources, processes of energy conversion, and the sheer use of force.

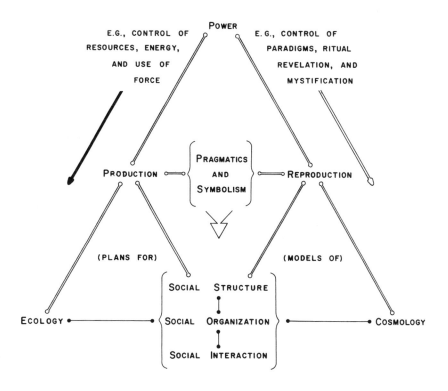

The "plans for" an economy of, say, increased commercial production based on timber extraction, cattle-raising, and sugarcane are actual blueprints for development that pervade every aspect of economy, ecology, and social life. On the other side we have paradigmatic control, such as when a bureaucrat recites his developmental rhetoric that people will become civilized, healthy, and wise as their wealth increases by development of commercial products; or when a shaman diagnoses a person's illness to be the result of one person's success at another's expense in the capitalist market. These "models of" society are themselves interpretive and reflexive; they give people metaphoric-metonymic bundles by which to render meaningful and mysterious the consistent and the transformed. The "superstructure" side of this diagram, then, regards ritual revelation and mystification to be part and parcel of the same processes of pan-human symbolization. Our duality deals with "energetic" and "psychic" forces (Adams 1975) vital to the study of power. A political economy of the state, powerful though its systems of control may be, cannot override the natural dynamics and properties of energetics; it cannot prevent entropy, or wasted energy, from occurring as a predictable complement to increasing efficiency. Nor can a political economy, even in its most sophisticated dimensions of planned thought control, overcome the cognitive and symbolic processes of cultural ordering (see, e.g., Turner 1975; Therborn 1980).

We turn now to the concrete in social life, to a small hamlet south of urban Puyo in Amazonian Ecuador which is subject to constant incorporation as Nueva Esperanza into the nation-state of Ecuador and objectified in indigenous thought as a projection of Nayapi Llacta into the nation-state. This is the site where magical frogs signal the coming of machinery, where a powerful shaman's advice is sought to understand the nation's political economy, and where inner reflection provides a means for coping with processes established by massive energy conversion attendant upon foreign-sponsored, but nationalist-sought, industrialization. This is but one of thousands of pulsating cultural microcosms around the rim of Amazonia wherein power is outwardly radiated and inwardly controlled—where the force of the expanding nation-state swirls and eddies and refracts in its indefatigable and painful penetration.

3

Social Organization

"Social life proceeds somewhere between the imaginary extremes of absolute order, and absolute chaotic conflict and anarchic improvisation. Neither the one nor the other ever takes over completely. There is an endless tension between the two, and also remarkable synchrony."—Sally F. Moore and Barbara G. Myerhoff, eds., *Secular Ritual* (1977), p. 3.

". . . within order, however uncomfortable one's position, one at least knows what the position is, while chaos, by definition, admits of no easy or constant definitions about anything."—Bruce Jackson, "Inversion in Action" (1979), p. 274.

Nueva Esperanza is a small but modern hamlet lying on the north side of Nayapi Llacta, about two kilometers in from the very edge of a 17,000-hectare communal territory. The existence of Nueva Esperanza concretizes the ideology of incorporation into the Ecuadorian nation-state; in turn, such existence depends upon the cultural and environmental resources of its Upper Amazonian Nayapi Llacta.

Today Nueva Esperanza features a school with twenty-nine students in its six grades. These young Quichua-speaking scholars are taught in Spanish by a *costeño* teacher who comes in from his home in Puyo on Monday and returns there Friday noon. In addition to the school there is a Dominican chapel and a "sporting club." There are only five family houses on the plaza and, if pressed, people say that many of their relatives moved away ("farther inside") due to "problems." The hilltop plaza looks southward over virgin and disturbed forest punctuated by *chagra*s toward the Pastaza River; eastward toward the verdure-canopied hills flanking the Puyo River; westward toward cow pasture with magnificent snow-capped Andean mountains as backdrop; and due north, where the jungle is broken by pasture, and where a gray-brown road slashes to within half a kilometer of the river that flows by the bottom of the hill.

On any given day Nueva Esperanza may be a beehive of activity, or it may seem virtually abandoned. It is characterized by a predictable flow of routine activities that depend, in part, on whether or not school is in session. The daily flow itself is punctuated by crises, breaches, restorations, rituals, festivities, intrusions, births, marriages, and deaths. Stable though Nueva Esperanza may seem to be as a little community in a beautiful location steadily incorporating into the regional culture of the nation of Ecuador, the hamlet and all others like it also represent a regime of chaos that mediates the antinomies of indigenous society and its system of ecosystem exploitation and maintenance, on one side, and national developmentalist, stratified, capitalist society, on the other. People flee the chaos born of contradiction; their flight reinforces the growing structure of antinomy that envelops them. To understand such strange, contradictory mediation it is necessary first to come to grips with the syncretic patterning of Upper Amazonia wherein the Canelos Quichua have emerged ethnically over the past few centuries, building upon previous cultural syncretisms and thousands of years of environmental and cosmological knowledge.

SEGMENTARY UNITY

Sacha and Chagra

Sacha means rain forest in the Quichua of the Amazonian region; it means "bush" or "uncivilized, untamed land" in contemporary Andean Quichua. *Chagra* is the swidden garden, the segment of jungle that is removed by males cutting trees, and restored to a system of growth by women planting manioc in what is called *chaquichishca panga allpa tucungahua* (dried leaf [litter] turning into soil), the underfoot leaf mat described in the previous chapter. *Sacha* and *chagra* are complex, contrasting cultural and natural forms unified by cosmological and ecological principles. The *chagra* is shifted periodically and allowed to grow back to forest. It is shifted as it becomes more diverse, and when its diversity reaches the point at which it is neither garden nor forest it is left to continue growing. Such old, second-growth garden sites/ new forest sites, known to be good hunting zones, are said to be a domain haunted by spirits.

Today, female-focused root-crop horticulture is basic to practical activities and symbolic expression. However, stories about events in *unai—*

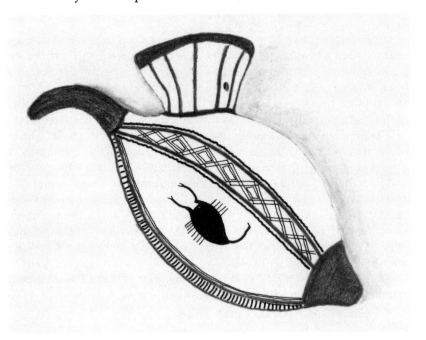

Sapallu (squash). Maker unknown, Sarayacu.

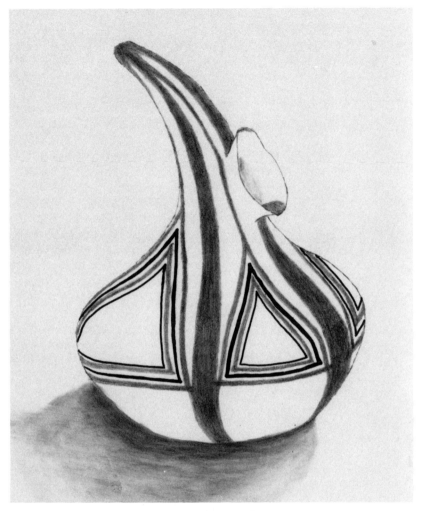

Pilchi (bottle gourd). Maker unknown, Montalvo.

mythic time-space—stress the male crop of maize and the female crop of squash. Such stories involve Jilucu, the whippoorwill-like potoo bird, and her moon-lover-brother-husband Quilla. Such origin myths of people involving maize and squash suggest an early Andean agricultural base. Nonetheless, other stories told on the *chagra* and in the forest, and all current practices on the *chagra* and in the forest, suggest a simple paradigm of contrasts and complementaries that stem from Amazonia.

Chagra is in the forest yet it contrasts with the forest. *Chagra* and forest depend upon water. But rain unbuffered is tremendously destructive. The water world—the hydrosphere—encompasses both *sacha* and *chagra*. The encompassment itself is the domain of Sungui, the

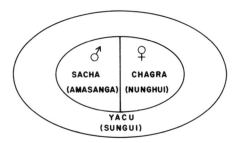

corporeal manifestation of whom is the anaconda. By extension, forest boas and even sometimes other snakes are thought of as manifestations of Sungui. Sungui is both male and female; as anaconda s/he may devour any living animal. Amasanga, forest spirit master, is also male and female. His many transformations (Amasanga *tucuna*) include not only a great tree (Ila supai), and the forest-cave-dwelling foreign peoples' spirit master (Jurijuri supai), but also the waterfall spirit (Paccha supai), and a spirit demon whose heart is carried outside his body (Ingaru supai). Amasanga's *sacha* world borders on and intrudes into the world of water and the domain of demons. Demons, who also may devour people, live in the water world and the forest world; but they are intruders—they are neither from the domain of Sungui nor from that of Amasanga. The word *supai* is used to tag spirits that are of their respective domains and to name intrusive demons.

In the myth segments where manioc gardens are created, Nunghui is walking in the jungle with her daughter, Junculu. Three men want to marry this daughter—Quindi (hummingbird), Acanga (hawk), and Sicuanga. "Which is the best worker?" wonders Junculu. They hear the sound of falling trees and much laughter in the forest—like a mighty worker clearing and clearing, so they go to see. There, on top of a hill, is Acanga (who is also called Atatau). He is picking up great rocks and heaving them into the forest, laughing all the while. The crashing and banging of boulders sound just like the felling of trees. Nothing is being cut, though, the forest is just being aroused. So Junculu says to Nunghui, "How can we make such an enormous *chagra*?" "Now we'll get a stick of manioc," Nunghui replies, and she and Junculu get lots of sticks—piles of them. Nunghui begins to dig with her palm-wood *tula*, and she digs and digs and becomes exhausted. Junculu

Nunghui with toucan-feather headdress. Teresa Dahua, *caserío* Nueva Vida, Comuna San Jacinto del Pindo.

Junculu. Faviola Vargas Aranda, *caserío* Río Chico, Comuna San Jacinto del Pindo.

says, "I'll now dig for you," and she digs half a *chagra* and can't continue. "When will we ever finish?" she says. "I can't work any more." But then she again attacks the ground with a *tula*; whack, whack—a great hole is made. Down goes Junculu into this hole, digging and digging. Nunghui says *"Suuuuuu* Junculu, *saquiringui"*; she blows on her daughter with her magical breath, saying "Stay that way," and turns Junculu into a large edible frog, and so Junculu remains, and so she is today. Junculu then says *"Suuuuuu* Nunghui mama, *saquiringui,"* and Nunghui stays as she is today—a harmless coral snake (several varieties classed by their niche—e.g., *jahua nunghui,* upper *nunghui,* who lives in the leaf mulch; *ucui nunghui,* inner *nunghui,* who lives in the mud-soil), with deadly venom but a mouth too small to bite even the little finger of a human. Quindi—the hummingbird—was made so by Nunghui; he became a male force in *chagra* dynamics. He may be Nunghui *cari* or Junculu *cari,* depending on the teller and the context.

Many myths pertain to forest spirit master Amasanga, and each has several variants. Most begin with Amasanga as Pasu supai, spirit of the *pasu* tree, high up picking fruit, and with a jungle woman, Sacha huarmi, below, either pregnant or with a newborn baby. A short version goes like this:

In *unai* Amasanga was Pasu supai; while he was up in the tree, he began to grow teeth, with which he would eat people, out of the back of his head. He was changing into Jurijuri. He dropped a *pasu* fruit down on top of Sacha huarmi—and some say on top of her child (which was his child), killing it. She, too, was growing teeth in the back of her head, and she was pregnant. Descending the tree Amasanga, as Jurijuri, and Sacha huarmi, as Jurijuri huarmi, go down under the soil, into a great lagoon, under the water, and then, moving like great earthmovers under the soil, they rumble on until they become located in a great cave inside of a big hill, where Jurijuri huarmi gives birth to a baby (after, in some variants, eating Amasanga). There, in the cave within the hill, jungle life expands as domesticated. This underearth, though, is foreign, in contrast to Nunghui's swidden garden domestication and in contrast to "our" hunting territory.

Forest spirit in male and female manifestations are givers of animals, of life, but they are also harbingers of death. A man may, for example, have a jungle spirit woman—*sacha huarmi*—whom he visits in a dream and who gives up much game to him. But if he takes her as wife he goes to live with her in a cave, in a hill, or under the water, and she devours him.

The forest nourishes and devours itself, and in its balance it depends upon the water for continuous nourishment, while at the same time

Amasanga with his blowgun—note the teeth growing out of the back of his head. Juana Catalina Chango, *caserío* Río Chico, Comuna San Jacinto del Pindo.

Amasanga huarmi, who is pregnant—teeth grow out the back of her head also. Juana Catalina Chango, *caserío* Río Chico, Comuna San Jacinto del Pindo.

providing its own source of that very water. It is forever perilously close to the domain of Sungui.

Sacha and *chagra* are discrete entities: the first is the object of male predation through hunting and gathering; the second is the realm of female domestication through planting and harvesting. Men cut trees on the *chagra* and hunt there too—they are *chagra* predators, in contrast with women, *chagra* domesticators. Mythically, women drive men, as animals, from the *chagra*. Both *chagra* and *sacha* are contained by the hydrosphere—by the ever-present, life-giving, potentially destructive force of the encompassing water world. These relationships are both natural and spiritual. To tamper with them is to produce culture, and to court disaster.

Huasi

This is the household, the oval structure symbolizing a contained universe divided into male and female parts. The male part may face

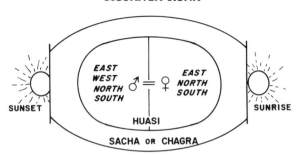

Huasi, male and female parts.

in any of the cardinal directions, but the female part may not face
west, the Andean land of sunset. The male side is *janaj*, up-river or
above, and the female side *urai*, down-river or below. Beyond the female
side, also called little house, *ichilla huasi*, is the woman's pottery shed.

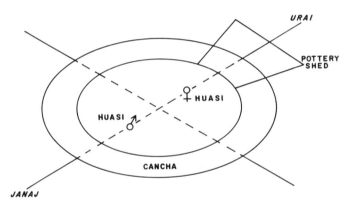

Huasi, up-river and down-river dimensions.

The *huasi* is analogous to a cell in biology. It is a nuclear, specialized
structure that contains all the general material to replicate society, the
material to transcend its internal form while projecting that form outward. The female *huasi* group, composed of wife-mother and her unmarried children, work the *chagra* together. The male *huasi* node is
husband-father, and he brings to the *huasi* its primary *ayllu* (kinship)
continuance just as, through mother-wife, *mama*, his *ayllu* continuance
is regenerated in the birth of their mutual children.

People visiting the household sit in the male area on a broken canoe
or on a bench symbolizing an anaconda. The male head himself sits
on a stool that represents the *charapa* (Amazonian water turtle), seat

Charapa—seat of power of Sungui. Apacha Vargas, *caserío* Nuevo Mundo, Comuna San Jacinto del Pindo.

of power of Sungui. When *ayahuasca* trips are taken, at night, in the female part of the house, an ancient waterfall or rain comes down over the top as shaman and patients sit on representatives of reptilian forms. The over-all cosmography suggests that *huasi* is analogous to the *chagra*-forest encompassed by water formation, a contained cultural universe within a tremendous hydraulic system of water above, below, and all around. *Cusca*, straight up, and *ucu*, straight down, are conceptualized from the center of the house. Drawing a line straight up and straight down through this center gives us the familiar *axis mundi* of Amazonian cosmology (e.g. Roe 1982). There is a clearing (*cancha*) around the house, broken only by a kitchen garden. The entrance to the house is *huasipungu*, whether by garden or clearing. Beyond the household is either *sacha* or *chagra*, the latter of which may be new or old. Earth below and sky above are encompassed by, and permeated by, water. The household is not only a replicative structure of the ecological one described above, it is also itself embedded in the ecological form and thereby bounded in its embeddedness by hydraulic power.

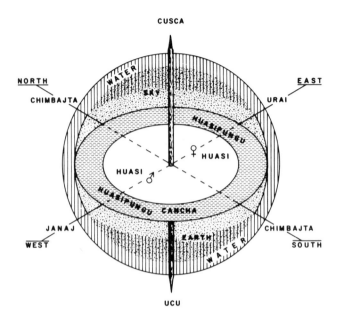

Huasi, various dimensions ordered around *axis mundi.*

Ayllu

With the *ayllu* or kinship system we come to the unity of segmentary oneness that binds the correspondences of *chagra-sacha* and *huasi* into one social formation. A powerful analogy is employed here to evoke the fundamental trope that unites the cosmos and biosphere, and places kinship and shamanism in their most enduring, mystical dimensions: *Runa ullu amarun tian* ("The Runa penis is anaconda"). A myth segment, regarded as obscene by the Runa and hence often told in somewhat circumlocutory formats, expresses this analogic trope that connects the natural world of sexual relations and indigenous kinship with the spirit world of Sungui, the water world, predation in garden and forest, and contained power.

Older and younger brother were on a *chagra* in the afternoon; in the evening they were talking and the younger said he wanted a woman. As the brothers later slept, a green frog came to the head of the younger, by his right ear, and perhaps its name was Piripiri. *Yucuna!*—the young man was having sexual intercourse with the green frog, against the warning of his older brother. The frog hopped; again and again it hopped. Younger brother's penis remained in the frog as it hopped and hopped away with the half-erect, half-limp penis still in it. The young man was *ungushca*, sick; the sickness was his penis because it had been pulled so long that he couldn't walk. It became *cauchullu* (*cauchu ullu*—rubber penis). Then the older brother went home to get help, but before he could get back Yacu puma (river jaguar—giant otter) was passing by in the river. He came to the younger brother and said, "What's happened?" And the youth said, "*Suni ullu saquirin*" ("Long penis stays that way") and sobbed, tears flowing. Yacu puma cut the penis with his machete; he cut it at just the proper length for humans to have. Then he cut up the rest of the elongated penis and put the pieces into his *ashanga* (basket). After that the younger brother went home to his *huasi*, while Yacu puma went down-river in his canoe, throwing the segments into every stream, every lagoon, each side of the big river, into the mouths of rivers and into the oxbow lakes. There the segments remain *amarun*, just as the penis remains *ullu* with the boy in his house. The male *ullu* in each *huasi* corresponds to the *amarun* of each river.

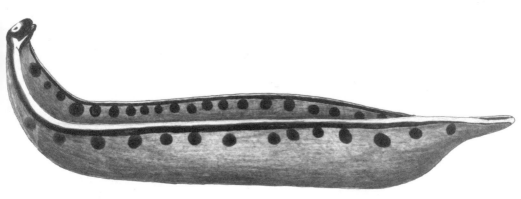

Yacu puma head as prow of *amarun cánua* (anaconda canoe). Apacha Vargas, *caserío* Nuevo Mundo, Comuna San Jacinto del Pindo.

Anaconda today comes out of the encompassing water domain—
out of stream, river, lagoon, or mud; as boa it comes from soil or
trees—to penetrate *sacha* and *chagra*, to hunt humans and other animals, and to devour them. The water domain itself is segmented into
distinct rivers and lagoons that often swell tremendously in rain-caused
flood. Men kill anaconda-boas and use their fat, brains, and jaws to
"make friends," to prevent an enemy from expressing anger, to prevent
one in authority from exercising his power. They never eat an anaconda,
boa, or any other snake, however. Shamans call the anaconda to the
huasi during healing sessions when cosmic ruptures have occurred and
when diagnosis is needed. To control the anaconda is to control power,
to unleash the anaconda is to unleash flood, to destroy the earth world
and its inhabitants.

Once material of this nature is elicited, people readily say that this
story of *cauchullu* explains the origin of the *ayllu*, the kinship of the
Runa. The Runa are one people, one system of male descent, but

Amarun motif around a pot for storing feathers, called *sicuanga manga* (toucan
pot). Pastora Huatatuca, *caserío* Unión Base, Comuna San Jacinto del Pindo.

the segments of the oneness have been cut by time and by distance. One Santi segment lives here, in Nayapi Llacta; another lives over there, in Río Chico; still another right nearby, at the Tashapi headwaters. Others are distant (*caru*), in Pacayacu, Sarayacu, and Teresa Mama on the Bobonaza River and Curaray on the Curaray River. Still others exist on the Conambo, Corrientes, and Capahuari rivers to the east, fanning north and south and even on into Peru. Wherever the *amarun* is found there too is our *ayllu*, for the human penis is anaconda.

Are there female *ayllu* too? The answer is yes, but people have to discuss the epistemology embodied in this question, and it is generally agreed that the *ayllu* must come by men through women. A man, with his penis, places an egg (*lulun*) in a woman, and the egg grows in its watery female womb into *lulun huahua llucshin*. That baby inherits his soul substance from his father and from his mother's father. A man calls his wife's father *yaya*, just as he calls his own father this. A constant constructionist occupation of the Runa is being sure that the soul substance (*aya*) from one generation to another is a replication, at least in part, of the segmentary unity through marriage occurring in past generations (see N. Whitten 1976; Whitten and Whitten 1984). The male child is extended into the *huasi* by the male substance of mother's father and child's father. As he grows he extends his soul substance out of the *huasi*, maintaining the *ayllu*. As the *ayllu* is maintained, so too is the *huasi* structure reproduced.

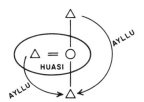

One can elicit at times, but not always, that *huarmi ayllu* is *sapumanda ayllu* (woman kinship is "from frog kinship"). Sometimes *junculumanda* is offered, sometimes not. Usually, the idea of explicit female kinship becomes mysterious, and analogies to evoke it just drift off. Tales from ancient time-space are called *ñaupa shimi rucuguna* (early ancestors' talk). A teller of such mythic texts is likely to jump to stories of re-generation involving fungi when explaining the origins of men and women, and the fungi allusions can lead in many directions. Yet another origin myth is set in a sector of ancient time-space when-where maize and squash were the crops of the *chagra*.

Jilucu, a potoo bird, had a beautiful lover who came to her *huasi* only at night. She wanted to know him better, so one night she painted

Two representations of *amarun* with break in pattern representing severed penis: (*above*) *amarun* motif with *yacu apahuais* (see Chap. 4)—Soila Aranda, *llacta* Sarayaquillu, Sarayacu; (*facing page*) *amarun* motif merged with zigzag and *charapa* patterns—Alicia Canelos, *llacta* Sarayaquillu, Sarayacu.

his face with *huiduj* (*Genipa americana*). In the pre-dawn morning she looked at the sky and saw her brother Quilla—the moon—there, with his face beautifully painted. She knew then that she had committed incest, that her children would be of both male and female *ayllu*, of potoo bird and moon *ayllu*, of which *ayllu* Manduru huarmi (red woman) and Huiduj huarmi (black woman) are sisters.

This myth segment is repeated again and again, and it is the dominant structure for ritual enactment in periodic festivals. The festivals begin with the bringing in of the outside world and the partitioning of the Runa world into Jilucu *huasi* and Quilla *huasi*, and they end when the power of the *amarun* is brought from the river to destroy (or devour)

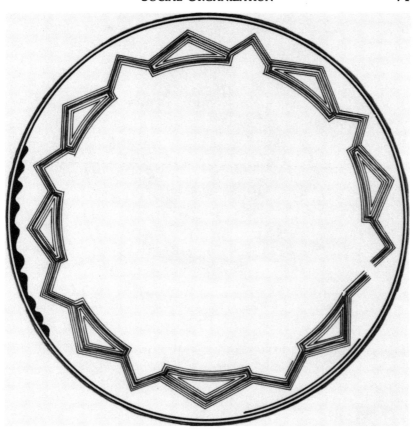

the earth world, and especially the invited foreigners. Through this ancient myth (which is also found in Asia, among the Eskimo, and in some areas of remote Mexico and southern South America), the solution to the continuity of male and female substance—male through female, female by male—is conceptualized.

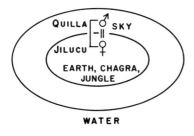

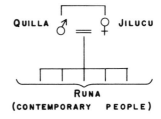

Jilucu (*left*) and Quilla (*right*) as two faces of the same festival pot. Alicia Canelos, *llacta* Sarayaquillu, Sarayacu.

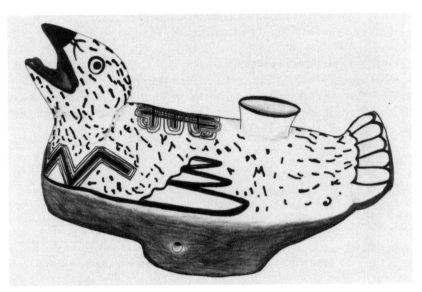

Jilucu. Apacha Vargas, *caserío* Nuevo Mundo, Comuna San Jacinto del Pindo.

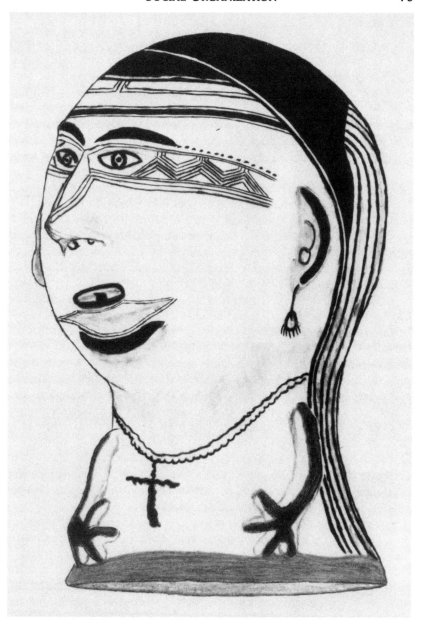

Quilla with face painted by Jilucu and wearing both toucan-feather earrings and Christian cross strung on *supai accha* (spirit hair). Maker unknown, *llacta* Sarayaquillu, Sarayacu.

Partimanda

The term *partimanda* is heard frequently among the Runa when they discuss one another. The term is a mix of the Spanish *partida* (division) and the Quichua suffix *manda* (from). Historically the term comes from the Spanish ecclesiastical and civil *reducciones* (centralizations, concentrations, and "reductions") of Amazonian people living in dispersed habitats. Often such peoples spoke different languages and made up different segments of a nucleated community dominated by a Catholic order. Peoples living in the dispersed residential patterns in Upper Amazonia themselves intermarried with individuals from other areas who spoke other languages. In fact, such intermarriage was even a requirement for the maintenance of social formations in some areas. For example, among many people in the Northwest Amazon a man was required to marry a woman from outside his own father's and father's father's descent group. Moreover, he had to marry a woman not only outside of such a patrilineal clan but also a woman who spoke a different language whom he would bring to live in his father's house (e.g. Sorensen 1967). By marrying a woman who was his mother's brother's daughter, a man could marry *a near relative* from a *social and spatial distance*. Whether or not native societies of central Amazonian Ecuador were ever quite so neatly structured is not clear, and we will probably never know what kinship system and ethnic system really preceded the present ones. We do know that the "reduced" segments of Amazonian societies brought together by priestly centralization contained, within each, members who were intermarried to other members who spoke different languages and who were related consanguineally to such other members as well. It is highly likely, as Naranjo (1977) and I (1976) have argued elsewhere, that the priests and administrators established their *reducciones* in refuge zones (such as Canelos) where residential nucleation for some portion of a given year, for some groups, was particularly evident before their arrival.

The concept *partimanda* today refers to where an individual's parents are said to have had their *quiquin llacta*, their proper territory. *Partimanda* is a geographic designation with cultural-ethnic-kinship implications. The cultural-ethnic implications can only be for the dominant cultural-ethnic-linguistic identity. Some bilingualism and biculturalism exist in every geographic territory that contributes members to the dynamic social system of Nayapi Llacta. *Ayllu* continuity is also represented by segments in every such territorial division. For example, Nayapi's grandson today says that he is from Nayapi Llacta. This is his *partimanda*. He has a large *ayllu* here. But his father (Nayapi's son) claims that Canelos is his *partimanda* and that, moreover, his mother is Achuar *partimanda* and his father's mother is Napo *partimanda*. In fact, everyone in Nayapi Llacta, and in adjoining territories as well, can trace parentage to some Achuar territory, to some Napo territory, and to a site on the Bobonaza River where peoples from the Napo and from the Achuar areas intermarried as *runapura*—humans among ourselves. In such marriages *ayllu* segments conjoined, creating small, complementary, segmentary unities amidst other such unities. Among these intermarrying humans of the Bobonaza system were other peoples speaking other languages. These include Zaparoan-speaking peoples, Jivaroan-speaking peoples, and perhaps some Tupian and Candoan speakers as well. As Christianity made tenuous inroads there developed a duality of ethnic patterning between the native person of the hamlet, of civilization, of Christianity—Alli Runa—and the person of the forest, of the animistic universe, of the spirit world—Sacha Runa. Alli Runa/Sacha Runa, I argue, are one and the same, the former facing the world of Christian conquest, its trade goods, destructive potential, and mystical power, the latter facing the indigenous world of ecosystem knowledge, society integrated by *ayllu* segmentary continuity, intermarriage, and mythology, and by its own system of spiritual power.

A convenient way to portray the dynamics of Nayapi Llacta today is by reference to a five-generational model of cultural-ethnic-linguistic identity and competence that ranges from the dispersed jungle settlement (domain of Sacha Runa) to complete participation in the town of Puyo (domain of Alli Runa). The value of such a model rests with two complementary facets of cultural tradition and ethnic affiliation of the area radiating out of Puyo in the twentieth century. One facet is that there are five distinct cultural traditions, each with its variants: Shuar, Achuar (both Jivaroan in language), Canelos Quichua, Quijos Quichua (both Quechuamaran), and Waorani (an isolate). Map 3 places these five cultural traditions in regional-territorial manner. Zaparoan-speaking peoples (Zapa-Záparo and Andoa-Shimigae) are salted through Canelos Quichua and perhaps Quijos Quichua territories. They figure into past Canelos Quichua cultural heritage, but do not play a part today as a traditional culture recast into an ethnic bloc. Waorani interaction with both Quijos Quichua and Canelos Quichua has been very reserved and often hostile until recently.

The primary streams of traditional culture and the primary emphases of contemporary ethnic affiliation that constitute Canelos Quichua cul-

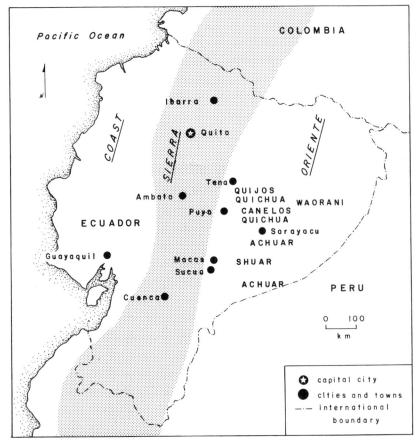

Map 3. Approximate Historical and Contemporary Locations of Native Peoples of the Oriente

ture stem from Achuar, Canelos Quichua proper, and Quijos Quichua peoples. To help conceptualize the contrasts and confluences in these three systems—each distinct yet intertwined—see Figure 2.

Although speaking the same language, with regional variations (described as Tena for the Quijos proper, Limoncocha for the lower Napo, and Bobonaza for the Canelos Quichua—Orr and Wrisley 1965), the Quijos Quichua (and here I include the Napo Quichua as well) and the Canelos Quichua are distinct cultures. The former seem to have had a *montaña* hearth, moving eastward as opportunities there presented themselves, and as pressures of colonization in their own area forced them out. By contrast, the Canelos Quichua seem to have had

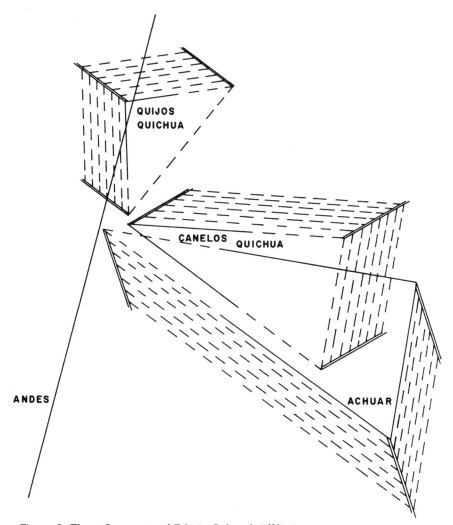

Figure 2. Three Segments of Ethnic-Cultural Affiliation

a more eastern hearth, and they moved westward according to a complex of factors yet to be thoroughly understood. In addition to historical
movement leading to convergence at the base of the Andes, Canelos
Quichua and Napo Quichua peoples clearly differentiate one another,
noting, at times, even the smallest of contrast sets (speech, ideas about
weddings, ideals with regard to marriage residence, group size, patterns
of agriculture—compare, e.g., N. Whitten 1976 with T. Macdonald

1979). So, looking at Figure 2 we should understand the Quijos Quichua and Canelos Quichua wedges to represent a clear and enduring distinction made by Quichua-speaking peoples of Amazonian Ecuador. Nonetheless, as we shall see, the people who belong to one wedge or the other intermarry. The next stream of traditional culture—the Achuar—is represented by the wedge that overlaps that of the Canelos Quichua. It extends more deeply and widely eastward, and penetrates a bit farther westward (not long ago up into the Río Topo and even today into the Río Llushín, right up into the Huamboya Mountains). From some standpoints, the Quijos-Canelos, as Quichua-speaking peoples, share many features (especially their language) with culture congeners of the high Andes. But in other features, the Canelos Quichua share more with the Achuar than with the Quijos Quichua. The message in this cryptic statement is that we—archaeologists, ethnohistorians, and ethnographers-ethnologists alike—have yet to come to grips with the deep, generative bases giving rise to the striking similarities and diversities that span the Andes and Amazonia.

A Model of Generational Mobility and Ethnic Structure

In this model I refer only to Achuar-Runa relationships. One could substitute "Zaparoan" for Achuar, especially if we could learn more of the Zaparoan social system. Recent history of Zaparoan-Achuar relationships stresses intercultural violence with Achuar achieving dominance. It is for this reason, and because I know more about the Achuar (thanks to recent research by Taylor and Descola), that this model is presented as Achuar-Runa. Bear in mind that this model is extremely general, designed primarily to gain a quick, and global, orientation to the relationship between cultural-ethnic contrasts as the contrasts relate to an ongoing process of complementary generational mobility.

Generation I

An Achuar (or Zaparoan) man or woman marries a Quichua speaker. He/she learns the language. If a man he normally moves to the area of the spouse's father; if woman she might move, but it is more likely that the man will move to her father's area. At this point it does not matter whether or not the man comes from Canelos Quichua or Napo Quichua language-dialect-culture areas. *Achuar culture dominates in Generation I regardless of residence site.* For men and women in this generation language is but a vehicle of communication and not a significant factor in cosmological insight. Should a man in this generation, however, become a shaman, or should a woman become a master potter, then the above statements must be modified, for in each unusual case (shaman-male, potter-female), cosmological manipulation (by use of two languages and two [transformable] sets of ideas about the cosmos and the world) is characteristic.

Generation II

Children learn Achuar as a first language and Quichua as a first language. They have true cradle bilingualism. They definitely migrate deeply into Canelos Quichua territory and marry at least into second generation and often into third or fourth generation. Maintenance of bilingualism (Achuar-Quichua) is a conscious act for the Achuar (i.e. they work at it) and secret for Zaparoans. Biculturalism, however, depends upon various motivating factors and can be secret for the Achuar. In other words, except for the maintenance of language competence, the Achuar in this generation are Canelos Quichua. Individuals in this generation are known in different ways in two geographical areas (e.g., in the Capahuari region and in the Canelos region). They maintain social ties and ecosystem knowledge in each of the two areas by periodic treks. Such treks, called *purina*, clearly cross demarcated cultural-ethnic-linguistic and topographic boundaries. Rumor and gossip about people in this generation often move into the shady area of negotiated killings. One is never sure of loyalty here and such people may well lay claim to a forest zone previously known for its no-man's-land-like qualities.

Generation III

This is the "pristine" Canelos Quichua generation, in which individuals are embedded in an artificial territorial division of a larger territory, *llacta*, as representatives of an *ayllu* segment intermarried in complementary ways with members of other *ayllu* segments. Marriage is either with another "pristine" Canelos Runa or with an Achuar migrant, but within a given siblingship, some brothers or sisters do marry into Generation II. Members of Generation III may also go out to marry Generation I Achuar, but it goes against the generalizations being made at this point for a Generation III to marry a Generation I and remain embedded in a Canelos Quichua *llacta* or *ayllu*. Such a Generation III–Generation I marriage constitutes an ethnic and social hiving off of the outmoving Generation III person. The children of Generation I-III, however, often return, as Generation II spouses, to Generation III life.

Generation IV

Men and women in this generation engage in systematic and sustained trade with alliances built up out of Generation III–townspeople (rural or non-Runa, quasi-Runa, or itinerant trader) relationships. These Canelos III–townspeople relationships themselves may involve some actual "mixed" progeny such that an "in" secret revolves around who in town is whose father in an area or kin group, who has a brother or sister in town known to other newer townsmen as non-Runa.

In Generation IV Achuar contacts are sustained and some "passing" in town takes place. Marriages with non-Runa take place and structural amnesia is legion. People in Generation IV participate in national culture as regionally defined. A sketch of these generalizations is given in the diagram below.

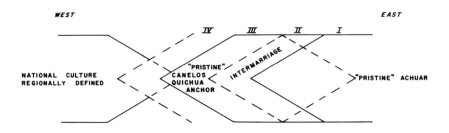

As drawn, this diagram of four generations of cultural-ethnic flow conjoins a number of extreme oppositions: Achuar/national; native Amazonian/Andean national; "Indian"/"white"; "savage"/"civilized"; and so forth. We return to this model repeatedly, elaborating as the story of Nayapi Llacta/Nueva Esperanza unfolds. For now, it is crucial to understand that the dynamics of the I-II-III-IV cultural-ethnic system are at work in every single family, in every *huasi*, in every *ayllu*, and in every territory.

Llacta

Llacta is the artificial division of a territory. As *ayllu* is a reference term for kinship, *llacta* is a term of the Andean social world that refers to territory. The Achuar have an implicit concept of such a dispersed, demarcated territory for hunting and for swidden horticulture (Descola 1981), but the Canelos Quichua name such a territory, associate it with an intermarried group of peoples (linked *ayllu* segments), and attribute its demarcation to mystical events involving shamanic activity and to occupational strategies adopted and deployed by interrelated, intermarried peoples. A *llacta* is often named after its founder (e.g. Nayapi Llacta); it is regarded as a present, demarcated spatial sector grounded in earlier events (*ñaupa llacta, ñaupa rucumanda llacta*). It is regarded as having people of the *llacta*, people whose *ayllu* ties are rooted there, and people who are new to the *llacta*—people who marry into *ayllu* segments rooted in the *llacta*. *Llacta* in Canelos Quichua refers to a minimal set of linked *huasis*, the members of which share *llacta* resources when resident in the *llacta*. As one goes further outward, conceptually, from a set of adjacent *llactas*, the concept *partimanda* again comes into play. A *llacta* is composed of a network of *huasis* linked by *ayllu* bonds on one side and by marriage bonds on the other. The *llacta* is an artificial division of the Upper Amazonian ecosystem and social system of the Canelos Quichua. Fundamental to the maintenance of an "integrated" *llacta* is a set of social and techno-economic strategies that maintains the structure of indigenous culture within its rain forest–riparian ecosystem. The keys to such maintenance are dispersal of population and the diversity of resources available to the dispersed population.

One mechanism of such dispersal is *purina*—intermarried *ayllu* segments of the *llacta* journeying together to a distant territory where they maintain another *chagra*, and where they hunt and fish and gather for part of the year. Another mechanism is temporary residence (from a few months to a few years) of a man or woman with his or her spouse's family. A third mechanism is population control within a *llacta* or expansion of the *llacta* territory attendant on population expansion.

NUCLEATED DIVISIVENESS

Caserío is the Spanish word for hamlet. The hamlet replicates feasible corporate features drawn from national culture and national society with an eye to increasing incorporation into regional administrative structure. A *caserío* is said by national developers to represent the stable, settled, agricultural, developing, Christian, civilized, "whitening" side of national life as opposed specifically to the unstable, nomadic, hunting-fishing-gathering, backward, heathen, savage, "Indian" side of Amazonian life. In the *caserío* people must draw from national infrastructure for capital support, just as they endeavor to maintain a meaningful set of lifeways and life-styles within a techno-economic relationship with the habitat that provides for basic subsistence needs.

Social and Ethnic Structure

For a *caserío* to grow and develop into a modern Ecuadorian political-economic structure it must accelerate its processes of nucleation. Nucleation of a community has particular features that impinge on all areas of life. The first of these is the imposed and unacceptable (from the Runa standpoint) dominant ethnic structure, which, in Nueva Esperanza, looks like this:

Here the Mestizo pinnacle represents the national ideology of racial mixture focused on the persons of the schoolteacher, the trader, and the administrators who come and go from Puyo on their various missions. It is the schoolteacher who instructs the children in the history of Ecuador, the indigenous tribes of the Amazonian region, and the glories past and ignorance present of all those for whom Spanish is not a first language. Mestizo-Zambu (Zambo becomes Zambu in Quichua) may run together as the Runa note hair form. If an outsider has kinky hair he is said to be "like a wooly monkey" (*cushillu shina*) crossed with a barley flour–chewing itinerant trader (*mashca pupu*). His origin in terms of the first expression is the Coast, in terms of the latter the Sierra, and often the history of such a person can be given quite accurately. Neither *mestizo* (usually *mashca* or *mashca pupu*—barley flour or barley flour umbilicus; or *ahualta* [*ahua llacta*]—highlander, but now also *mishu*) nor *zambu* peoples are regarded categorically as acceptable outsiders. They are intrusions from an Andean-coastal world that is not of the cosmogony that imparts soul, spirit substance, and acceptability in *unai* to these people. Representatives of this modern sector of the Andean world came with the Spaniards as conquerors; they sought to dominate the Runa. They did not evolve out of ancient time-space; they are clearly "here," but not "from here." They are forceful, coincident ubiquities. The nature of their soul substance is questionable.

At another transformation, we arrive at the ethnic structure indicated below as one variant of several analogous structures of many *caseríos*. An acceptable outsider (in some contexts) to whom the Runa may turn for adjudication of a problem is either someone regarded as indigenous-nonindigenous mixed, called "half human"—*chaupi runa* in Quichua (if he comes from the highlands or from near the border of Peru), or *costeño* if he comes from the Coast, and especially if he has some *zambo* features.

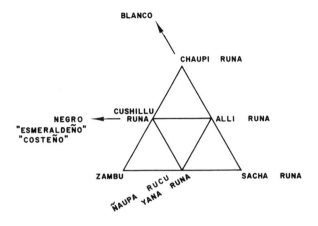

In this national paradigm writ small, and segmented into distinct features, Canelos Quichua culture would represent, in Generation III, the anchor of the *caserío*'s social formation. Its dominant *ayllu* or *ayllus* would be "properly" from the *llacta* of which the *caserío* is the modern nucleus and prominent *ayllu* spokesman, as up-river people (*janaj runa*) would provide the binding contacts with the outsider, near-human, teacher or trader. Achuar of Generation I (as down-river people — *urai runa*, or *uraimanda runa*) as in-marrying affines and Achuar-Canelos Quichua of Generation II are definitely present (also as *urai runa*). Generation IV people live in Puyo or elsewhere off indigenous territory, and visit the *caserío* as outsiders during festivals.

One could easily write of indigenous *caseríos* in Amazonian Ecuador in terms of *blanco/indio* asymmetry, leaving out the *negro-zambo* dimensions of the triangular paradigm except as they impinge on the nature of *mestizaje* itself. It is an error to do so, an easily constructed oversight. The triangular paradigm is manifest in *caserío* life and thought, though reference to the darker side is more allusive, sometimes hidden, often given jokingly, or spitefully and hatefully.

Throughout Canelos Quichua territory one who has kinky hair may be referred to jokingly, endearingly, or pejoratively as *zambu*. Whether or not hair form represents a variant of Amazonian genotype is not germane here. Black people did enter the area during the Amazonian rubber boom, from Brazil and from the Ecuadorian-Colombian coast, and others have entered since. Runa and Achuar-speaking Quichua refer to black people who are Spanish speakers as *cushillu runa* (wooly monkey people). They refer to Quichua-speaking black people in various ways, one of which is *ñaupa rucu yana runa* (early-time black people), and often refer to and nickname in address as *zambu* the children and grandchildren of the few black people. When speaking Spanish a person may pejoratively refer to one with kinky hair by recounting physical features, pretending not to remember the person's name. For example, María Santi once tried to get me to remember someone whom she didn't like at all. She said, "You know, that fairly dark person (*media moreno*) who lives near you—the one with the kinky hair, the one who lived on the Coast for a while, the *zambu*." Not long before, Plutarco Vargas, the object of María's pejorative string of ethnic slurs, had asked me about María in much the same manner. He said, "You know, that Peruvian, uncivilized (*auca*) person whose father is a friend of yours—the one who brought another killer in from Peru to live near us."

María's father was Achuar in Canelos Quichua Generation II, and she had just married a Generation I man. Plutarco (who is Generation II Achuar as well, but whose hair is curly) speaks Spanish very fluently and frequently associates with schoolteachers and other authorities in Puyo. María's father and Plutarco are in different *ayllu*s and it is said that there is some feud between them that dates back to Achuar and Shuar reciprocal killings generations before. In referring abusively to one another to me, each drew from the pole represented by the *zambu*–Sacha Runa base, as represented in the diagram above (p. 83). In this gossipy context, especially since the conversation took place in Puyo rather than in any *caserío*, and certainly not in *huasi*, forest, or *chagra*, both María and Plutarco could identify in the urban context as *choloficado* and as Runa: as civilized and as human. Both work to "demote" the other from Runa and "civilized" categories, and again, by so doing they evoke the horns of the pejorative designata that thrust out of urban Ecuador into the *caseríos*.

The concept blackness crops up in interesting ways in the *caserío*, but one must be in a *huasi*, or a *chagra* or forest site, to hear such a story.

Huayulumba Supai

This *supai* is not normally thought to be connected with any of the spirit masters discussed above. In Quichua, *supai* is the only word used for spirit masters and spirit beings. In Achuar this sort of being is called *iwianch*, which translates easily as "demon." It is a being who is intrusive upon domain order. Huayulumba supai, whose name comes from a spiny fern thicket, does not crop up in mythology, and its name does not seem to derive from Quichua or Jivaroan languages.

This demonic figure lives inside a circular entanglement of vines from which hang soul gourds (*aya pilchi*). He has a mass of hair, is dark, and beats a large drum which he holds close to his chest. He beats this drum and dances near a *caserío*, or in an abandoned household site abutting the plaza, early in the morning, while parents work in forest or *chagra*. As he drums he dances in a non-Runa way; children gather in a circle around him. They are drawn to him; he is their *curaga*. The old people knew how to treat the Huayulumba supai—they would build a platform over his vine nest, within which he danced with his long hair, pour gasoline on the nest and hair, and burn the Huayulumba supai to death. The Huayulumba supai, it is said, is "like us," but his hair is long and kinky. And he drums a different beat. Shamans send him to kill us.

This is not much of a *supai* story, as these stories go. What is important here is that contextually the story triggers other stories that refer to the concept *negro* as this concept is used for humans. In fact, the two synonyms for the Huayulumba supai are *callpachin* (makes one run, frightening) and *negro supai* (black demon). When a person using such terms is pressed, the analog is quickly given from the national ethnic-social worlds as "like an *esmeraldeño*." Let me give two examples of how this out-of-place bit of folklore about a *negro supai* syncretizes to an expression of the ethnic paradigms discussed above and in the previous chapter.

A Runa living near *caserío* Rosario Yacu, whose nickname just happens to be Indio, was pulling a vine in the jungle—hauling it—having cut it from a tree. The vine stopped moving. Indio pulled and tugged, but it didn't move. He turned to look and saw an *esmeraldeño* standing on the vine—a black man just standing there. It terrified him. He turned away, pulled again, looked around, and the *negro* was gone. This event really frightened Indio.

José awoke one morning and saw a small black man, an *esmeraldeño*, leaving, walking away from the site where Enrique used to live, from an area where the *aya pilchi* was growing round and round. A few days later José told Venancio and a week later Venancio told me. The next day I mentioned this to Enrique while we sat in his new house ten minutes' walk from the plaza of Nueva Esperanza. He looked at me and said "*ñuca causai*" ("my life force"), and then he explained that the *negro* came to his new house from his vine-infested lair because of new, living, shiny black stones he had acquired from an Otavalo shaman from the northern Ecuadorian Andes. Then, having oriented himself by reference to the stones, the *negro supai* returned to where Enrique used to live. Then Enrique's son spoke up and said that a *negro supai* may be sent by a shaman to kill. Enrique is in the process of becoming a powerful shaman, and toward that end a dark demonic force may well be thought of as his coming "life" (or a part of it). At the same time, there has always been some mystery surrounding one of the immediate ancestors of this family, and several family members may be referred to pejoratively (or endearingly) as *zambu*. As we talked, Enrique reflected further, and then he said, in Spanish, "Perhaps black people have penetrated our forest from time to time, from various areas. They left their eggs and made people darker."

The demonic figure of Huayulumba supai, and the stories that transform him by association into a human with the characteristics of a black person identified with the rain forest–riparian-coastal province of Esmeraldas, completes the triangular paradigm of ethnic disunity that is manifest in the *caserío* Nueva Esperanza, just as it is in the nation of Ecuador as a whole. Blacks and Runa in Ecuador are associated with a bifurcate jungle pole of jungle/urban opposition. *Negro/indio* is just as polar as are *blanco/indio* and *blanco/negro*. But the quality of the oppositions with regard to control of resources is strikingly different.

The jungle Quichua and black *esmeraldeños* are both completely competent with regard to rain forest and riverine ways, and, especially in the latter category, with urban ways as well. One competent in the ways of the city or town, who is black but urbane, will, in a black area, be tagged *zambo* or *mulato*. Because Runa with frizzy hair are viewed as less stereotypically indigenous (more "national") in towns and cities in Ecuador, such people are also often tagged by their indigenous relatives as *zambu*.

Indio and *negro* pulling against one another in the forest is certainly a transparent, negatively ascriptive analog to their mutual existence as competent people at the bottom of the class hierarchy at the antipodes of national "civilization" and at opposite poles of the dominant, triangular ethnic structure. We return to this ethnic structure much later. It is simply introduced here to give the reader a glimpse of the complete ideology of dominance that permeates the ethnic structure of a small *caserío* normally classified as a "progressive indigenous village" in national terms. Within that progress lies a dominant expansion of pejorative ethnic stereotyping, fear, and the potential use of nonindigenous life forces for shamanic control of a changing universe.

To return briefly to the diagram on page 83: on the left angle we have the *mestizo-zambo* mixture giving us *costeño*. *Esmeraldeños* are *costeños*, and many people from other parts of the Coast manifest negroid features, in the eyes of the Runa and in the eyes of *mestizo* and *blanco* nationals. The Coast lies to the west, beyond the Andes.

Moreover, the Runa concept of "sea," which they designate by the Spanish term *mar*, places it farther *east* from Upper Amazonia—in Amazonia proper, the land-water system of the river sea described in the previous chapter. Mythically, the sun went into a cave at the headwaters of the rivers that run eastward. He went down into the earth and emerged out of the river sea (Amazonas), leaving behind him white salt and rainbow-colored seed beads that peoples from deeper Amazonia traded westward to the Runa. On making his way westward, Sun became tired and he retired over the Andes, sinking again into the water world that encompasses and passes through the earth world. Runa don't know this myth of Indi well. To learn it, they say, you must talk to those more ancient people—the Achuar and others—who come from far down-river, from Amazonas. During the Amazonian rubber boom, peoples with *zambo* features came both from Amazonia and from the Ecuadorian-Colombian coast. These darker peoples came out of the land from beyond the outsider Andeans—by extension they were *lamarmanda* (from the sea). They penetrated Runa territories and left progeny there. They represent, by this reasoning, the destructive power of the water world, the power called upon by shamans. Dark phenotypical features became tenuously attached to a concept of potential destructive power, something to be *controlled*.

Thus far I have described the social system of Nayapi Llacta/Nueva Esperanza holistically by reference to the universal pattern of ecology, social structure, and cosmology, taking encapsulated information about each to present the cultural conjunctions and disjunctions that result from the coincidence of contradictory formations. We move now to the area of activities and organization that draw from and contribute to structure and that serve as both centrifugal and centripetal forces with regard to ecology and cosmology.

SOCIAL ORGANIZATION AND SOCIAL PRAXIS

In its early days, after having split off from San Jacinto, Nueva Esperanza was characterized by a buoyant excitement; its members worked hard together to bring the outside road in, to build a school, to expand the forest-swidden territory. They were united within the *caserío* and against outsiders, but part of their unity involved establishment of relations with outsiders. There was ample room for the sons of Nayapi and Lluhui, their in-marrying sons-in-law, and their daughters and daughters-in-law. Lluhui cured within this kinship group, and outsiders from the rain forest and Andes also came to him. One of Lluhui's sons spent a great deal of time in Puyo; two others worked for some time near Quevedo on a coastal plantation, while other sons and daughters of Nayapi primarily worked their *chagra*s and maintained their subsistence existence. With the death of Nayapi and later Lluhui, Nayapi Llacta became more and more a site of overt tension between strong men, punctuated by demonstrations of unity as the brothers and their residential in-laws took stands against other comparable units. One group hived off to form another *caserío* in 1969, and it, too, requested that a road be built to it. At times, *caseríos* united against other comparable larger groupings. The *comuna* itself, though shot through with internal dissension, also took unified stands against the outside world. The basis for social unity and disunity is tied to the idiom and reality of kinship and marriage, constrained by the availability of forest-*chagra* space, and elaborated upon by processes of complementary opposition that, in turn, stem from the dominating structure of economic, social, and ideological antinomies.

Kindred

Runa are born into a nuclear family that consists of husband-father, mother-wife, and the spouses' children. As the children grow, some stay and some leave. Although men in Nayapi Llacta want many of their sons to remain, and although women expect to see most of their daughters leave, the actual movement of real peoples depends on many factors. Moreover, leaving and staying are themselves relative to the vicissitudes of marriage and residence after marriage, tied to the flow of people through generations described above. As the household expands a kindred forms, the locus of the kindred being the husband-wife pair who founded the household. The men and women who settle within a half-day's walk from the founding couple make up a localized kindred from the standpoint of the household founders. Those who live farther away make up a dispersed kindred. Kindreds that expand in a territory so as to create a *llacta* system focus upon men who can manipulate paradigms so as to mend what might be called rifts in a cosmic network. In anthropology we call such men shamans (see the following chapter; also N. Whitten 1976, 1979; Ohnuki-Tierney 1980a, 1980b, 1981). A *llacta* is like an expanded *huasi* with a shamanic node, and a *caserío* is like a large house built in town rather than in a forest or *chagra*. Shamanic nodes are complemented in the feminine dimension by women who are master potters (see D. Whitten 1981). When the shaman dies the *llacta* may become completely reorganized. When the *llacta* is characterized by a modern *caserío* nucleus, as is the case with Nayapi Llacta, then each of the household heads—each the conjoined male-female node of a new kindred that overlaps at least minimally with the other growing kindreds — claims, in one way or another, to be leader of and spokesman for the *caserío*. The *caserío*, in short, grows into a divided town house. The *caserío* is profoundly egalitarian within a stratified national system. There are as many positions of high status or rank there as there are persons capable of filling them (Fried 1967). But at the same time there is a limitation on high status that all members of the *caserío* share vis-à-vis national ethnic ideology.

In the first generation of hamlet growth the *llacta* founder is shaman and kindred node. In the second generation of that shaman's expanded kindred, the shaman's sons and son-in-law (in the model case) are unified by their ties of consanguinity in the cases of sons A1, A2, and A3, and in terms of affinity in the case of son-in-law B. But in Generation III (reckoning from the founding shaman), all three of the As and B have their own kindreds; they represent separate segments of the same *ayllu* represented in the *caserío-llacta* by different emergent nodes. The number of possible members is reduced by inter-cousin and inter-generation marrying, usually out of the *caserío-llacta* and into kin groupings representing a replication of previous marriages. Each kindred is a tangible manifestation of a lattice of intermarriages and intercalculations of genealogy that ramify through the entire culture area and beyond. There tends to be, in *caseríos* such as Nueva Esperanza, a concentration of consanguineal males who compete with one another, each allying with an in-marrying male affine, *and* a concentration of affines who are also in competition with one another. The kindred stems from an apical male founder, so brothers and sisters of the founder and his wife/wives claim that the kindred is an *ayllu* with satellite members in-marrying from other *ayllus*. But some of those "other" *ayllus* are, genealogically speaking, the "same." They are "other" when they come from a great distance, or from across ethnic space.

To marry "close" but "far" is but to substitute geographic or ethnic
distance for genealogical distance. Such substitution is then discussed
in the idiom of "past time."

Let us consider Achuar–Canelos Quichua intermarriage for a moment, referring back to the generational mobility model given on pages
78–80. The kinship systems of the Achuar and Canelos Quichua are
very different—jarringly so on first inspection. The former is shallow
in genealogical depth, quite rigid in terms of a rule that insists on a
man moving into his wife's territory on marriage; it stresses the advantage of polygyny for strong men, and favors marriage of two brothers in one family to two sisters in another. The kindred clusters around
a "great man" (*uunt*) whose sons stay home instead of marrying out.
Cross-cousin marriage is prescribed within the localized kindred. The
kindred node is not a shaman and kinship and the shamanic world
seem not to merge or diverge as co-occurring sets. The Canelos Quichua
kinship system, by contrast, stresses time depth, uses Andean terminology reminiscent of both Cuzco and Ayacucho, places stress on the
in-movement of women, emphasizes that men should stay in the vicinity of their father's household after an appropriate period of service
to the father-in-law. Shamans and their sons also seem to hold their
sons-in-law in the shaman's territory. Monogamy is also the preferred
marriage arrangement, and the domain of shamanism cannot be separated from the domain of kinship (compare, e.g., ·N. Whitten 1976
and Whitten and Whitten 1983 with Descola 1981). Marriage within
the localized kindred is proscribed. Moreover, kin terms and concepts
tie the Canelos system to Andean ideas about higher and lower groupings (up-river–down-river: *janaj runa–urai runa*), and notions of *llacta*
and *ayllu* can also become quite intertwined, as in the Andean world.

Nonetheless, Achuar and Canelos Quichua move back and forth
with a fluid facility into one another's cognitive universe, as denoted
by intermarriage (see Taylor 1981). Returning to the model of generational mobility from Achuar to "pristine" Canelos Quichua for a
moment, we can say that the inner form of the kindred remains essentially the same, and that the following transformations take place:

A. Matrilocality is dropped in Generation III and is ambiguous in
   Generation II.

B. The rule of kindred-territorial endogamy in Generation I is transformed to its opposite (prohibition) in Generation III. Ethnic and
   geographic distance, together with the Canelos Quichua concept
   of replicating past alliances through marriage, establish the cognitive basis of a marriage system whereby intra-kindred marriages

take place if the kindred is dispersed across ethnic or geographic space.

C. The lattice of kin and marriage ties between Achuar (Generation I) and Canelos Quichua (Generation III) are such that those in Generation I and III can both obey their own rules while marrying in the same way. That is, male III and female III can marry as non-cousins by following cognitive procedures established in Canelos Quichua kinship reckoning, but they can also marry as close cousins by following the cognitive procedures of the Achuar system.

Through marriage and contrasting forms of kin reckoning of marriage partners, Canelos Quichua culture, including the Puyo Runa and the residents of Nayapi Llacta, continuously incorporate the ethnic opposite (I) as part of their ethnic focus (III) and project that focus into their sector of the nationalist system (IV).

Not only do the Achuar–Canelos Quichua systems interrelate, but the Canelos-Napo (Quijos) systems do too, and all three of these sets of interrelationships contribute to the kindred structure in Nayapi Llacta/ Nueva Esperanza and all cognate *llactas-caseríos*. A large kindred — one including all of the descendants of a particular apical pair and

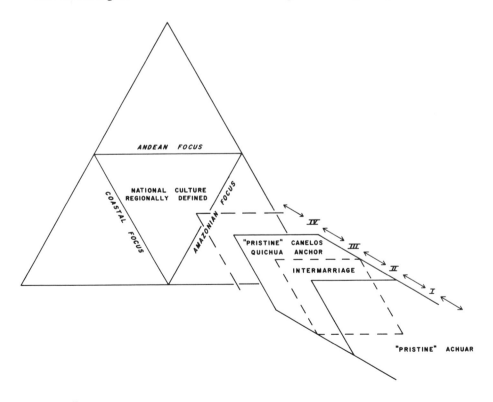

their in-marrying male affines—is called *muntun* (from the Spanish *monton*—pile, bunch) in the Napo area (see, e.g., T. Macdonald 1979). The people of Nayapi Llacta know this term, but they don't normally use it for their own overlapping groupings. In the Napo area whole *muntun*s may migrate together. In fact, one such *muntun* is currently in the process of marrying its children into Nayapi Llacta and adjacent *llacta*s, with the idea that parents and others will soon be entering.

From the standpoint of Nayapi Llacta, the expanded kindred of a founder can stay spatially localized only so long as the *ayllu* segments maintain some tenuous alliance among themselves, and with the affinal *ayllu* segments within Nayapi Llacta. In sharp contrast with the Napo *muntun*, the idea of moving as an expanded group—keeping the group stemming from the same nodal pair intact during migration—is looked upon as preposterous by people in Nayapi Llacta. There, as in other parts of Canelos Quichua culture, stem kindreds hive off into personal kindreds when spatial movement or rearrangement takes place. If movement is to occur, it is with small groupings, the largest of which would be a brother and sister married to another brother and sister, together with their children (the minimal two-*huasi* unit representing two *ayllus*):

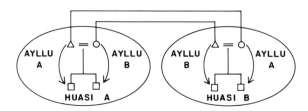

The very smallest unit that has been spontaneously discussed, by men, is the male kindred node together with his youngest son. The smallest unit for a woman is mother and eldest daughter.

In a system where everyone is related to everyone else in various ways, calculable by various means, and where the cellular structure is relatively autonomous, there are unending possibilities for opposition and alliance. Factionalism in Nueva Esperanza is endemic and schismatic, but alliances crosscut the factions. Herein lies the process of unity in a system of complementary opposition. For example, Abraham (A) and Venancio (B), as strong men, may be on bad terms with one another. They started out as friendly partners a week before, when they went to Puyo together as members of a *caserío* commission to

speak to the governor about the new cement bridge they seek to replace
the palm-log one over the Putuimi River. When they came home with
a new contract guaranteeing money to pay Runa workers (their sons
and sons-in-law), they brought with them three gallons of 160-proof
cane alcohol to celebrate. They got drunk and, without really knowing
how it happened, wound up slugging one another. Rather than apol-
ogize the next day, they made disparaging comments about one another
to their wives, who then repeated the comments to their daughters or
daughters-in-law. Abraham and Venancio are the classificatory sons of
brothers (one Achuar, one Canelos Quichua), so they regard one another
as brothers by extension. They call one another *huauqui* in Quichua,
or *hermano* or *primo* in Spanish. But now that they are not on speaking
terms (though living only forty yards apart), they exaggerate the ethnic
and geographic distance of the cousin bond and emphasize the close-
ness of marriage to respective in-laws (both of whom have Achuar
parents). Where before the spat a strong unit was composed of men
A-B-C-D, A and B now see the A-B relationship to be attenuated and
seek to develop two opposing groups—A-C-E-F contra B-D-G-H. If
there should be other bad relations between F and H or E and G, the
factional structure of Nueva Esperanza could shift; but if, for example,
F and H were "close" and E and G "neutral," then the contretemps
born of a drunken fistfight could be patched up. There are varied bases
for complementary opposition, and the opposition between factions
can generate alliances across an attenuated linkage.

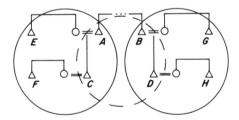

In the above diagram the alliance between A and B is indicated in
dashed consanguineal lines; the "new" alliances are circled in solid
lines and the attenuated alliance in dashed lines. If a genuine A-B
opposition develops in Nueva Esperanza, and if the *ayllu* segments
(AC and BD) conjoin with alter affinal *ayllus* (ACEF contra BGDH),
then the idiom of kinship would be manipulated as A "remembers"
and cognitively activates more intense official ties with E, while B and
G also "recall" close ties.

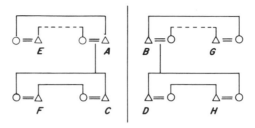

Here A doubly links E and F to him as in-marrying affines, as B does the same with G and H. Now, if E, F, G, and H are Generation II Achuar, marrying into the father-in-law's territory as is the Achuar custom, then things could get serious, especially if F or C, D or H had inherited a killing debt in Achuar territory generations before (as Nayapi himself had done). What might seem at first to be a temporary choosing of sides might take on a sinister, deeper cast that could lead to the forcing of some of the lower generation right on out of the *caserío* and *llacta,* and even the territory. But if, on the contrary side, older feuds between the forebears of F and C or D and H had occurred on the Copataza River, then there would be a mixing of loyalties, a crossing over of antagonistic boundaries as actors seek to use a new (and trivial) conflict to gloss over an old (and serious) one. Then the opposition would not be as severe as it might appear, even though F and C might make it seem so to "make stronger friends" with one another.

The kindred, as an operating unit, must be understood in terms of alliance and exchange expressed through the idiom of kinship and marriage. Alliance with one another due to shared antagonisms complements a system of exchange of like commodities between people who wish to signal cooperation. The ultimate expression of alliance is found in the exchange of marriage partners, and this exchange is made outside of the localized kindreds of the *caserío.* Therefore, "ultimate" exchange bonds creating alliances between *huasis* divide the *caserío.*

National developmental processes continue to bring new ideas, forms, opportunities, and threats to Nayapi Llacta, funneled through Nueva Esperanza. The varied bases for factionalism increase proportionately, but they continue to be mediated and exacerbated by the kindred through the idiom of *ayllu* continuity and marriage alliance, and constrained by the need for territory and the competing systems of resource management. For a brief example, D in the foregoing diagram is studying to be an Episcopal priest; F wants to be a Catholic catechist. C, in turn, was baptized by a *chaupi runa evangélico* a month back in the Chingosimi River, where he shouted "hallelujah" and vowed to forsake his recent craving for *trago.* Each of these men has a vision of imminent economic wherewithal and each is now learning about new forms of cosmic power with *Dios* (God) at the pinnacle, with a *blanco* missionary as His messenger on earth, and with the indigenous missionary as the pinnacle of Christianity among his family of heathens. Factionalism that ranges from forces originating in killing vendettas in Achuar territory to the competing ideologies and financial possibilities of Western, mission-borne Christianity can enter into a mere drunken fight between classificatory brothers. These factional bonds, the oppositions and alliances that they signal, and the ways by which each is mediated and exacerbated continue to be expressed through the idiom of kinship and marriage, of which the kindred is the localized and dispersed action set.

Minga

As *ayllu* refers to kinship and *llacta* to territory, *minga* refers to goal-oriented collective action. It, too, is an Andean indigenous term. But unlike the concepts *ayllu* and *llacta*, *minga* is also nationally constituted, as part of the legal charter of every *comuna*. The Ley de Comunas was enacted in 1937 to promote and control *campesino* (peasant) rights of usufruct, organization, and juro-politics (see, e.g., Iturralde 1980: 19-22). By national law and by indigenous ideological consensus, every Runa living on the Comuna San Jacinto del Pindo must collaborate with members of a *caserío* on a weekly *minga*. According to the law of the *comuna* as interpreted by the officials of the *comuna*, collaboration need not be with one's own *caserío*.

Every Tuesday morning the Runa of Nueva Esperanza come together in a formal work group. When the *caserío* was new, one or another of the sons of Lluhui would let loose a falsetto call around 5:00 A.M. (sometimes earlier). He would release his breath in a controlled labiodental fricative followed by a strong *u* vowel that split the darkness: *duuuuuuuuuuuuuuuu*—holding as long as possible but not cracking at the end. The call would first be answered by male *ayllu* members with various nature-splitting shrieks of hilarious response — *wheeeee, whyaaaaay*. Such sound would travel through the pre-dawn viscosity of water-saturated air through male *ayllus* into and out of the dispersed *huasis*. After several other exchanges of friendship, people would eat their breakfast and begin to gather on the quadrangle. Women would clean the plaza of weeds with their machetes, and men, governed in a consensus manner with a low-status *vocal* (spokesman) naming a previously agreed-upon project, would set to a hard task such as cutting logs for a corduroy trail, building a palm-log bridge over a river, or erecting a new national edifice on the plaza edge itself. By 10:30 or

11:00 the women would be done and would bring *asua*—mildly fermented, yeasty manioc mash mixed with water—to the men, carrying the mash in bottle gourds or leaf bundles, and serving it in calabash shells or ceramic drinking bowls. Men and women would discuss present and future actions as they worked or rested, keeping the political context unremoved from collective activity. Politics stayed on the move, so to speak. Women would go to their homes by 2:00 P.M. to prepare a later afternoon meal while some of the men played volleyball.

As the *caserío* developed and grew, only one or two men would let out the opening shout and usually no one would answer. Collective discussions took place more and more in a formal, removed setting— in the school or sporting club —where public policy became bogged down with escalating political rhetoric. Since 1981 it is common to hear only one man shouting away, *"Hey hey hey hey, minga, minga, minga, minga,"* and then playing the radio. Other radios are turned on too, some tuned to Radio Pastaza, coming out of the chauffeur's union in Puyo, for coastal and Andean music. This is followed by the world news as presented from Quito by Radio VozAndes, the most powerful station in South America today, controlled by the North American Evangelist World Radio Mission. Other radios are tuned to the Shuar Federation or to Radio Macuma, beaming out of Shuar territories. These stations (the first supported by Salesians, the second by North American evangelists) mix Ecuadorian martial music with indigenous Shuar songs and chants (see Belzner 1981; Salazar 1981).

First to arrive for the *minga* now are those who are most marginal to the *llacta*, in-laws who live far from the plaza and sons of plaza dwellers now living from an hour to nearly two hours' walk away. Very slowly do the principal men arrive, and some of the women don't bother to come at all. The *minga* gets started by around 9:30 A.M. if it isn't raining, and men and women work, as described above, until about 11:00. Invidious sanctions are applied to one another nearly constantly, and for the men the concept of capacity—*ushana*—is continuously invoked. *"Mana ushangachu!"* shouts Felipe as his brother stumbles—"He can't do it!" All laugh, and when Felipe drops a 200-pound log prematurely all laugh again.

Although the line of squatting women advancing with machetes slicing a sixteenth of an inch into the plaza's sun-baked hardpan surface may at first appear to be a system of unbroken solidarity, the truth is that the line is broken into minimal groupings of *huasis* adjacent to *ayllus*. María and her daughters Alicia and Ursula work next to María's daughter's cousin Rebeca and her (Rebeca's) daughter Elisa. They are more or less in the center of the line, having had no recent fights with anyone. At either end of the line is a woman not speaking to the woman at the other end. Mother–daughter–daughter-in-law constitute the minimal segments, and daughter-in-law may not even be present at the *minga*, if she is new, not resident in her mother-in-law's house, or if her husband is away. If her husband is not on good terms with several other men, then she definitely will not come to the *minga* at all.

Everyone is glad when the *minga* is over; no one today really wants to have a formal meeting in school that they all agree they must have. Indeed, unless a visitor from Puyo is present to call the meeting, there normally won't be one. Moreover, even when visitors do come and call a meeting, it sometimes does not take place. *Minga* day is the day for outsiders to visit the *caserío*. A public health team may come to vaccinate children; the bishop may come to count Catholics and to ask for a daughter to be "civilized" for a few years in a Puyo convent-school; a German photographer may arrive to take pictures of "typical Indians"; and an inspector of schools may arrive to see how the teacher is getting along in his "tribal" station.

For awhile, in Nueva Esperanza, people worked with great force to override their escalating interpersonal antagonisms by sharing *trago*, raw cane alcohol, which they purchased from Veracrúz or Madre Tierra, or on the Puyo-Shell road, for about 75¢ a gallon. Two things occurred: the first was such heavy drinking (sometimes continuing for days) that serious damage to interpersonal relations occurred within as well as outside the *huasi* unit; the second was escalating all-out brawls wherein some individuals were so badly beaten that they required hospitalization. Interpersonal, reciprocal grievances thereafter were aggravated in the extreme. By 1981 Nueva Esperanza was using just a little *trago* at its *mingas*—perhaps a quart or two for forty to sixty adults—and often none at all is brought forth. Manioc *asua* is still served, sometimes being brought in plastic pails or even paint cans, but sometimes in traditional leaf bundles to be served in calabash shells or ceramic bowls.

Where the kindred represents the indigenous action set in both organizational and idiomatic dimensions, the *minga* represents the merger

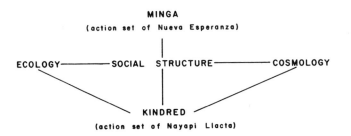

A few months before the completion of a road to a native hamlet, men pause near the end of a *minga* to discuss seriously what their (Runa) policy should be with regard to their territory. Each spokesman assumes a role of outsider, as he offers advice to insiders about public *caserío* policy.

of Andean-indigenous and national-poor-nonindigenous action sets of the hamlet. Where the kindred articulates the ecological and cosmological paradigms, forces, and constraints, the *minga* endeavors to mask ideologically the asymmetrical ethnic structure and make *caserío* collaboration "total." Where kindred ties bind segmental rifts through processes of complementary opposition, the *minga* promotes schismatic, noncomplementary factionalism.

Occasionally a household head will call a *minga* in the Nayapi Llacta system to clear new land for a *chagra*. He calls on those whom he is reckoning as his active kinsmen and affines. No one, so far as I know, would be invited just because he shared a common opponent with the *minga* organizer. Much food and drink is served in such a *minga*. *Trago* is normally served before the work starts, and then a large feast is prepared for the end of the day's exhausting activities. The *trago* may be served late in the evening as most participants go home. Only when those taking part in a household *minga* continue drinking and the drinking scene moves into the Nueva Esperanza *caserío* have I known fights to result. These fights have been the worst that we have either witnessed or heard about, equal in their intensity and worse in their aftereffects than those occurring after weddings (see Whitten and Whitten 1984).

The *caserío* is a chaotic place. People are in flight from it today. One pole of such flight is the relative security of Upper Amazonian cultural ecology with its nurturing components of *sacha-chagra-huasi-ayllu*. The other pole is found in Puyo itself, where a full-scale microcosm of national economic, social, ethnic, and political structure exists. In its chaos the *caserío* mediates and exacerbates the forest-swidden-riparian Upper Amazonian socially egalitarian system of complementary oppositions as this system is encompassed by nationalist, developmentalist, capitalist plans and practices, on one side, and the nationalist urban scene as this scene is beset by counter-national forces, on the other side.

NUEVA ESPERANZA AS A SOCIAL SYSTEM

Nueva Esperanza is ethnically stratified in the cognitive sense, and egalitarian in the social sense. In a way, every man in the plaza area is a community leader, depending upon how he can attract people from the outside. Each *huasi* segment articulates in its own way to *chagra*-forest and to town life. And each *ayllu* segment is linked mythically and in contemporary time-space to its alter segments through marriage and to its cognate segments through kinship. Each *huasi* in

Nueva Esperanza is alienated from some others of its analog *huasis*. The *caserío* represents the localized system of alienation that prepares one for that which is faced in the national system. Flight to town and flight to forest-*chagra* lead to encounters with others similarly engaged. The whole system holds together due to ties developed away from the *caserío* rather than within it. The complete, multifaceted, face-to-face interrelatedness of those within the *caserío* plus mutual alienation from and mutual dependence upon the contradictory modes of livelihood prepare the members of the *caserío* for a radically changing "real world."

Every family in Nueva Esperanza makes its own adjustment to Upper Amazonian cultural-ecological adaptation and adaptability to an urban ambience. In this process of continuous adjustment, of continuous structural maintenance and adaptability—of consistency within radical change—one could conclude that the *caserío* might as well not exist. Some *caseríos* have been abandoned for ecological, economic, and social reasons. Indeed one today, only two hours' walk from Nueva Esperanza, functions only on *minga* day or during festivals. Why does Nueva Esperanza exist at all? What is it that binds the people in Nueva Esperanza to a hamlet structure that satisfies neither their cultural-ecological needs nor their urban aspirations?

First, the people of Nayapi Llacta are limited in their options. Hamlet structure is a requirement of national political economy; without this nucleated residential structure the people would not have a "place" on the *comuna*, and the *comuna* would not have a viable system by which to demonstrate its continuing existence in the political economy radiating out of Puyo (see N. Whitten 1976). Political economy articulates with cultural ecology; but the economy/ecology systems are fundamentally incompatible with one another. The coincidence of oppositions adheres in multiple, contradictory ways by means of a mediating formation. This formation—the *caserío*—becomes one of continuing perturbation as well as mediation.

Second, as a consequence of the first, the hamlet formation provides all of its members with a clear sense of common, external opponents in both the indigenous and nonindigenous worlds. It gives an urban, national, stratified locus to *llacta* egalitarian territoriality which, in turn, gives an egalitarian rural locus to stratified, urban life. Third, alliances shift more rapidly in the *caserío* than in the dispersed settlement pattern. One can seize the moment in *caserío* life to get back at an opponent, or to escalate a quarrel to a level where outside adjudication is called for by other *caserío* members. Such adjudication may keep a quarrel from ramifying, though it usually does so at the expense of increased escalation. Finally, *caserío* life encapsulates the system of complementary oppositions and thereby provides a ready mechanism (or locus) to create a higher level of contradiction and a higher level of complementarity. Such raising of levels and the creation of antinomy is an inevitable consequence of the contained mediated coincidence of incompatible formations. This encapsulation, which raises the level of contradiction, generates visible and tangible antinomies that throw into sharp relief salient dimensions of the Upper Amazonian cultural ecology and the stratified, bureaucratic world of nationalist, capitalist developmentalism.

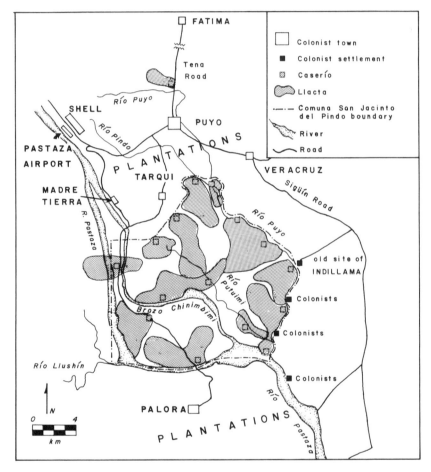

Map 4. The Greater Puyo Area of Abutting Frontiers, with Puyo Runa *Llactas* and *Caseríos* Indicated

The world of the Runa is poised between two orders, each of which controls its ramifying chaos in different ways. The *caserío* (or *centro* or even *comuna*, as it is often now called) formation replicates the systemic, chaotic order of the nationalist world, caught up as it is in processes of international dependency. The *caserío* brings the urban world to it, contains it, and forces it back out, and its residents get caught up in these nerve-racking centripetal-centrifugal currents. The *caserío* feeds upon an outer, developing political economy, and its wastes permeate its expansive cultural ecology. It also feeds upon its artificially divided sylvan-swidden-riparian resources, in a system of ecosystem management that is restorative.

Tarqui, Madre Tierra, Fátima, or Veracrúz are national frontier towns facing out from their anchoring urban center—Puyo—toward the poverty of sugarcane fields and tea plantations that abut the brush zone of barren vegetation, which the residents of these conflict-ridden rural nuclei of an urbanizing nation mistake for the fertile, though hostile, forest. The *caseríos* of the Comuna San Jacinto represent an indigenous cultural-ecological frontier zone that faces back at the system of urbanization and urbanism. On the rim around Puyo, and in the rim around Amazonia, we find a polar system of converging and conflicting frontiers organized into a system of segmentary unity and nucleated divisiveness. Yet consistency reigns in this intercultural system of chaos, for the Runa have developed a way of creatively utilizing disorder to reproduce order.

4

Beauty, Knowledge, and Vision

"The shamanic system . . . can be said to be mankind's oldest religion, the ultimate foundation from which arose all the religions of the world. Further, as archaic specialist and 'technician of the sacred,' the shaman is clearly father to the priest."—Peter T. Furst, "The Roots and Continuities of Shamanism" (1977), p. 21.

"Poised delicately between defeat and success, forever entangled in the mire of the underworld and the shining clarity of spiritual enlightenment, the healer is in the constant process of ascending a hierarchy of purity and power from which he can be easily toppled. Receiving power 'from above' is contingent upon giving it 'to below,' to the afflicted. It is only through helping the afflicted and thereby engaging with the powers of evil that a healer can ascend.

"Power comes from this chain of reciprocal exchanges. And these exchanges of reciprocity, so it would seem, assume connections going back to the beginning of time through the spirits of generations of Indian shamans and folk Catholic saints. The phenomenology of yage [ayahuasca—soul vine] is basic to this, because the wisdom and the worlds it reveals, so sensuously and vividly, cascade into ever-widening cycles of understanding of cosmic history and one's place in it."—Michael T. Taussig, "Folk Healing and the Structure of Conquest in Southwest Colombia" (1980), p. 255.

Around the rim of the Pacific basin there exists an ancient cultural complex that has its locus in the Siberian menders of rifts in cosmic networks. In fact, the word *shaman* comes to us from the Tungus language of Central Asia and Siberia. These northern healers of nature, society, and the supernatural-supercultural ate sacred mushrooms called fly agaric to induce states of ecstasy. The history of this mushroom, by the way, has been traced all the way from Siberia into India and identified as Soma, the god of ecstasy (Wasson 1968; Lévi-Strauss 1983 [1976]). The concept of the regenerative power of some mushrooms today ranges from India around the Pacific rim and crops up among the Canelos Quichua. The shamanic complex may be 50,000 years old, perhaps entering the Americas with the first inhabitants to cross the Siberian-Alaskan land bridge (see Furst 1977). Although the people of Nayapi Llacta know of a hallucinogenic mushroom (which some say is red — the color of fly agaric — and others say is white, like tobacco), and although they attribute many regenerative powers to various fungi, they do not take any mushrooms for visionary experience (they say that some of the ancients did eat such mushrooms, however). Rather, they use two powerful hallucinogens, Datura and Banisteriopsis, together with dreams and insights, to obtain direct, firsthand experience with the cosmic network, as this network extends through and beyond their jungle, swidden, territorial, social, and cosmological formations.

Around the rim of Amazonia there exists a ceramic complex related to Central Amazonian and coastal-Andean traditions. Its locus in Upper Amazonia is in the women of various cultures, and the ceramic tradition is especially elaborate and exquisitely beautiful in the very areas where European colonial rule held sway, but where the indigenous people still survive. Recent work in Ecuador suggests that there are networks of ancient co-traditions that have waxed and waned across the contrasting, rugged, but "compressed" topography of Amazonia-Sierra-Coast, focusing and florescing in various areas from time to time. Since the colonial era, going back into what is still an inchoate past, and continuing today, one such florescence is seen in the Canelos Quichua women potters. It would appear that the ceramic tradition of these knowledgeable, skilled, reflective, and vision-filled women originated in Central or Upper Amazonia, penetrating other traditions in Amazonian Ecuador centuries or perhaps a millennium ago — probably through the area where the Villano River empties into the Curaray River — and spread southward and westward as native cultures and their peoples were obliterated northward on either side of the Napo River.

At the very base of the Ecuadorian Andes, male shamanic tradition has long been syncretized with female ceramic tradition; the result is

a male-induced–female-induced conjoined system of cultural transmission that relates private imagery to public imagery, vision to knowledge, thought and reflection to practical action. To understand this
syncretic tradition that provides consistency in a system of radical
change, and that utilizes disorder to reproduce or create order, we must
come to closer grips with the Canelos Quichua concept of power that
includes ideas about knowledge and vision, about "our" culture and
"their" culture, the sense of parallel transmission of cultural knowledge,
a paradigm of ecological imagery, and a fundamental contrast in two
hallucinogen-induced forms of visionary experience.

POWER

The verb *ushana* in Canelos Quichua means to be capable, to be able
to respond to contingencies in life. Usually one hears the term as a
negative, invidious reference to the capabilities of another person.
Someone who can't carry through a task set by himself for himself is
characterized as *mana ushangachu* ("he/they can't do it"). *Utipana*, a
synonym for *ushana* in the Napo dialect, is sometimes used in the sense
of cosmic power. When Lluhui died in Nayapi Llacta in the late 1970s,
there were clear rifts in social and cosmic orders that lasted for some
time. In the course of a brief stay there a month after his death, I
reported occurrences to my friends (the shaman's kindred and affinal
survivors) ranging from strange noises and vibrations to a brief period
of possession while dreaming; *utipanamanda* was given as the source
of such disturbances, and people said that they came from "beyond,"
where fire and water merged. A couple of years later, I was unable to
elicit *utipana* as a term for anything other than *shuj shimita*—
another word in another language.

Ursa (or *jursa*), from the Spanish *fuerza*, is the most frequently heard
positive term of capability, and the adjective *sinchi*, strong, is affixed
to a noun denoting capacity. To have capacity is to prove oneself; the
term for proof is *camai*. Proof must be tangible; one must not only
succeed in a task, but produce something that another can feel.

For example, one who says he senses a beauty (*suma*) within himself
can prove this by playing a flute or by singing. In both cases another
concept enters—*samai*, breath. One's *samai* carries with it something
of the force of one's will, *shungu*, and something of the invisible (to
humans when awake) and yet tangible proof of inner strength. The
proof of the strength of one's breath for communicating musically
through a flute can make the person receiving the musical beauty reflect
on the evocative meaning of the unsung words and the heard melody,

and perhaps they make him sad, perhaps happy. When one plays a poignant song its beauty evokes love, sadness, or melancholy, and "proof" (*llaqui*). As the song goes out from the singer it is *llaquichina* (to make [one] suffer, to make [one] long for, to make [one] love); and when the qualities are communicated to, and received by, the hearer, the song is *llaquirina*. When a "to-make-one-happy" (*cushiyachina*) song is played, the recipient who becomes happy is *cushiyarina*. *Camai*, proof, a tangible manifestation of *samai*, breath, and *llaqui*, also as proof, are concepts that imply reciprocation in interaction. They must be recorded by alter from ego and ego must be aware of alter's reception. For another example, a shaman's corporeal heart-throat-stomach area (his *shungu*, his will) contains especially sharp and dangerous objects that protect him but that can also be blown out as projectiles. When one gets hit with such a projectile it is proof of the strength of a shaman; the projectile is in a shaman's class, *sami*. When a shaman dies, hard proof of the strength of his tangible breath appears as small snails (called *samhuai*) near his grave. Because a shaman's-class projectile is stronger than a non-shaman's class, proof exists of reciprocal asymmetry. A shaman of the same or higher class must be consulted for a cure and for redressing the wrong of the reception of a missile from another. Shamans also keep many stones (*rumi*). Each *rumi* in the shaman's class, *yachaj sami rumi*, contains the life force, *causai*, of a deceased shaman, of a spirit, or of a soul (or of some combination). One proves that a *rumi* is shaman's class by blowing gently on it with one's own breath—*fhuuu, fhuuu*—if condensation appears on the shiny surface, the stone "has breath; it is powerful shaman" (*samai tian sinchi yachaj*). Such stones are "like soldiers" (*soldado shina*). The shaman with his phalanx of animated shaman's-class stones is like the center of a military formation.

For a third example, a woman making a pot must control the breath of the fire, *nina samai*, as this heat leaves a pot after firing. If she does not do so the fire's *samai* will cause the vessel to crack or burst as it cools. The completed pot is her *camai*, her proof of ability to control clay, water, fire, and breath, and also, with the forces of clay, rock, fire, and water, to produce color, design, and form. Finally, for a fourth example, actual song unmediated by a musical instrument projects a particular synthesis of mythic time-space, knowledge of *sacha* and *chagra*, interpersonal-intersubjective reality, and skill into the cosmos across space and through time. Songs are received by those to whom they are sent, by souls and spirits, and by powerful shamans.

These examples show something of the associationally complex cultural elements with which the people of Nayapi Llacta work to maintain a sense of inner strength and integrity.

Testing a shaman's stone with one's breath. If the stone is alive the tester's breath causes dew to appear on the stone's surface.

A man plays his *juliahuatu.*

Two men reciprocate the proof of their shamanic status during a festival.

Control of clay, water, and fire.

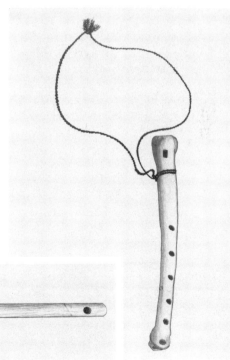

Ceramic representation of *yachaj sam-huai*, maker unknown (*upper left*).

Festival *corneta* with Amasanga face. Such trumpets are presented to indigenous authorities at festivals. When they are blown everyone is said to suffer. Maker unknown, Sarayacu (*upper right*).

Juliahuatu, transverse flute played by all men (*lower left*).

Yachaj sami pijuanu, shaman's class bird-bone flute (*lower right*).

Knowledge, Vision, Thought, and Reflection

The conceptualization of power among the Canelos Quichua is paradigmatic. There is a consistent patterning to certain key concepts; the patterning is anchored in a social status; and the social status is named. Moreover, the semiotic paradigm—the patterning of sets of concepts— that helps us understand the conceptualization of power in Canelos Quichua culture deals with the contrast between "our" culture and "other" cultures as well as with the means whereby the threshold between ours and other can be moved or crossed while maintaining the contrast. The shaman moves the threshold between our culture (and the plane of existence of our quotidian world) closer to the edge of other cultures and other worlds. He himself passes from our culture and our world to others, and he returns, thereby exploring the other while maintaining and enriching the dynamic inner integrity of ours. The shaman maintains and manipulates series of analogic relationships such that novel interpretations may be presented on an enduring symbolic template. The shaman, in the traditional Canelos Quichua system, is a person who, above all others, has mastered the art of forging concepts of beauty to the bidding of an unusual power to heal. The shaman is also the node of the *ayllu* and *llacta* system, and the broker between indigenous culture and the outside world. The shaman is called *yachaj*, one who knows. The word derives from the verb *yachana*, to know, to learn. In order to "know" and to continue to learn through one's growing mastery so as to respond to the vicissitudes of ordered and disordered worlds, the concept of *yachana* must be balanced with another concept—*muscuna*—which means to dream, to envision, to be insightful. *Yachana*, as knowing, has a real "depth" to it, and this depth manifests itself through various forms of "proof." For example, if one sees a deceased relative in a dream, one may, or may not, "know" what the vision is. Is it a soul, or a spirit taking the form of the soul; or is it the relative? A *yachaj* "knows" by degrees; and the more he knows, the stronger he becomes.

One of the proofs of increasing strength of a shaman is acquisition of a special shaman's song, *taquina*. Only when the shaman is strong enough to ward off in-coming projectiles of all other shamans can he actually sing out the song (send it out through his *samai*). When the beauty of the *taquina* is received by other shamans, they blow (*shitana*) back at the singer to test his strength. This is not the tangible blowing (*pucuna*) of, say, a dart through a blowgun. Rather, it is a dangerous blowing of unseen tangibility. If he is now "strong one who knows" (*sinchi yachaj*), he may sing his shaman's song without harm to himself

Iputindi (scorpion), tangible proof of shamanic sting. Apacha Vargas, *caserío* Nuevo Mundo, Comuna San Jacinto del Pindo.

or to *huasi* members; the fearsome beauty of the heard song proves the shaman's strength. He then may continue shamanic activities privately, within his own family, or more publicly, by curing others from his *ayllu* and, eventually, as he becomes stronger, people from other *ayllu*s and from other cultures.

Ricsina is yet another verb that deals with knowledge in a somewhat different way, in a more immediate sense. It means to know, to experience, to perceive, to comprehend. This sort of knowing is experiential, and it must be backed up by depth and also balanced with vision. One who is central to the reception of information—a *curaga* in the past—could be known as *ricsij runa,* a sort of know-all, see-all

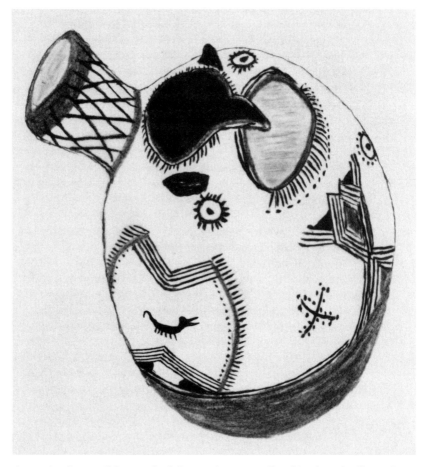

Apapa (owl), tangible proof of shamanic power. Eucebia Aranda, *llacta* Sara-yaquillu, Sarayacu.

person. There has never been such a person in Nayapi Llacta, though the concept exists in the Quichua-speaking world.

There are a number of terms that develop agglutinatively from *yuyana* in Quichua, one of which is the reflexive *yuyarina*, which means to think, to reflect. As Sibby and I came to understand more, and as our questions began to reflect paradigmatic relationships, some of which our friends found compatible with their own thoughts, some of which they found utterly erroneous, and some of which they found made them re-think some of their ideas and ask others about relationships that made sense but were far from their consciousness, a few people who had studied us said we were *yuyayuj runa*—sort of professional students. A true insider, however, balances his thoughts and reflections with his immediate and deep knowledge, and—always—with his visionary activity. People who reflect upon Canelos Quichua culture (as we do) may be classed as *shuj shimita yachai* (or *yachan*), "other speech-knowledge." By contrast, to so reflect and work within the semiotic paradigm of Canelos Quichua culture one is *ñucanchi yachai* ("our cultural knowledge") or *ñucanchi ricsiushca runa* ("our people's perception").

The following model helps conceptualize the systemic relationships discussed above:

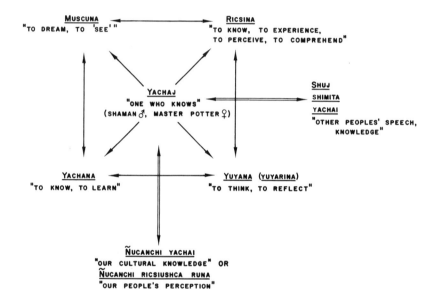

Here the *yachaj*, or more properly *sinchi yachaj*, has attained a level of control such that he is sufficiently powerful to balance his knowledge with his visions, to relate his visions to cultural knowledge, and to relate his thoughts and reflections to knowledge and to his visions. To know more about that which is within, the shaman must increasingly know more about that which is without. The shaman becomes a *paradigm manipulator*. He continuously reproduces cultural knowledge, continuously maintains the contrast between our culture and other culture, and continuously transcends the boundaries that he enforces. His work must, in part, be based upon experiences with other peoples speaking other languages. Such people (Achuar, Quichua-speaking peoples of the Napo area, Quichua-speaking people of the Sierra, other indigenous people of coastal Ecuador, nonindigenous people) give to the shaman "other speech-knowledge" (*shuj shimita yachai*). The shaman at the same time maintains native paradigms and expands the paradigms by drawing from his knowledge of other cultures. The shaman controls the process of syncretism.

Master potters, all of whom are women, do the same thing. Although it is less common to hear this, one may refer to a genuine paradigm manipulator—a woman who is able to evoke both inner cultural knowledge as a synthesis of vision and experience, and one who can also evoke systematic relationships between such knowledge-vision integration and other forms of integration—as *yachaj huarmi*. It is also the case, as far as we know, that every master potter is related closely to a powerful shaman. In some cases the shaman is a father, in some cases a father-in-law, and in many cases there is a complex of shamanic males and master potter females. An example of the latter occurs, for example, when a woman who is the daughter of a powerful shaman marries a man who is the son of a powerful shaman. Her mother and mother-in-law are both master potters and she learns from each. Her husband, in turn, could be an incipient shaman, or a local political leader, or perhaps both.

Yachaj qualities exist in most men—perhaps in all. Most men must be able to "see" that there is something wrong within a *huasi*, and may actually "see" projectiles when they take soul-vine brew. At a certain point, however, in obtaining shaman's-class status (*yachaj sami*) one must acquire a *taquina* from another shaman. His breath then must be balanced with "proof." He becomes *sinchi yachaj*, powerful one who knows, and he both anchors and manipulates a cultural paradigm. Few men reach this level. Today in Nayapi Llacta the powerful shaman Lluhui is dead. Three of his sons privately regard themselves as *yachaj;* all cure within their families and all have close relationships with shamans equal to them and more powerful than they are. At least two of these men have acquired a *sinchi yachaj taquina*, but only one is strong enough to sing out, and he does so only secretly within his own house.

The daughters of Lluhui are all potters, and one is a master potter. Unlike men, who place themselves, their *huasi*, and their *ayllu* in danger with *taquina* songs due to their built-in system of potentially uncontrolled, reciprocated "proof," women's proof lies in the control of the breath of fire, in the control of color, of water, of clay, of form. Ceramics emerge as a tangible form of beauty, and the designs and colors evoke and motivate dynamic and syncretic syntheses of deep and immediate knowledge, thought, reflection, and vision.

Parallel Transmission of Cultural Knowledge

One could visit Nueva Esperanza repeatedly and never realize that shamanic activity took place there, but one could never enter a household and fail to notice the Upper Amazonian ceramics used to store and serve *asua*. Finding a woman who is a master potter gives one the first clue about where to find a nodal relationship with respect to kindred continuity, broker relationships with other indigenous cultures and with the urban system radiating out of Puyo, and complementary opposition and schismatic factionalism.

The woman's role in paradigm manipulation faces inward, drawing sustenance from ancient knowledge that has been imparted to her by instruction, by demonstration, through secrets, and through extensive impartation of private imagery drawn from myth and song by other women. The potter works in her own site, often in the middle of the house, but her supplies, which include red and white clays and black rock dyes, different clays that are mixed for different purposes, and tree resins, come from different places. Female-to-female networks of exchange that range widely, some across territories where men are hostile to one another, have their material manifestation in the ceramic product of the female master potter. Seated on a split-bamboo mat that faces away from the Andes, she sculpts an array of ceramic pieces that represent the cosmos, the mythic ordering of social life, imparting always something of the novel, something of herself, and something of the insights that link private thought and reflection to publicly acknowledged intracultural knowledge. She works from dawn to dusk, thinking songs and sometimes singing. Within a few days of such sustained activity she is managing a very complex system that includes the building of a large storage jar, several delicate drinking bowls, an effigy jar, and a figurine. As she works—sculpting, painting, firing, working clay—she reflects upon the complete array that she is making, and she imparts something of this reflected universe to other women who watch, help, and learn. Ceramic manufacture is especially elaborate in preparation for a festive event, when a deliberate rift is made in the fabric of *ñucanchi yachai* in the form of invited intrusion from the right side of the semiotic paradigm given on page 117.

An *internal* disjuncture of *ñucanchi yachai* within a cosmic network from human to spirit, through cosmos, and back to human triggers the activities that create a situation in which prominent male paradigm manipulation takes place. Here a shaman, working in the woman's sector of the household, faces both inward and outward. His paraphernalia includes a split calabash shell for drinking the *Banisteriopsis caapi* hallucinogen *ayahuasca* (soul vine); a smaller container for snuffing tobacco water, a cigarette or cigar for blowing cleansing smoke on whatever he wishes to "see into"; and an array of stones which themselves contain the life force (*causai*) of contained spirits, each with its own soul. Within him exists an array of hard spirit substances that form a shield (*lurira*) to protect his body. These substances are brought into his throat to help him diagnose the cause of illness, and they may be projected outward on his breath if he chooses to blow harm at an enemy. When these inner substances are so blown as projectiles they are *supai biruti*, spirit darts, or just *tsintsaca* (from the Jivaroan *tsentsak*, dart). One who has felt the hard, living proof of sent evil (*shitashca*) approaches the shaman and asks for help in exchange for pay.

The shamanic seance takes place just after dark and may go on until dawn. The shaman is seated (*tiarina*) on a carved stool that symbolizes the Amazonian water turtle. While he is seated and after he has drunk, spirit forces come to him in their corporeal manifestations. Then other spirits come to him and a spirit shaman appears standing (*shayarina*).

As spirits appear standing to the shaman while he is seated on his stool, he also travels to other lands where he appears standing to the spirits. To so appear standing is to be poised, to be ready, to be capable, to feel power. While still seated the shaman sings of where he is going and where he has been and of the power to see and to cure that he has obtained. He identifies the cause of illness as an object (perhaps a spider encased in blue mucous within one's kneecap) and as an agent (the shaman living on the Llushín River) and as an agent's client (Jorge, who claims to be a friend of the afflicted one's father), and, if he is paid to do so, he calls a demonic spirit; while seated and in a state of possession he sends forth a harmful projectile of his own.

In the traditional Canelos Quichua system, before the introduction of a large-scale ethnic arts market, and before the introduction of new forms of power and social control based upon relationships with the urban market, we can easily describe the system of cultural transmission as a parallel one. Taking the master potter female–shaman male as the conjoined node of a kindred it seems quite clear that cultural paradigms are manipulated in one way by pottery manufacture and in another way by shamanic activity. In such manipulation shaman and potter evoke, mystify, and clarify in complementary ways. For example, a man may look at this design around the shoulder of a pot and say

simply that it is an anaconda. But the woman who made it may wish to evoke a particular *amarun* manifestation that suggests to her daughter or daughter-in-law a whole series of relationships involving territoriality, ethnicity, and kinship. Similarly, when after taking *ayahuasca* the anaconda appears to the shaman, he cannot see it well; but women working with him snuff tobacco water and clarify the image, even speaking for it: "I am person Yacu mama." In their activities the shaman faces both outward and inward (in terms of our culture–their culture) and the potter faces primarily inward. This activity of parallel transmission can be diagrammed in terms of parallel concentric circles below.

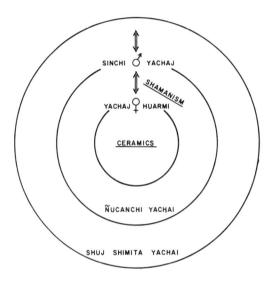

The force field created by the shaman protects the people while at the same time drawing additional strength from the outer world. The world to which shamans turn for power must be outward as well as inward, but the world to which women turn is expansively inward. For example, when a shaman flies to the right bank of the Pastaza River to engage the killing spirit force of the legendary Chirapas, he makes them different as he crosses the boundary between them and us, and takes the power of them back to us. But if a woman trades today with people from that same area for her clays and her dyes, then she makes them like us, for marriage and kin ties are manipulated so that material flow in the female domain is a manifestation of existing social ties.

Today in Nayapi Llacta we can still describe the system of cultural transmission as a parallel one. But in Nueva Esperanza, the microcosm of urbanism and urbanization, women too are facing both inward and outward as they manufacture ceramics for the burgeoning ethnic arts market as well as for their own use. This transformed parallelism is represented in the diagram below.

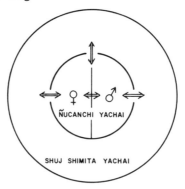

In the creation of a *llacta* a clear shaman node exists. But as the *llacta* grows in personnel and nucleates into a *caserío*, the strong shaman node eventually disappears. Few such men currently reside on the Comuna San Jacinto. Most powerful shamans today are of the *ayllus* of Nayapi Llacta residents, but they live in other places, some of them in Puyo, or in one of its satellite towns, some in Achuar territory, some in Canelos, Pacayacu, Sarayacu, Montalvo, or Curaray, some in the Napo region. *Yachaj* status, however, has been obtained by three brothers and one brother-in-law in Nayapi Llacta; each of these men has also taken over important brokerage functions between Puyo and Nueva Esperanza, working in very different ways and often in conflict with one another. The wives of each of these men is a potter; one is a master potter. Each of these women is also making pottery for sale in Puyo, and trying, in competition with other women, to attract exclusive patrons from Puyo, Baños, Ambato, and even from Quito.

As women and men transmit not only traditional culture and ancient syncretisms in a parallel, mutually reinforcing and mutually reinterpreting fashion, they also transmit, in a continuing if transformed parallel fashion, much of the new syncretic formations as both males and females intensify their own gender-specific ordering of cultural domains, while expanding those domains by exchange and interaction with bearers of other cultures. In the process of expansion sensory perceptions of "us" and "them" drawn from paradigms of ecological imagery are constantly invoked. This imagery locates the cosmology of Nayapi Llacta solidly within the Amazonian culture sphere, but also with syncretized elements of the ancient Andean world and the world of Hispanic conquest, and the invidious, pernicious exclusion of the peoples of Nueva Esperanza from the national system.

Paradigm of Ecological Imagery

The cosmos of the Canelos Quichua is permeated by concepts such as mythic time-space (*unai*), to which we allocate special fields of science in the Western world. To even attempt "cosmography"—description of a world-view—is to impart structure across vastly different cultures, technologies, and ways of thought. For example, concepts such as *unai* and *ñaupa* are left to hard-science specialists in the "theory of relativity" in modern U.S. universities, while the social scientists all too frequently seek their metaphors in physics now abandoned by post-Einsteinian scholarship. Our task is to present aspects of cosmology systematically so as to comprehend something of the ordering of chaos, and the use of disorder to maintain or reproduce wanted and unwanted consistencies. Toward this end I draw on bits and pieces of Canelos Quichua thought that help in understanding a largely implicit structuring of the cosmos. No one Runa, I am sure, would see things in exactly this way. But those who have watched Sibby and me try to understand, who have taken pains to instruct us, to develop devices of learning for us, and who have reflexively followed our process of learning, understand how we could comprehend their vision and knowledge of the cosmos and biosphere in this way.

Let us begin with the concepts *aya* and *supai*, which I define in English as soul and spirit respectively. Everything that is living or once lived (*causana*) has a soul. The soul's existence is both dependent upon its living substance, *causai*, and potentially independent of it. A *supai* is a living spirit force, being, or image which itself has a soul. Sometimes one hears that there is no difference between a *supai* and an *aya*. For example, take the great tree with massive flying buttresses called *ila*. One learns in time that the *ila* is a soul, is a human, is a spirit. One also learns that it is a *sacha supai runa—sacha supai aya tian* ("jungle spirit person—it has [is] jungle spirit soul"). Many such souls/spirits are prefixed by one of three adjectives: *sacha* (forest), *chagra* (garden), or *yacu* (water). And such spirits with forest, garden, or water prefixes may also be regarded as *tucuna* (transformation) of a highly allusive concept of spirit force specific to one of the three domains. I call such concepts *sign images* (Fernandez 1974, 1977; Whitten 1978); each may be described as a master spirit or as a key symbol. The master sign images are called Sungui, spirit master of the water domain (of the hydrosphere), Nunghui, spirit master of garden soil and of pottery clay, and Amasanga, spirit master of the forest.

The terms (and associated concepts) of Sungui and Nunghui are found in Jivaroan, Zaparoan, and Candoan languages; they are not

Yacu supai runa (Sungui), *left*, and *pai aya* (his soul), *right*. Apacha Vargas, *caserío* Nuevo Mundo, Comuna San Jacinto del Pindo.

Quichua. Amasanga (Amasank) is an Achuar image but does not figure into Achuar cosmology as prominently as in Canelos Quichua worldview.

Sungui and Nunghui may easily by contrasted. Sungui's manifestation, the anaconda, is frequently described with the suffix *mama;* as such s/he is Yacu mama, *curaga* of the *yacu supai runa* (water spirit people) and the force behind fish proliferation. Sungui represents the water world in all of its manifestations. He is male and female, his corporeal manifestation being the anaconda that hunts humans in order to devour them. His seat (*bancu*) is the Amazonian water turtle (*charapa*). When sitting on his turtle stool Sungui is a powerful shaman—his form is male-human and he is cloaked in the many colors of the rainbow; bright yellow and bright red make him a thing of shimmering beauty. This beauty, by the way, is likened to the basic black, white, red, and yellow colors of the toucan. When Sungui is standing he "appears" as the rainbow, a phenomenon of nature that may signal the unleashing of massive force from one end of its arc to the other. The word for the rainbow in Amazonian Quichua is *sinchi amarun* (strong anaconda).

With the concept of Sungui we encounter a consistent set of analogies with the Runa shaman, with the origin myth of *ayllu,* and with the observations that the nodal figures of the *ayllu* are powerful shamans. *Tucuna* in Quichua may be translated as "become," and in Canelos

Quichua as "transform," and *tucurina* means "to end everything." Both of these concepts are linked to Sungui. In the first, it may be said that a shaman person is an anaconda transformation; that the anaconda changes into one's soul; that the anaconda is a human penis. In the second, the *amarun* may be brought forth ceremonially to end the world (*tucurina*) in a great flood.

Within the global container of Sungui live many denizens from which human powers are descended. These are the *yacu apahuais;* all have external skeletons, ancient signs of the Asiatic–New World shamanic complex (Furst 1976). Their imagery is controlled by women, who may say that they are *yacu apamamamanda* (from water grandmother). The *yacu apahuais* are also regarded as spirit darts and as "our flesh." Examples include armored catfish, shrimp, clams and mussels, water bugs (called *yacu apatara*—water roach), helgramites. These hard creatures from the water domain, many of them edible, symbolize the descent of tangibility of cutting, stabbing, and shielding power. They are feminine forms of early shamanic power coming from the global water container into the lives of humans today. Yet they are made of, or contain, human flesh.

Potentially destructive force is linked to Sungui as torrential rains promoting flood, erosion, and landslide. Perhaps syncretized with Andean concepts is the idea, expressed only in times of crisis, of the ultimate merger of fire and water producing thunder, lightning, earthquake, volcanic eruption, and flood. Also linked to the domain of Sungui, and to a myth of the sun, is the concept of *rasu tamia* (ice rain), also called *nina tamia* (fire rain). Such hard ice-hot rain, it is said, comes to the Runa when God (*Dios*) is punishing them. We could take this to be a recent syncretism with Christianity, or as yet another truly ancient set of beliefs radiating out of Asia (see the discussion of the "Thunder Complex" in Blust 1981: 299-308, and the discussion of "Negrito" versus Austronesian origin or as ancient syncretism). Sungui is potentially unleashable nature (or nature occasionally unleashed) imbued with natural shamanic strength. Sungui must be controlled.

Nunghui is also often described in Quichua with a suffix *mama*, especially in Chagra mama and Manga allpa mama. It is these latter two forms that lead me to gloss her (she is always female) as a spirit master of garden soil (Chagra mama) and of pottery clay (Manga allpa mama). Her corporeal representations are the "harmless" (but deadly) coral snakes with mouths too small to bite humans. One species of these snakes is found in the leaf-mat litter (*chaquichisca panga allpa tucungahua*), where it is called *jahua nunghui*. Another lives underneath, in the actual soil (*allpa*); it is called *ucui nunghui*. Nunghui is, above all else, the spirit of domestication, of culture. Nunghui does not control

Interior (*above*) and exterior (*facing page*) of a *mucahua* in the form of a compote. The motif is that of *yacu apahuais*. Alicia Canelos, *llacta* Sarayaquillu, Sarayacu.

Rumi curu (helgramite). Apacha Vargas, *caserío* Nuevo Mundo, Comuna San Jacinto del Pindo.

Luchunga (shrimp). Apacha Vargas, *caserío* Nuevo Mundo, Comuna San Jacinto del Pindo.

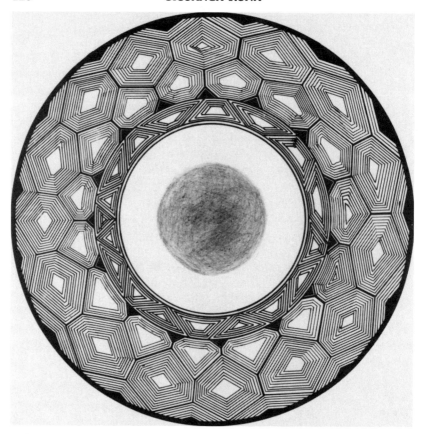

Interior (*charapa*), shown *above*, and exterior (*jahua nunghui*), on *facing page*, of the same pot. Delicia Dahua, *caserío* Río Chico, Comuna San Jacinto del Pindo.

nature. She exists within a *chagra* set within a forest cleared by men. She domesticates plants, helps women grow domesticated root crops, and imparts to women the secret of conversion of clay and water into ceramics by the mediation of domestic fire.

Amasanga, whose domain surrounds that of Nunghui, is, in turn, surrounded by the domain of Sungui. Amasanga is not only the spirit master of the rain forest in Canelos Quichua cosmology but also the personification of the antithesis of national urban culture, as this antithesis is borne to the Runa by priests, businessmen, explorers, or other purveyors of Western "civilization." My opinion is that the specific

forces pertaining to the forest have become syncretized by negative
analogy in the face of centuries of Western proselytization that stressed
the concept of the jungle, its people, and its properties as metonymic

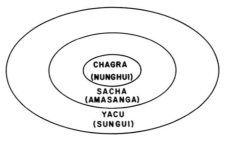

sets of invidious contrasts to "civilization." Whether or not I am correct
in this assessment, Amasanga *tucuna*—Amasanga transformation—
today includes these:

Sacha supai runa	Jungle spirit person (a synonym).
Sacha Runa	Jungle person (see Whitten 1976 for full analysis of multiple meanings).
Jurijuri supai	Foreign people's Amasanga; Amasanga of the Machin Runa. He is master of monkeys and lives in underground, urban centers.
Ila supai	A great tree.
Allpa supai	Soil or under-leaf-mat spirit.
Paccha supai	Waterfall spirit.
Uyarij Runa	Noisy (and brightly and beautifully dressed person); derives from *uyarina*, to hear.
Ingaru supai	A "demon" person who carries his heart on the outside of his body; a child will walk with him into the forest and return unharmed the next day, and without fear.
Palu supai	"Pole spirit." The word *palu*, from the Spanish *palo*, means both a pole used for orientation in a Datura quest and a poisonous snake.
Sacha mama — Sacha chagra mama	Feminine spirit of forest garden — she domesticates wild plant analogs to human plants — deer manioc, quail sweet potato, catfish taro.

The concept of *control of nature* imbues Amasanga with special character, though he is regarded as outside the domain of human domestication. He contrasts with Nunghui and with Sungui. However, Amasanga and Nunghui are from the domain of Datura; Sungui is not. The corporeal representation of Amasanga is the black jaguar. This forest creature embodies the sense impressions of yellow-red (orange) and shadow (black). Whereas humans see a reflected vision of their own *aya* through their shadow, Amasanga's *aya* is prominent in the black jaguar, where one must look closely to see the hidden jaguar's color underneath, so to speak, his tangible external shadow. Jungle cats were as ancient people chased from the *chagra* by Nunghui in some mythic texts, by Manduru (red woman) and Huiduj (black woman) in other myths. In each of these texts the woman domesticator, who chases

Sacha supai huarmi mask. Clara Santi Simbaña, *caserío* Río Chico, Comuna San Jacinto del Pindo.

Sacha chagra mama face on a *sicuanga manga*. Rosaura Hualinga, Río Llushín.

the jaguar away as it comes from the forest to hunt on the *chagra*, uses the jawbone of a peccary placed upon a stick, which animates the jaw to go *tuc tuc tuc* around the *chagra*, scaring the cat-men. The soul and spirit of the forest belong to the forest, not to the *chagra*.

In the forest Amasanga controls the weather; thunder is his drumming, and lightning is his as well. Strong wind (*urcumanda huaira samai*) is his breath, coming from a cave within a hill or from the hill itself. He is the *curaga* of animals and his pet is the bush dog. He helps

Sacha allcu (bush dog), mascot of Amasanga. Teresa Dahua, *caserío* Nueva Vida, Comuna San Jacinto del Pindo.

Two representations of a peccary: (*above*) Apacha Vargas, *caserío* Nuevo Mundo, (*below*) Juana Catalina Chango, *caserío* Río Chico, both of Comuna San Jacinto del Pindo.

humans create things out of jungle wood and animal skins. For example, when a man is making a canoe Amasanga helps by not allowing the log to split; and when a man makes a drum (to "walk like Amasanga"), Amasanga works inside as the man works on the outside. Man does not domesticate nature by his wood-working. He shapes it, and with Amasanga's help partly controls and partly "plays" with it.

Amasanga is parallel to Nunghui as *sacha* is parallel to *chagra*, but Amasanga also surrounds Nunghui as forest surrounds garden and is, in turn, surrounded by the hydrosphere, domain of Sungui. For this reason we can consider the parallelism of Amasanga and Nunghui either in terms of each being a separate entity surrounded by water or as a concentric parallelism (see pp. 121, 129). If, as suggested above, Amasanga is a syncretized sign image, then we could see the nature/culture (Sungui/Nunghui) dichotomy as a fundamental contrast mediated by Amasanga. Amasanga seems to be a set of syncretized imagery built reflexively out of Western denigration of the rain forest and indigenous dependence on its ecological relationships. The relationship of Amasanga imagery to that of Sungui and Nunghui is that of control over the power of nature on one side and lack of control over the power of domestication on the other.

The Sungui-Amasanga-Nunghui set of sign images is paradigmatic in that discussion of any one of these images invariably evokes thoughts of the other sign images. For some time now we have dealt with the paradigm given on page 117 in terms of the twists and turns of knowledge, thinking, reflecting, experiencing, and learning, skirting the issue of *vision* (*muscuna*).

Visionary Experiences

The Runa of Nayapi Llacta, like people everywhere, dream when they sleep. They actively seek meaning in dreams, using the concepts set forth in the paradigm to guide them. Dream imagery as sense experience (*muscui*) is related to the universe of souls and spirits, to *unai*, to known history, to cultural, ethnic, and social space. Like their cultural congeners of Amazonian South America, the Runa also gain visionary experience by use of a soul-vine brew. In this use the Runa are either guided by a shaman or take the shaman role themselves. Unlike most Amazonian peoples, but in concert with many Andean, MesoAmerican, and North American native peoples, the Runa of Nayapi Llacta also use, in a culturally prescribed manner, one of the most dangerous hallucinogens in the world—Datura (specifically *Datura suaveolens* cultivars).

My intent in this section is to sketch the cultural patterning of visionary experience by reference to the contrasts between *ayahuasca* and *huanduj* trips. Such structuralist reduction is not an end in itself, but rather a strategy of description that allows us to perceive the means by which ordering of visionary experience, which articulates correspondences from coincidental planes of existence, provides the information necessary to understand the ordering of chaos in Nayapi Llacta/ Nueva Esperanza.

Dreams are part of life. As such they themselves are manifestations of life. They are real but not tangible under ordinary circumstances. Their origin is problematic and they provide the stuff from which creativity and imagination born of reflection are made. One's *causai* exists in corporeal and non-corporeal dimensions; its reflection, in the latter, is seen when awake in one's shadow and in one's eye. These reflections, in Runa thought, are said to be just that, even though they may be called *aya* or *alma*. The fundamental mystery of simultaneous existence of both flesh and soul is not overcome with any sense of soul detached from body. Detachment and attachment are complementary facets of life processes. The *aya* (soul)/*aicha* (body) contrast is analogous to the *shayarina* (standing-appearing)/*tiarina* (sitting-being) contrast. The former is a reflexive form of *shayana*, to stand, the latter of *tiana*, to be. Let me explore this analogy briefly in a very mundane, everyday setting.

I am going to visit Tselctselc in his house; he and I are *compadre* to one another, and I've known him for over a decade now. When I am a couple of hundred yards from his house I call sufficiently loudly so that he, and all in the vicinity of his household as well, can hear: *huuuuuuuuuu*. And he answers: *whaaay*. I walk steadily to his house, and when I see him sitting on a stool, as always when he is so forewarned, I ask *"Tianguichu, gumba"* (from *tiana*, to be present)—"Are you there, *compadre?"* and he answers *"Tiaunimi, gumba"* ("I am here, *compadre"*). Then, while I am still a few yards from the house, still walking steadily, I say *"Pactamuni, gumba"* ("I am arriving, *compadre"*), and he says *"Shamui"* ("Come"), *"Yaicui"* ("Enter"), and then *"Tiari"* ("Sit down"). Etiquette having been observed, we talk. Both of us must be sitting on something that itself is on the floor; we sit on a *bancu*, which, for the household head, is carved in the form of the Amazonian water turtle; for the visitor it is a long bench symbolizing the *amarun*. As we talk we drink *asua* served by Tselctselc's wife, Faviola, and we drink a good deal of this yeasty, mildly fermented manioc brew from a lovely ceramic bowl, decorated on the exterior with designs representing Sungui and on the interior with more embellishment of forest, water, and *chagra* motifs. Only when our bellies are full of *asua* do we stand, move around, walk as we talk. If others enter the house we again sit until everyone has drunk, until all are full.

Ecological imagery is with us, the *huasi* contains us, we are rooted, so to speak, in that *huasi* by our mutual sitting; we are real, corporeal; we are not "standing-appearances" to one another. To be "standing-appearing" is to be "seen" there, in contrast to "being" there. We are real to one another in a waking world, and one of our subjects for conversation is often a dream. By discussion we may decide on the source or origin of a normal dream, called *puñusha muscuna* (sleep-dreaming).

If our bodies remained well, if interpersonal tensions did not cause us to be suspicious of our neighbors and friends, if we but lived in a static world where the pattern of life was not forever disrupted by births, deaths, loves, hatreds, alliances, vendettas, then, perhaps, there would be no need for radical readjustment. But today we are flesh as well as soul; our *ayllu*s contain real people. The visions we encounter in today's world, and the difficulties we encounter in bringing our knowledge into line with our thought and reflection, require trips beyond the *sacha, chagra, huasi,* and *caserío.* We go as we are and we hope to return stronger. There are two mind-altering vehicles for such a trip: the first is Banisteriopsis; the second is Datura.

Ayahuasca

A man or a woman is advised to take *ayahuasca* by a shaman. The shaman so advises when, in a discussion with someone who has an illness, he feels the need for a deeper experience with patient, on-lookers, and sectors of the cosmos, before making a complete diagnosis and before healing. The shaman always takes *ayahuasca*; the patient may take it if he or she is an adult; and on-lookers, who never number more than three or four, may also take it. *Ayahuasca* is a vine that grows in the jungle, and shamans plant it near their homes. It may also be called *quilla huasca* (moon vine). The vine stem is split and cooked, together with leaves from another Banisteriopsis species or psychotria called *amarun yaji* (anaconda *yaji*). The word *yaji* is not Quichua; it comes from Tucanoan or other Northwest Amazon languages and is used widely throughout Upper Amazonia for the brew itself. No red paint is used in *ayahuasca* trips, but it is not uncommon for the shaman, or another in his household, to still have black paint on his face or body. The black paint, from *huiduj* (*Genipa americana*), is painted on in the evening, after being cooked, and it does not show up until the next day. *Huiduj* and *ayahuasca* must be cooked; each is associated with the moon, which, in turn, is associated with disorder, and with Runa origin and continuity.

Seated on his *bancu* in the woman's part of the house, which is faintly illuminated by flickering flames, the shaman drinks. He feels intoxicated and begins to "see" as he hears the roar of rain or waterfall encompassing the house. As large images appear before him, a woman who has snuffed tobacco clarifies the first visions and speaks for or as the "vision": *"Yana puma runa mani"* ("I am the black jaguar person"), *"Yacu mama runa mani"* ("I am the river woman person"). The woman who so "sees" is usually the shaman's wife, herself a master potter, who is known as *muscuj huarmi* or *sinchi muscuj huarmi*, and may be called *yachaj huarmi*. Both black jaguar and black anaconda appear as pairs; the former comes first as co-shaman from the forest domain, the latter then appears in black manifestation as canoe-vehicle for the forest spirit master as shaman. The black anaconda is from the water domain, the world of Sungui, who is himself a shaman. Yacu mama in the form of a colorful anaconda or fish examines the Runa shaman's *shungu*, his will, and silently converses with him. The will has two manifestations—the inner essence that contains the shaman's motivations, strengths, and purposes, and the flesh of stomach, heart, and lungs. The shaman converses with Yacu mama, and as he gains her knowledge about his will and about his patient's affliction, his body swells. Then, sitting on his stool, now puffed up fat with visionary potency, the shaman converses softly with the patients. He calls for his leaf bundle (*shingu shingu panga*, named after a jungle cat), and it is given to him by his wife or daughter. He drinks again, shakes his leaf bundle to create a spirit wind, and "sees" the snake tongues flickering from its lanceolate leaves. He sings out his *taquina* song and more spirits of the forest come. Spirits of *events* come too—some are other indigenous peoples, some are animals marching as soldiers in the Peru-Ecuador war or as a karate expert who taught soldiers in Shell a few years back. As these images come they dance, swinging left, then right; they are beautiful, and they are strong. While still sitting on his *bancu*, the shaman flies into the air and travels to other lands. While sitting he sings of his travels through space, which varies in its viscosity. Out of this air come killing missiles sent by other shamans, and he defends himself, swinging from side to side, using a shield of Sungui or a deflective move of Amasanga. He returns to where he is, still singing of where he has been, and he "sees" the evil in the patient in the form of a cutting or stinging creature encased in blue mucous in the patient's stomach. Again he drinks, and he sucks, noisily, again and again, taking the evil from the patient into his mouth, holding it, allowing his own spirit helpers from his *shungu* to examine and to take the soul of the evil substance from it; he then blows the evil substance, devoid of soul, into a tree outside of his house, and there it stays. He then examines everyone in the household, and cleanses them with the breeze from his leaf bundle.

Sinchi muscuj huarmi.

Drawing of *sinchi yachaj* sitting on a *bancu* and swelling with knowledge as he communicates with Yacu mama. Drawn by Alfonso Chango, Colonia Cuatro y media, Vía Napo, Pastaza Province.

If the shaman goes on with his seance performance he next calls the undersoil spirits of the forest in triple, feminine form, and they come to him *under the house;* there, unified as a single, powerful, killing spirit, they sit on him as their *bancu.* They then possess the shaman; he is *bancu.* Through him they as one do what he has just done, and then they divine the causal agent who initiated the action leading to illness, and "he" as Jurijuri—soul master of other people from other cultures (the spirit on shaman on *bancu* on ground with spirit force under the ground)—sends a killing missile out to rend the air with slight, high falsetto, but audible sound (*quich huiaj*) and to break into the biological, social, and spiritual network of the agent and his shaman—into their bodies, protective shields, and into their *ayllus*—to do killing harm.

Before dawn everyone is home; the disorder of night created within the *huasi*—as the shaman stays seated on his *bancu* but appears standing to the spirits, while the spirits appear standing to the seated shaman until, finally, both spirits and shaman are together seated in one cosmic connection to project death—does not carry into day. The sun brings order out of the waters to the east. Day is a time of its own order/ disorder. Ruptures which occur are usually mended at night by shamanic activity, just as this activity creates its own ruptures that then require a mender. Rupture that cannot be so mended demands that one enter the cosmos alone, to risk everything for a secure grasp on knowledge and a heightened ability to "see."

Huanduj

Huanduj icon. *Caserío* Río Chico.

The decision to take *huanduj* is an individual matter and the drug is usually ingested alone. If a second person is present, however, companionship is precautionary: there is no guiding helper who is of this world. Both the person taking the *huanduj* and the companion, if there is one, paint themselves with red, uncooked *manduru* (*Bixa orellana*) dye. The *huanduj* must not be *yacu huanduj* but rather *alli upina huanduj* (good drinking Datura, as opposed to water Datura). The *huanduj* has been previously acquired from a close friend from a distant *llacta,* one who usually is not a relative. It is planted and then "found" in an old *chagra,* where the distinction between *chagra* and *sacha* is difficult to make. A great *ila* tree is addressed as *amigo* (friend) in Spanish, and the tree is asked to help the seeker. A barked pole is placed in front

Cuando descubrían
alguna planta valioza.
Se sentaban a meditar
que hago con esto.
sentado en un árbol
caido.

Ancient person discovering *huanduj*. Drawn by Alfonso Chango, Colonia Cuatro y media, Vía Napo, Pastaza Province.

of a lean-to, the forest is cleared of brush in a particular direction, and sometimes poles stripped of their bark are placed there too. The pole and the *ñambi* (trail) help the taker, as does the great tree; indeed, the forest itself becomes a helper. The *huanduj* is drunk around noon, when the sun is high and the world is ordered. It is squeezed from the inner bark and drunk with water taken from a bamboo stem, not from a river or stream.

The taker sits in front of his house, looking toward his pole and his trail; within ten minutes he passes out completely and falls back into his lean-to. Oscillating between an extremely agitated state and unconsciousness, the taker sees things that are distant as though they were right there, and he sees people and things nearby as though they were far away. He sees clearly, though, and he converses at great length with friends and close ones. Amasanga arrives, usually dressed in a shimmering black-purple robe; he is in two bodies, a tall one and a short one. (Some say that in this context Amasanga and Sungui are one and the same.) He helps the *huanduj* taker to see rifts in the social fabric and penetrations into his body. The taker sees his enemies and his friends, and he knows how to differentiate between them. He also sees into the future and takes note of coming crises. Then Amasanga, turning to the taker's body, sucks out the intruding projectiles, cleanses him completely, and gives him counsel on coming crises, opportunities, and misfortunes. There is no danger while one is in the expanded universe, where souls, spirits, and humans, living and dead, are one; but there is danger when one begins to leave the cosmic theater. By midnight the taker begins to move; he staggers and falls. The spirit master of the rain forest helps him so that no injury occurs, and eventually, as the sun rises the next day, the taker finds his way to his own *huasi*, even though it is a couple of hours' away from the site of his *huanduj* experience.

On his return the person is an absolute disaster within the quotidian household. While others attempt to go about routine tasks, he still sees the world of spirits, of the dead, of the future, of souls; he stumbles and falls and crashes, laughing when he should say *ayaów!* (ouch!) and frightening people. Gradually he sees the surroundings as others see them, and he sees the expanded cosmos as well; the latter continues to recede as the former comes into sharper and sharper focus. Only when about three days have passed in a state of agitation and confusion does the taker go to the river and bathe, and then he is "back," but with a new level of knowledge and a new level of "seeing."

BRIEF CASES

Discussed below are cases where a few people of Nayapi Llacta/Nueva Esperanza actually utilized many of the elements presented in this chapter to create order from disorder, and in so doing maintained a sense of continuity in a setting of radical change.

The Characters

Taruga married Elena in 1973; he, the son of Sicuanga by a previous marriage (his mother died later in childbirth), is from Nayapi Llacta. It is his *quiquin llacta*. He met Elena in Puyo, where she had come to work in the house of a *comerciante* in order to send money home to a small hamlet outside of Archidona. Her family is part of a large *muntun* that periodically travels between the Archidona *llacta* (the territory of which was then owned by a *blanco*) and a site on the Napo River, just up the Río Payamino, which the *muntun* was trying to acquire

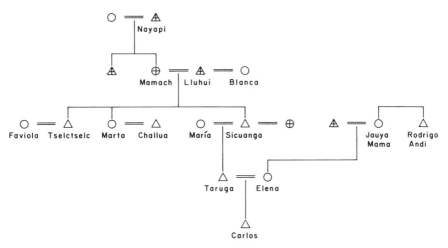

legally from the Ecuadorian Institute for Agrarian Reform and Colonization (IERAC), with the assistance of the new National Institute for
the Colonization of the Ecuadorian Amazonian Region (INCRAE). The
whole *muntun* attended the wedding in Nueva Esperanza, tempers
flared, fights broke out, and most of the *muntun* departed the same
day. Little by little, though, other alliances were formed by men and
women visiting back and forth, and by 1981 three more people from
Nayapi Llacta had married into Elena's *muntun*. Sicuanga, Taruga's
father, was one of several sons of Lluhui, a powerful shaman. He was
instrumental in the decision to send Taruga off to work in the oil fields
near Montalvo for two years back in the late 1960s, reciprocating with
his son for the financial aid given to his father by presenting him with
the territory of the *llacta* that he had occupied when Carmen, his
Achuar wife, had been living. After Carmen's death Sicuanga himself
had gone off to work on a coastal plantation and then returned to
Canelos, where his father, Lluhui, had lived prior to moving, with
Nayapi, to the area south of Puyo near the Curiminas Yacu River. There
he again married, returning to Nayapi Llacta in 1969. Sicuanga's wife,
María, is a master potter from Canelos; his sister, Marta, is a master
potter from Nayapi Llacta proper, and his widowed stepmother, Blanca,
is a master potter from Papaya Llacta on the Upper Conambo River.
Lluhui himself had spent considerable time in his youth in Archidona,
on the Conambo River, and in the town of Ambato in the Sierra,
learning about other cultures. In fact Elena's mother, called Jauya Mama
(in-law mother), has a living brother, Rodrigo Andi, who was in the
same shaman's class as the late Lluhui. Jauya Mama is also a potter,

making fragile black pots and eating ware in a style that contrasts with that of the Canelos Quichua peoples.

Today Sicuanga and María live off the plaza, about 300 yards due west; Marta and her Achuar husband, Challua, live on the plaza; Blanca lives off the plaza about half a kilometer due south, and Taruga, Elena, and their seven-year-old son, Carlos, live about six kilometers southwest, in the area designated the "second line" of Nayapi Llacta.

Taruga's Dream

An hour and half's hard trek from *caserío* Nueva Esperanza, Taruga and Elena today live near the center of their two-hectare *chagra*, set in rain forest that appears virgin to the uninitiated but was partially cut some twenty years or more before by Sicuanga. They are in their second house now, a large, roomy, quadrangular structure on top of a hill looking over the rain forest with good, filtered spring water twenty meters from the house and a stream to bathe in at the bottom of the hill. Sleeping on the upper story on the west side of the house one clear night in late May, 1981, the time when the guama tree fruits, Taruga saw, in his dream, a great horse coming to the house.

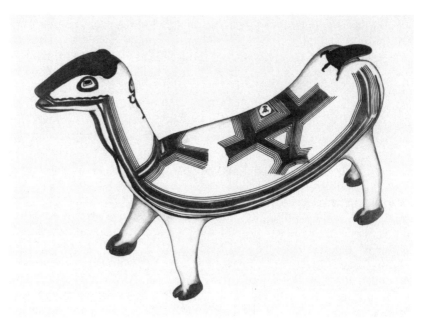

Taruga. Maker unknown, Sarayacu.

He was looking toward Palora, on the right bank of the Pastaza River, when he saw the horse coming. Palora is an urban area, but not long ago it was the territory of the Jivaroan Chirapas. There had been some strange killings near Palora over the past few months, as poor people from many areas struggled for land on the edge of the expanding tea plantations and cattle ranches.

The horse was coming from Palora right toward him. On either side were the troops, and behind the horse there were still more troops, all marching toward his house, and he saw them coming in his dream. The horse was as high as his second story—it could look right at him as he looked at it. Taruga was sitting up, looking at the great horse. It snorted as horses do, with nostrils flared and raised: *plffffffff*. Taruga snarled back at the horse like a jaguar, *ssssgggghhhh*. He woke up. He had a fever. He first blew smoke where the horse had been, and then went down to the ground and blew smoke all around the house. Then he returned to sleep and dreamed of a lagoon where he was paddling a canoe; he crossed to the other side, gave a new hand-operated coffee-bean decorticating machine to an in-law there, and received, in turn, a beautiful headdress of toucan feathers. Also, in that dream he "knew" what his *taquina* song would one day be: *unaimanda sicuanga taquina* (toucan shaman song from mythic time-space). The next day Taruga still had his fever, but Elena said it was getting better. She, too, told of how he snarled like a jaguar, how he blew smoke right off the second floor into the air, where the all-too-real horse dream-image, with its flanking and following troops, had stood and snorted, before Taruga descended to the ground to cleanse the entire house and surrounding air with his white tobacco-permeated breath.

Taruga was concerned about the dream all day, as his fever subsided. He told me of many young men in the *comuna* who, like himself, were not shamans but were known to be strong to one another, and were so known to residents of Puyo. He fears no one, he says, not even the great horse coming toward him like the president of the *comuna*, whom he had recently crossed politically in an *asamblea general*. The president might hold the dominating authority of office, backed up by regional, juridical, and political control, and be represented as the mighty force of a warhorse, but he, Taruga, the red brocket deer, had the powerful breath of a jaguar and the shaman's song of the warrior toucan with which to blow away that formation of authority and control.

Taruga's Trip to Visit Rodrigo Andi

On June 1, 1981, Taruga, Elena, Jauya Mama, an unmarried sister, and one of Taruga's young cousins decided to go to Ahuano, on the

Napo River, to visit the *sinchi yachaj* Rodrigo Andi. Taruga had tremendous confidence in himself, but just too many bad dreams were coming his way, and although his fever had subsided and he knew his future shaman's song, little Carlos had twice been stricken with fever and diarrhea. He had been treated in Vozandes Hospital in Shell, and a powerful shaman on the road to Napo had also sucked a spirit protrusion from his heel. Nonetheless Taruga was uncomfortable, and after consultation with his father, Sicuanga, he decided to drink *ayahuasca* with another powerful one, at a greater distance in space, culture, and ethnic identity but at the same time closely related to him as a member of his wife's *ayllu*.

This group left Puyo on the 9:00 A.M. San Francisco bus, taking with them the green wooden decorticating machine that Taruga had purchased in Puyo as a gift for his brother-in-law. They also took 450 *sucres* to pay necessary fees. They talked to the shaman all one day, learning that he was now treating not only occasional Andean visitors, but also posing for pictures (and occasionally selling bottles of *ayahuasca* mixed with alcohol) to tourists from the United States, Germany, Italy, Spain, and other lands. As evening drew near all talked quietly in the shaman's house, as don Rodrigo himself rested. Just as dusk descended over the Napo, with the frogs beginning to peep and the skyline of the mighty Andes standing in black relief before the great red ball as *indi* crossed over to *indi yaicushca*, and as the whirlpool that grinds and polishes two- to four-pound pebbles where the Arajuno enters the Napo swelled in intensity, a motor was heard coming down-river. In ten minutes a commercial cargo canoe arrived and in it were two North Americans with a great deal of recording equipment. While Taruga and Elena listened, the *gringos* talked to don Rodrigo, and he agreed to let these outsiders sit in on the curing session and to partake in the *ayahuasca* drinking.

At 8:00 P.M. all had drunk, had become intoxicated, had talked. The following information comes from the recording made by the two North Americans (Crawford 1979) and from discussion of the recording with people in Taruga's family, Elena's family, and with others who subsequently listened to the record that Neelon Crawford made on this particular occasion.

On his *bancu*, seat of Sungui, don Rodrigo chants *sumá, sumá, sumá, sumá* (beauty, beauty, beauty, beauty); because he is bottling up his sounds, closing his vowels, and "tightly" releasing his *samai* it sounds as though he's chanting *tomá, tomá, tomá*. He also chants *tarí ri rí ri rí ri rí* (from which comes the term *tariri*, "shaman" in several languages), which demonstrates that don Rodrigo has the killing power of the Jurijuri (Jirijiri in Napo Quichua, Jirijri in Achuar) supai, the undersoil, cave-dwelling master of monkeys and foreign peoples that sends his *huaira samai* (breath of the wind) out from his mysteriously lighted inner cave and across the jungle.

Don Rodrigo sings that he is pleased with the beauty of the spirit of *ayahuasca* herself, and with the merged beauty of the spirit world and the strength to kill. He talks and sings of the appearance of a male jungle spirit person, who then arrives. This spirit being is first un-identified as it arrives dressed in red and yellow toucan feathers, with bandolier-like seed-bead adornments. He swings his entire body from side to side, side to side. Don Rodrigo, sitting on his stool, becomes the spirit, singing, playing, seeing, ready to travel beyond to bring more spirits to him. He experiences a flying sensation as though he were a great condor, soaring, going out, coming back, and he sings about this.

Danger exists everywhere for the shaman as he experiences flights; now he must fend off flying death in the form of spirit darts and lances. He chants about what he is doing—singing that he is protected by a powerful shield of Sungui. As the spirit darts come toward him, first from one side and then from the other, he swings his body and his shield rhythmically, as in a dance, and as he swings he blows out, *suuuuuuu, suuuuuu*. The darts glance off the water-power shield and are blown away by his *samai* full of its spirit forces. He sings that the shield itself is made up of powerful medicine and spirit substances that come from a drugstore. The shaman is at one and the same time fending off killing missiles with his Sungui shield and becoming a doctor who buys medicines in a spirit drugstore on the Napo River. This ancient Sungui–modern doctor continues to call the beautiful, killing forest spirit Jurijuri to him as he chants that he has now acquired the power of Sungui, which came to him out of a great lagoon, and that he has strong medicine with which he can cure. And the shaman continues to sing that the spirit of the forest is arriving and that it is dancing, adorned with *sicuanga* feathers, *sicuanga* bird bones, and a beautiful *sicuanga* headdress. This unnamed vision dances and ar-rives—standing right in the place of the shaman himself, where he is seated on his *bancu*. Now a force field of dancing, warrior-spirit power occupies the same space as the chanting shaman, though they are on different, complementary cosmic planes (one sitting-being, the other standing-appearing).

The spirit brings ten machines (*máquinas*)—among them X-ray, blood-pressure apparatus, stethoscope, large bright surgical light—with which to cure the patient, little Carlos, son of Taruga and Elena. The spirit is making quite a noise, jingling and rattling and laughing, and he is dressed like a beautiful Sicuanga Runa. Now the shaman acknowledges the spirit as Uyarij Runa, noisy person, and as *sinchi yachaj*, powerful shaman.

Don Rodrigo identifies the beautiful, noisy spirit still further as Runga supai, water-jaguar spirit (Napo Quichua), or giant otter spirit. As the spirit arrives he snorts, rattles his teeth like a peccary, and makes the jaguar's cough associated with the Jurijuri spirit. Now, as the Runga supai is with the shaman on the *bancu* (standing-appearing versus sitting-being has become ambiguous), don Rodrigo chants of power drawn from the spirit and human waking worlds and from recent history. He chants that he has spirit cannons with which enemies will be killed, and that an ancient hill has been pulverized. Then he sings of airplanes around and above—circling, blitzing, buzzing, making a tremendous noise. There are all types: small one-engine planes and big military ones, company and commercial planes, helicopters and Herculeses. "Here I am," he sings, "a shaman sitting in the center of aviation control, peaceful with the spirit power, while all this noise and destruction go on around me in the air. And it is beautiful."

"From down-river the soldiers are coming," he continues, referring to the power of invasion during the war with Peru in 1941. "A beautiful line of marching soldiers, all swinging from side to side, left to right, right to left, moves up-river. All are water-jaguar spirits; more come from the south, and I, as *yachaj*, contact them with radiograms. They come here and are with me on my *bancu*, a Spanish seat of pure gold." Now the shaman chants that he is arriving at a high hill where there are many *muja huarmi supai*, which are special oblong-shaped, basin-like water spirits. There the water-jaguar spirit comes dancing and singing as Amasanga huarmi, the forest spirit in feminine form. Then the shaman stops singing; he yawns, whistles, talks a bit to the two foreigners, and accepts a cigarette from one of them.

After more whistling the shaman takes out a *pijuano*, a vertical, shaman's-class flute, and again plays his *taquina*, noting with care that the *gringos* are still recording his music. Quietly, almost but not quite so that those present can't hear, don Rodrigo now hums two tones mm-mm mm-mm. These sounds, it is said, are the only ones that humans made in *unai*. At that time humans crawled around as babies, and all other life forces were "human." The hum, or whistle, of the two tones is the sound analog of swinging from side to side; each brings the Runa world and mythic time-space into the same cosmic dimension with known history and the spirit domains. With ancient and contemporary now one, and with a unity of history and now, don Rodrigo has taken the steps necessary to establish a force field around himself and his Amazonian water turtle seat of power; he again begins to sing.

Beauty and spirit-killing powers are again chanted, and then he summons the underwater feminine power as a chief, *curaga*. And again the spirit comes as Uyarij Runa, the noisy spirit, making the sound of the jaguar, which evokes the fearsome Jurijuri supai. The shaman is now gathering the power to kill, for only when he possesses this power will he be strong enough to cure his patient of the killing darts sent to him by a shaman working for a malevolent agent. Instead of calling a spirit shield he now summons a spirit lance with a steel tip and refers to himself as a warrior, chanting the sounds of the Shuar peoples to the south, who visited him in order to purchase spirit darts to use against their own enemies. These Shuar, he chants, were Chirapas who lived just beyond Palora, just south of the Pastaza River. He sings as the dancing water-jaguar spirit and enjoys both the beauty of vision and the noise accompanying the vision. Now there is no longer ambiguity about the seat of power and the control of power from the world of spirits. Don Rodrigo himself *is* the seat of power for the powerful spirit, and the spirit chants through him. The shaman has become *bancu* for the spirit shaman.

Although those present still see the shaman chanting, he himself knows that the chants are coming from the spirit, and he is now the spirit's anchor and vehicle into the waking world of humans. The spirit chants that he will cure, that he is part of a *bancu* (here the shaman himself has become the *bancu*). In addition to the qualities of noise and vision the spirit now chants of strength. The spirit shaman sings that he is like a sun pope, a spirit force of the sky that corresponds to the Pope in the world of Catholic Christians. Then the spirit sings that he is the Tsalamanga *curaga*, chief of the mystical water spirits of the deep, cold Andean lakes. He descends into a lake of beautiful ice inside of a mountain, where he sits on the seat of power there, still swinging from side to side, dancing and singing. Note here that the shaman, as *bancu*, is still seated-being in his house on a high bank above the Napo River, but now his spirit possessor, who has traveled while seated on the shaman to the Andean lakes, is *also* seated-being in the Andean lake. The shaman with his spirit is anchored solidly in two domains, but as himself (shaman) he remains anchored where he is. There is tremendous danger in this procedure, for if the shaman loses his grip within his household—loses his ground, so to speak—he will die.

The spirit, speaking through the shaman while still within the icy Andean lake, next asks the Tsalamanga spirit if he can have a horse to ride; he wants one that looks like the sun (a palomino). When he returns to the Napo, he says, he will be riding a dancing horse, rhythmically swinging from side to side, right to left, left to right, dancing. He will also return wearing a sweater and necktie and be master of all these Andean things that have come from other native Quichua cultures, and also from foreign sources.

Now the spirit, singing through don Rodrigo, chants of his and other powerful, sentient, living stones. Spirits are coming to him from such stones in the form of sharp, dart-like projectiles. He grabs them, first from one side, then from another, swinging rhythmically from side to side, taking from the left, then from the right. Where, in the first *taquina* rendition, the shaman was defending himself with Sungui's shield from the incoming darts, the spirit shaman, working through the shaman, is now capturing the darts in the form of sharp stones and keeping them for future use. Behind the incoming spirit projectile stones the Uyarij Runa once again appears-dancing, and he is beautiful.

Now don Rodrigo, still possessed by the spirit, sings of the Chirapa Jivaroans from the right bank of the Pastaza River. He says that he is chief of the Chirapa, and will take the ancient specter vision of them however this vision may come. He sings that while he is dreaming, the ancient specter comes to him all dressed in white, black, red, and yellow toucan feathers, with a pure *sicuanga* shoulder-bone adornment which Achuar killers wear. All the Chirapa women are brought to him, he sings, and this is both beautiful and powerful. He alone controls their feminine beauty and forces. The song ends, and don Rodrigo instantly snaps his attention back to what is going on around him. He says that foreigners have come to record his song, and that he has sung well; he shushes a baby who is crying. Then he turns to Elena, who is holding Carlos, and asks her some questions. Taruga enters the conversation and tells of his dream of the horse. Again don Rodrigo drinks *ayahuasca* and offers more to Taruga. He intersperses playing his *pijuano* with making comments and queries; long into the night the flute sounds and conversation goes on. At about 1:00 A.M. don Rodrigo plays his violin, calling once again to the spirits whose help he will need in his diagnosis and curing. He says that the tape recorder has captured his spirit songs, and that the music is good.

He then asks Taruga to put Carlos on the long *bancu*; Elena does so, and don Rodrigo examines the child with a practiced eye. He sees the source of trouble quickly—spirit dart-like projectiles, many of them, lodged in his little stomach. Taruga vaguely sees them too and sighs, *haaaay*. He bends over the child's stomach and noisily sucks out a dart, blue mucous and all, taking it into his mouth and rolling it around. His own spirit helpers come up from his *shungu* to examine the inner substance of the dart and to take the essence from it, thereby increasing the shaman's power by the addition of more spirit substance. The shaman himself is left to dispose of the remaining substances, and he does so by blowing them into a rock on the edge of the great whirlpool that can be heard clearly from his house.

Elena now tells the shaman that little Carlos was with her in her manioc garden when she went there to harvest for the evening meal. "A stick broke and hit his side, and he fell," she said; "the wound kept hurting and now he is nearly dead." Taruga asks don Rodrigo, "Can you see the one who would do this?" "Yes," says the shaman, Elena's uncle, "I can see him; now I'll do the same to him."

The next day the *gringos* left, and the day after that a number of gallons of blue paint arrived by cargo canoe from Misahuallí, a cordial return of outside material for inside knowledge previously requested by don Rodrigo. Taruga and Elena stayed a week, helping don Rodrigo paint a new addition to his house, where, he said, more tourists would be received, and where he would make more money. Carlos became healthy and Taruga and Elena felt that now, indeed, their merged *ayllus* were more secure within their *huasi* on the second line of Nayapi Llacta, for they had strengthened it, by outside shamanic performance in a distant *llacta* by a powerful one with strong ties to Elena's *ayllu*, and to the outer worlds.

Sicuanga's Journey with Huanduj Supai

Sicuanga, María, and their children listened with interest to Taruga and Elena's report of don Rodrigo's curing session with Carlos. They reflected on the northern shamanic power of Napo "ones who know" and on the killing prowess of Jivaroan peoples to the south. Sicuanga quietly said that his father had come from the south before living on the Copataza River. Later, out of Canelos, he journeyed to the Napo area, where he met and married Sicuanga's widowed mother, Mamach, bringing her back to Nayapi Llacta and re-uniting there in that new territory the ethnic antipodes of Napo Quichua and Shuar, stereotypically perceived as civilized, subjected, and conquered Indian (Napo Runa) and savage "Jívaro" headhunter in the eyes of Puyo's residents. Sicuanga was pleased that his son and daughter-in-law had been able to cure their son, who himself was the embodiment of the social and spiritual essence of the founding *ayllu*, by recourse to Napo shamanic activity no longer securely available at home. But he was also uneasy, for the replication of structure—the tenuous, disordered, transcendental conjoining of opposites—by human volition invariably creates rifts elsewhere.

A month later Sicuanga was clearing a new *chagra*, making a big one for María to plant manioc in, for he expected to be named *prioste*—

carrier of the sumptuary charge—of the festival at Nuevo Mundo in a couple of years, and he wanted to do right by those who would be invited and be served massive quantities of manioc beer. He had chopped away at a massive tree all one day until his body not only ached with each chop, but also took him at times to the edge of visionary experience with the combination of exertion and lack of solid food. He had drunk three gallons of strong chicha—*ucui yacu*—the pale drippings that María got for him by putting a screen between her fermenting manioc mash and the bottom of the pot. Just as the tree began to fall, images flashed before his eyes of a world asunder, and as the great tree crashed and the forest resounded, taking four smaller ones and a mass of jungle tangle with it, a large sector of a palm log flew up into the air and came crashing down upon him, rendering him unconscious. He thought he had died, and as he became increasingly conscious of being still in the forest that he sought to fell, and being pinned there by the *chonta* section and other sylvan limbs that it had carried with it, he was sure that both of his legs and arms were broken, that he was useless, that he had been felled there along with the forest trees, to be the home of beetle and fly larvae. María was there with her machete and she cut and cut and dragged him free, but still he hurt and he was frightened. For two weeks he lay in his bed at home and he dreamed, thought, and reflected on life. His bones, it seemed, were not broken; but still they hurt. He decided to make a journey beyond the quotidian world, not one controlled by a powerful shaman human but rather one controlled directly by the forest master spirit.

One Sunday in late August, while most of the residents of Nueva Esperanza were in Puyo to shop and visit with peoples from all over the Oriente and elsewhere, Sicuanga walked westward on the nearly invisible trail that cuts through the forest between Rosario Yacu and the second line of San Jacinto that fans out from Ishcai Tucushca Chingosimi. There he cut south, and in twenty minutes he arrived at the bottom of a high hill. Thirty-five years before, on that spot, Lluhui had given him one dart for his small, new Achuar blowgun, obtained in trade by Lluhui just for him, and had told him to kill just one bird with that dart to "prove his breath" and to return the bird to him. Sicuanga had been afraid of failure. He walked around quietly, and then he saw a dozen birds, a covy of small, lovely finches, chattering. They alighted ten feet from him and suddenly he felt strong and accurate. He raised the blowgun, focused on one, blew strongly (*sinchi pucushca*), and the dart went straight through the tiny bird. He went to it and held it gently by the beak, slowly smothering it, the dart still through its tiny body, until its little eyes rolled up, the eyelids closed, and its living force with its soul departed. Then he took it to Lluhui. All this Sicuanga remembered at the base of the hill that Sunday in August. Then he climbed the hill thinking of other hills to the east, north of Canelos, near Villano, where the wooly monkeys would now be growing fat in the tops of the trees, for it was that time of the year when cool misty drizzle (*huira tamia*) came and when they gorged themselves on a particular palm nut, becoming nice and fat.

Arriving at the top of the hill, he decided to cut his special spirit or soul trail southward, and he gently trimmed the trees of their low vines, epiphytes, mosses, lichens, and parasitic plants to make a swath about ten feet across and thirty feet long. When he was satisfied with his *supai ñambi* (spirit trail), he made a lean-to facing due east. Then, taking another trail through the jungle, he walked home, taking care to follow the ridges and look for signs of game. He passed through the rear end (*chagra siqui*) of María's and his *chagra*, where his brother had discharged a cash debt to him a decade before by planting plantains, and wandered a bit in the second-growth forest. There, in about ten minutes, he found his *alli upina huanduj* that he had brought with him from Canelos in 1969. The last time he had drunk Datura was in 1967, deep in the forest just south of Villano, where María's father and mother and their family went on *purina* each year. After that drinking journey María and Sicuanga had decided to migrate from Canelos back to Nayapi Llacta: there were just too many malign influences coming their way, and Sicuanga decided that he needed both the safety of a stronger residential *ayllu* structure and the security of a *llacta* founded by his powerful shaman father.

The *huanduj* was still growing, although it hadn't been cut and replaced for some time now. He continued on home, arriving there in the late afternoon. As the pickup trucks arrived from Puyo and Tarqui, one by one, unloading his brothers, sisters, and in-laws in groups reflecting current alliances and oppositions, he listened to the conversations, chuckling at the various voicings of rights and wrongs, knowledge and ignorance, of the urbanized Runa returning from Sunday market, some with new wares, some with a belly full of *trago*, and all with new stories to tell about the bustling national activities so prominent in the urban center at the doorstep of Nueva Esperanza. He drank *asua* and talked softly with María, his children listening. "On Wednesday I will travel with the spirit of Datura. I'll go alone, without a helper; I will go far, to distant gardens, distant forests, to waterfalls, rivers, and faraway cities. I will not go to the United States to visit my *compadre* as my father did when he died, but I will go far and learn much, and then I will return here to my *huasi*."

Sicuanga spent Monday and Tuesday walking in the forest; he bathed
in every stream and river within a fifteen-kilometer radius, thinking
and reflecting, alone in the forest he knew so well. Twice he checked
his hut, chuckling over the fact that he could have made a much
sturdier one—but the hut wasn't for him, it was only to protect his
flesh from rain and perhaps from falling branches when his body
thrashed around in the throes of the uncontrollable powers that would
be released within it as he, as his *aya*, traveled with the spirit master
of forest substances.

Tuesday afternoon his sister Marta came to see him, and Challua
accompanied her, playing his three-hole transverse flute as he approached the house. Both Marta and Challua had painted their faces
with *Bixa orellana* for the visit since they were to enter a household
of one about to enter the world of the forest spirit master. The everyday
ritual of arriving and being seated over, Marta asked if Sicuanga would
like a small *mucahua* from which to drink *huanduj*. He thought about
it and declined. This trip would be his alone; he would make his own
drinking cup from forest materials. Totally relaxed, at peace with themselves in the knowledge that a loved one, socially entwined in more
ways than they could count with each of the people drinking *asua* in
Sicuanga's house, was soon to journey from setting to setting through
a network connecting them right there to other seen and unseen aspects
of the cosmos, Marta, Challua, María, Sicuanga, and their children
passed the evening away and then retired in their respective households.

Sicuanga arose at 4:30, bathed, painted his face with *manduru*, and
left his house at 5:00, walking steadily, eating up ground and making
time; by 5:30 he had broken off eight nine-inch segments of Datura,
each about the size of a nickel in diameter. He replanted three of the
sticks and took the other five with him, arriving at the site where he
would drink Datura at 6:00 A.M., just as the sun rose. The jungle was
very misty, light coming in through the canopy the way it flickers
through tiny windows and peepholes that are opening and closing.
Many birds were around, but the sweat bees hadn't appeared since
no exertion had been expended. Everyone always says that one drinks
huanduj at noon, but Sicuanga knew that this was silly—what one
does is begin the trip at noon—so he would drink soon. He checked
the *sacha huasi*, swept inside it and then swept the ground outside,
going on down the trail that he would soon travel with the forest spirit.
He fashioned a drinking cup (*purungu*) from a palm leaf held together
with palm spines. Then he turned to the great *ila* tree and embraced
it, saying in Spanish, "Help me, friend; help me, friend." He split the

Datura stem, taking the inner green pulp, and put this, as mash, into the drinking cup, setting the cup on the frame that he had constructed especially to hold it. María appeared, together with her youngest daughter; both of them had painted their faces with *manduru* as well. It was 8:30 now, and they were on their way to the *chagra*, María said. Sicuanga accepted her explanation, even though she was about four kilometers off course. "Go ahead to the *chagra*," he said gently, "and then go home." He spoke softly; she looked at him and left, walking steadily, quietly, peacefully. She passed through the *chagra*, not exerting herself by working that day, and went home.

Sicuanga brushed himself off, checking his clothes. They were the ones he liked the best, those that he wore to Puyo on Sunday: red-and-black checkered dungarees with flare bottoms, white shirt, dark blue jacket, dark socks and polished leather shoes. He made a cut in some nearby bamboo, catching a cup of pure water in his *purungu*, mixed the water with the *huanduj*, and drank it. Then he sat down on some palm leaves, looking eastward in front of his lean-to, and composed himself with open mind and peaceful soul. Suddenly he remembered that he'd forgotten a couple of things. He jumped up, put the barked pole six feet out in front of him, and put the *purungu* back on its rack. "How could I forget something so important?" he asked himself. Sitting down again, now slightly harried and not so composed, he remembered the time that he had organized a hunt for a special festival, rented a Datsun pickup truck, bought powder, caps, shot, fishline and hooks, and got all the way to the town of Diez de Agosto — twenty-five kilometers from Puyo — with eight men and provisions, ready for a two-day trek into the forest, before he realized he had forgotten his own gun! He chuckled over the memory of how he'd rushed back home, borrowed money from his *compadre*, and rushed back again to the taking-off point.

Then Sicuanga died. He fell right backward into a black abyss. His body twitched, like one suffering a dreadful poisoning, and then ceased to move. It was now 9:30 A.M. Marta and Challua arrived during the first few minutes and stayed behind a tree near the lean-to, watching. They saw Sicuanga try to get up, thrash around, and then, at 10:20 A.M., they saw him lurch up violently, crash into the frame, wham into his pole, and a tree branch crashed down upon him. This worried Marta and Challua tremendously. Challua lifted him, talking to him the way one speaks to a drunk in Puyo: "You're drunk on Datura, *compadre*; you're in the forest drunk, *compadre*." And Sicuanga fell again and Challua put him in the lean-to and Sicuanga thrashed out of it and began to giggle and look at his fingertips as though grasping

Drinking *huanduj* from a *purungu,*

a man waits for the effects of this potent hallucinogen.

Then he "dies."

Thrashing around, he leaves the lean-to and his sister stands ready to help.

His brother-in-law helps him back to his lean-to

and puts him inside;

but he reemerges and crawls down the spirit trail,

where he again sits, seeing spirits, as flesh and soul continue to separate.

tiny things. "It is good," said Challua; "he is seeing spirits." Marta then examined his head and found that the skin had not been broken by the fall. *"Aliman,"* she said. "It's good." For an hour, until about 11:00 A.M. or shortly thereafter, Sicuanga alternated between complete unconsciousness and hallucinations. Flesh and soul were separating and reuniting frightfully. School let out in Nueva Esperanza for an hour and three of his children came racing to the spot, their faces painted red; they too watched from a distance, and Sicuanga saw them, though they were hidden, as though through the wrong end of a telescope.

From this point on the description of this trip is as Sicuanga later told it repeatedly; as a public event of a private trip, the imagery refined into exegetical text.

The pole in front of Sicuanga spoke to him a little before noon. In Spanish it said, *"Ya viene gente,"* and when he looked it said again, in a mixture of Spanish and Quichua: *"Gente shamunchi"* ("People are coming"). People were indeed coming, and Sicuanga could see them. His friend the pole stayed in front of him. The *gente* wanted to carry him but he couldn't move. His body was dead. Huanduj supai appeared before him. He looked like a great tree, but he was human, a person. He was the owner and chief of the Datura. There were two of these Huanduj supai, and the pole, his friend. During the day Sicuanga saw many things, and he moved, thrashed, fell, and was dragged back by Challua. Sicuanga sent Challua home before dark; like a drunk, he said in Spanish, *"Vaya no más compadre; déjeme aquí,"* and Challua went home.

At midnight Huanduj supai returned and said, "Walk like a jaguar." Sicuanga grasped the ground with his fingers, nails deep in the leaf mat, like a jaguar, clawing. He sat up and looked around, snarling; the *supai* said *"Jacu"* ("Let's go"). He walked a while and came to a lagoon in which there were many anaconda—*jatun jitamare* was the name of the lagoon. Then he came to another lagoon, and another. He came to three lagoons, one after the other. Whenever he stumbled Huanduj supai would steady him; there were two of them helping him. He found himself walking around a lagoon, and the spirit said, "We'll go under the water here," and Sicuanga went under the water in the lagoon and came out again, peacefully. Huanduj supai said, "You do well." He invited Sicuanga to go to another house, a great one, almost a city; it was Sacha Runa *huasi* (jungle person house). Sicuanga went into this great house and sat on a long *bancu*. The spirit was talking; it said "Here are peccary," and a tremendous herd appeared. He said "Know them," and Sicuanga did. Monkeys, game birds, jaguars, anaconda appeared, and Sicuanga knew them. "Good," the spirit said, *"jacu"*; and they left.

Mundu puma (world jaguar, from the Spanish *mundo* and Quichua *puma*) was down inside a cave in a high hill. There were lots of jaguars there. All of the animals were there. The spirit said, "Your friend [the *ila* tree] made this. We old ones—the captains, the *curagas*—live here." Then Sicuanga returned; he wanted to drag a big tree trunk with him, back to his little lean-to on the hill, because the *supai* had ordered it. He staggered and fell, but he did not hurt himself. The *huanduj* was passing, but he could still see as Huanduj supai sees.

He looked at Curaray, 100 kilometers away, on the edge of Waorani territory, and he saw that some people there were doing bad things to him, making him ill, making trees fall upon him when he cut them. The spirit showed him the exact person sending evil his way to harm him, and said to him, "You will be well, the other who is sending evil will be hurt. The next day he will die. You will live peacefully." Then Huanduj supai again said *"Ya viene gente,"* and María appeared. She asked what he was doing and he said "Walking." She made him sit down while she examined his body; the *supai* agreed that she should do this. Flesh and soul were together and he'd been falling everywhere in his state of extreme agitation.

As María examined his body the *supai* did too, and Sicuanga saw as the *supai* saw: he saw round, golden worms—a great many of them—in his right leg. "He" (it is never clear at this point in such telling whether "he" refers to *supai* or Sicuanga—the ambiguity is deliberate) took them out by hand and put them in a tree. The *supai* said, "Let's use a machete and scrape them off," and they did; they chopped them all up with a machete. Then they inspected the other leg and did the same with the worms in it. María watched all this, though she couldn't see the golden worms.

Sicuanga and the *supai* returned to where he had drunk *huanduj* and the *supai* said, "You are peaceful and well; take your things and go home," and Sicuanga did, with María helping. Many *sacha supai runa* came too, and they arrived at his home well before dawn. But then the spirits took him back to the forest. They took hook and nylon fish line and he tried to put a worm on the hook, to fish, but he couldn't do it. The *sacha supai runa* encouraged him. They picked the worm up again and again, but he couldn't put it on the hook; he was too drunk. The spirit put the worm on the hook for him, threw it in the water, and told Sicuanga that a fish was coming, that it was biting the worm: "Pull!" Sicuanga did pull, following instructions, and he caught a fish. He caught fifteen fish of all kinds—pike-cichlids, other cichlids, characins. Then the *supai* said, *"Ya viene su compadre Oswaldo; vamos."* Oswaldo said to him, "You're walking now, let's go below." And they went to another lagoon and caught more fish, almost thirty of them.

Huanduj supai said "Enough, let's go," and they arrived back home. Then the *supai* said, "Your wife is arriving," and María came into the house carrying manioc from the *chagra*.

The spirit went farther away, and farther and farther; now Sicuanga could see his surroundings more clearly, his soul and body were returning to waking life, to quotidian reality. The spirit spoke again, clearly: *"Sinchi runa mangui, mana ushangaunachu unaita causangui"* ("You are a strong man, [but] no one has the power to live in *unai* where you are now"). Then Sicuanga knew that he was well, the *huanduj* was passing, he had emerged from *unai* to live strongly in this world. If he had the capacity to live in *unai* then he would emerge from the *huanduj* world dead. By exercising control over the *huanduj* power of death, Sicuanga would live on.

Now Sicuanga was reflecting back on the conversations. The *supai* had told him: "You want to blow darts at enemies. Don't do this; repress your urge." And Sicuanga did this. Some people had already come to Sicuanga's house to be cured, even though he could not yet sing his *taquina* song. The *supai* said to him, "More such people will come and they will pay you; don't charge too much." Then the *supai* said, "Come back and drink *huanduj* one more time." And Sicuanga will, eventually. He was healed, his limbs were perfect, there was no more pain, he was strong. Then, as an afterthought while emerging from the *huanduj* world, he saw the wife of Nueva Esperanza's schoolteacher robbing him. But he also saw his own wife entering the room just as the professor's wife grabbed his pants and shirt. María was wearing two revolvers with a cartridge belt of bullets to frighten this wife—the *zambita*. Sicuanga saw the curly-headed darker woman hide, so María took care of Sicuanga without having to kill her. Sicuanga thinks that it was really the *causai* of his wife that arrived like that and scared the professor's wife's *causai*, because María can't remember doing it, even in a dream.

PUBLIC DIMENSIONS OF PRIVATE IMAGERY

Selective and selected facets of Taruga's dream and his visit to his shamanic maternal uncle, and of Sicuanga's trip with Huanduj supai, are known to everyone in Nayapi Llacta. The reduced formations that individuals and small groupings there construct of such events are in turn elaborated upon. The semiotic structure of knowledge, vision, thought, and reflection creating the thresholds and portals between our culture and other cultures, together with the "negotiated proofs" of the capacity to respond that develop out of such a structure, provide a symbolic template that can be endlessly elaborated. Reduction and elaboration are but complementary facets of an ongoing process of adaptation and cultural change, just as they are complementary facets of structural maintenance.

Sicuanga's visionary "afterthought" while on the threshold of emergence from the *huanduj* world has a personal significance, and a public one, with which people are quite concerned. María's oldest daughter and her next oldest were not sent to the school in Nueva Esperanza; they "accompanied" her to her *chagra* and were well schooled in *chagra* maintenance and in feminine fundamentals of Canelos Quichua life. Under Ecuadorian law, which increasingly governs life in Nueva Esperanza, these girls must go to school. Illiteracy today in Ecuador is illegal. By maintaining the structure of feminine relationships at the core of Nayapi Llacta, María was breaking the national law governing Nueva Esperanza.

In 1980 the teachers in Nueva Esperanza were from the Coast; they were from poor families, friendly, accustomed to living in a rural area, and got along well with the Runa there. They even brought their father to many festivities, and he, too, got along well with the Runa. Gently, by persuasion, María agreed to have her second oldest daughter enrolled in the school in 1980, so that she could gain minimal literacy. After all, she still had her oldest daughter to "accompany" her in the *chagra*. Privately and publicly all agreed that it was best now to have girls formally schooled, so that "they would not be ignorant like their parents."

But privately and publicly people were also very pleased to hear of Sicuanga's afterthought. Many chuckled over the story, and retold it a number of times. The *causai* of María, a woman who as yet knows little Spanish, "saw" what the teacher's wife was really doing to María, and by extension to all of them. She was exercising a new control, thereby taking something from them. Moreover, this *causai*—this living substance of the Runa woman—frightened the *costeña* living among them, just as the *negro supai* frightened Sicuanga's brother Indio. As long as the dynamic tension expressed by the verbs *callpachina* (to make run) or *mancharina* (to make tremble) radiates outward from the allusive symbolism of insider-outsider relationships, the contradictions that permeate lifeways and social organization in Nayapi Llacta/Nueva Esperanza are tenuously contained.

5

Duality of
Power Patterning

"Power (*Macht*) is the probability that one actor within a social relationship will be in a position to carry out his own will despite resistance, regardless of the basis on which this probability rests."—Max Weber, *The Theory of Social and Economic Organization* (1964), p. 152.

Nueva Esperanza, Scene 1, 1981

At 4:00 A.M., on the morning of June 28, 1981, Challua awoke in a cold sweat. He had dreamed in Spanish, and still thinking in that language within his quadrangular tin-roof house on the southeast corner of Nueva Esperanza, he knew that his land, and therefore his life, was genuinely threatened. He had taken a new bank loan two years previously, offering in his name, and in the name of his adult children, fifty hectares of land of the San Jacinto communal territory, in exchange for 60,000 *sucres* ($2,000) to be used to purchase cattle. He had loaned some of the money to relatives, given three of the bulls away to potential in-laws, and used some of the money to try to get a divorce settlement for his eldest daughter; generally he had managed his bank loan about as badly as could be imagined from the standpoint of rational economics. Today he had to face the general assembly of the communal territory and the bank officials who would attend that meeting, right here in his own hamlet, New Hope. Assuming his most humble persona, he sat quietly in his house as people moved by, and at 11:00 A.M. he walked to the meeting across the small plaza, where, after being publicly harrangued by white bank officials and elected indigenous leaders alike, he simply stated that he would pay back the loan in steady installments, knowing full well that to do so would mean the loss of all the social capital he had built up over his fifty-five adult years. On that day Challua knew the effect of national control over every aspect of his being, and he felt the sheer force of a new capitalist order of existence.

Nayapi Llacta, Scene 2, 1981

At 4:00 A.M. on July 5, 1981, Challua awoke with a surge of energy flowing through him. He arose, took his muzzle-loading shotgun, crossed a small stream, and walked the high ridge in the dark, feeling with certainty the contours of the jungle around him, knowing confidently that the murmur of water below the ridge was but a reminder of the rushing of cataracts where the anaconda with whom he had earlier spoken in a dream, using his native Achuar language, replenished his growing shamanic strength. As the mediation of the forest spirit master Amasanga was remembered from a Datura quest the year before, and as the surgent power of Sungui, the water spirit master, as first shaman, came to him a month ago (when his new father-in-law, Abraham Hualinga, sucked magical darts from his left leg as they drank *Banisteriopsis caapi* together), Challua knew that he was strong. He saw an owl monkey and laughed; "I'll shoot you when we need meat, Jurijuri," he said in Quichua, bringing to mind the foreigner's forest spirit master, who in some contexts one must fear. At 7:30 A.M. he returned home, where his wife had a large breakfast of fish and boiled manioc waiting. He sat on his seat of power carved in the form of a water turtle and his wife served him bowlful after bowlful of *asua*, which he gratefully drank. He talked long and loud, and as he talked people came and went and were pleased with the strength in his voice, the projection of a common "proof" of power in his breath. He talked of trees as though they were people, of the imagery of his mind when he could "see" every bit of his territory and every bit of Amazonian Achuar territory far away, from whence he had come and to which he could always return. He spoke in Quichua, and then he sang high falsetto in Achuar. All who listened to him, or heard about this day at second hand, knew that Challua had cut the bonds of bank officialdom. He became the antithesis of the man who had walked slowly to the assembly meeting. He was quintessential human in touch with all of the forces of forest and water, and his wife, Marta, was quintessential *chagra mama*, the enduring basis for productive activity.

In the last chapter Sicuanga hovered for a while on the threshold that exists between the world of spirits and the world of everyday, mundane life, to which he did indeed return. This chapter opens with two vivid, private experiences of Challua, Sicuanga's brother-in-law, that began in a dream and led to subsequent patterned, personal activity. Just as Sicuanga's threshold-vision became a public event, so too did Challua's experiential encounters with different fields of force. The public events that Challua's activity triggered reveal contrasting sides of a set of contextually motivated stances vis-à-vis control of resources. The first shows Challua's consciousness of nation-state control of capital resources and his consequent appropriate behavior in a juro-political meeting in Nueva Esperanza. The second demonstrates his acute awareness of cultural-ecological control over productive resources within Nayapi Llacta and in other Upper Amazonian settings. Both of these control systems constitute the bases of felt, acknowledged, recognized, contradictory power systems that are conjoined not only in the technological and economic process of development-sponsored change, but in the very core of Challua's and Sicuanga's psyches.

The experience of taking Datura and going on a trip with Huanduj supai is a rare and profoundly private event. Nonetheless, tales of such a trip, from falling into death through prophetic insights constructed on the threshold of re-entry, are likely to be told to the most casual visitor. Indeed, such tales sometimes pervade intra-*llacta*, interpersonal talk. That which is "seen" privately during a Datura trip becomes part of public discourse, grist for every symbolic mill that condenses experiences born of antinomy to manageable, revealing proportions, while at the same time allowing for unending allegorical play that re-introduces multiplicities of meaning, evocative imagery, and charged emotional responses.

To enter completely the world of spirits by drinking Datura is to cross over the universal threshold from life to enter the portal of death. No one can cross such a threshold often, and many Runa do so only once, few more than three times. The most powerful images (*muscui*) are *huandujmanda*, from Datura. The world of spirits and souls, of which *muscui* provide glimpses, are omnipresent. Those living Runa who have unusual insight, and who can even control their own process of dreaming, projecting the resultant inspirations into creative artistic work, are known as *sinchi muscuj runa*, or, more often, *sinchi muscuj huarmi*, the vision-filled, image-oriented, knowledgeable woman who is master potter, complement to the male shaman and in control of the beauty inherent in the household micro-universe.

168

Passage into the domain mediated by *ayahuasca,* while extremely difficult for most, is effected quite regularly by a few men. These are the *sinchi yachaj,* the strong ones who know, who are at the center of a paradigm of internal consistency (*ñucanchi yachai*), and who regularly take the Canelos Quichua peoples to the very edge of contrasting, external consistency. These *sinchi yachaj,* like the *sinchi muscuj huarmi,* must be governed by tremendous visionary powers, but they are also guided by the ability to move between worlds that exist simultaneously on differrent planes, and to intuit, interpret, and manipulate the correspondence between such planes.

THRESHOLDS

A threshold is "a beginning point of something." Literally, it is a piece of wood or stone placed right in front of a door. The concept of threshold signals the idea of entrance, which in turn evokes the concept of transformation as one passes from one domain into another. For humans to be in another domain is to become, however subtly, something somewhat different. To at least a very minor degree one "is" as s/he is "situated" in a social interactional context. In everyday life the Runa are not always aware of their various public personae, but they become intensely aware of the self in relation to immediate and distant others during *ayahuasca* sessions and during festivals. In mythology, the self is radically different in each of the fantastic houses that it enters.

Quotidian but symbolically significant passages are made regularly as Runa go in and out of one another's households and in and out of their own *huasis,* crossing the boundaries of *plaza, chagra, sacha, llacta.* They can and do speak of such passages as moving through an entry— *pungu*—and even label entries in terms of social or spiritual personae. Examples from a swidden garden include *ñucanchi pungu* (our entrance), *supai pungu* (spirit entrance—something normally invisible but existing on another plane), and perhaps even *mashca pupu pungu* (barley-gut, non-Runa Ecuadorian entrance—one placed at an easy-to-find trail to assist non-knowledgeable people so they won't become lost).

When a couple marries, the social passage from the status of youth to that of household founder is supercharged in terms of altered social relations. In fact, the transition of a man and a woman to marriageable age is signaled by overt, formal house-entry awareness. Children come and go in and out of houses, and into parts of houses, as they please. Then, for years, young men and women live on the threshold of marriage, during which period they go only to certain houses in which they are situated by specific gender-related tasks. Marriage itself is a process of transition embracing about three years (N. Whitten 1976; Whitten and Whitten 1984), after which more formal entrance and departure to any household accepting the couple takes place. While on the threshold of marriage itself, youths and their parents move upward in command of knowledge formations. As knowledge signals power acquisition, they thereby segment off from others in the same kindred who are similarly engaged, and the oppositions sketched in Chapter 3 become pervasive. The entire hamlet remains on the threshold of fission and dissolution as each expanding kindred strengthens its position in Nayapi Llacta/Nueva Esperanza, and in urbanizing Puyo.

Before marriage young men may feel that they have become very strong (*sinchi*) and that they are imbued with force (*urza*). Such a feeling of surgency leads to fear when illness strikes, for the youth reasons that the personal projection of self-oriented strength may have led to an encounter with an invidious, shamanic, greater strength. The concept of strength development in the microcosm of the reflective self generates, we could say, a growing consciousness of the developing individual and collective power of comparable others. Some young women reach striking heights of artistic ability with ceramic manufacture prior to marriage, combining skill associated with a given *ayllu*, learned from a mother or mother-in-law, with great personal creativity. Such women also feel especially vulnerable when illness occurs, and like the men they seek shamanic guidance as well as maternal protection. Then, for years after marriage, man and woman readjust their micro-universe of founded *huasi* in multiple and shifting relationships vis-à-vis parental *huasi*s until, perhaps in their forties, a deep recognition of their transformed life situation within biosphere, noösphere, and cosmos provokes more conversation about such symbol-laden concepts as *muscuna, ricsina, yachana,* and *yuyana*. By this time, on quotidian and spiritual planes, each adult *huasi* member is deeply embedded—on terms that he or she has negotiated—in both Nayapi Llacta and in Nueva Esperanza, and the nature of the embeddedness may differ in each of these sociosymbolic settings. It is with such highly embedded individuals of Nayapi Llacta that we frequently hear these verbs used as adjectives to identify the self related to significant others. Putting them together, as we did in the preceding chapter (p. 117), we arrive at the off-centered ordering of the threshold of change and the control of change represented below.

Everyone is *ricsij runa*—one who sees—but no one today is *sinchi ricsij runa*. A person with such a status did exist in Quito in past centuries, as sort of a powerful see-all (see Salomon 1980), and many

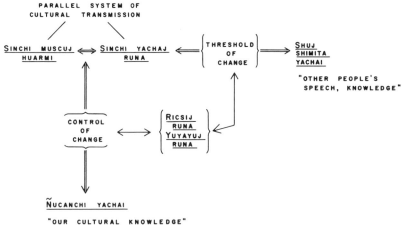

Runa say they have heard of such a status elsewhere, including Quito, in "ancient times." Such an indigenous person controlled human and material resources within a nonindigenous power structure. But this indigenous control does not exist today. The Runa of Nayapi Llacta say, "We are all very strong, for with the spirit masters we control forest and *chagra* and we know our waterways and terrain." But *sinchi ricsij runa* is not a status here. Everyone is also *yuyayuj runa*—one who learns, "for we not only learn from the old ones who knew more, but also from those of other cultures, of other languages" (for example, through the school system and through continuous encounters with those who come from Puyo, Ambato, Quito, or elsewhere in the republic, and from other nations). But again, *sinchi yuyayuj runa* do not exist here, for this concept implies going ever outward into other systems. Being able to "see well" and being able to "learn well" places everyone on the threshold of change, for as highly intelligent, perceptive people, they are rapidly assimilating an enormous amount of information about other lifeways, much of it necessary for survival as questing human beings in a transformed Upper Amazonia.

Sinchi yachaj and *sinchi muscuj huarmi* do, however, exist conceptually in Nayapi Llacta as special statuses. They conceptually anchor Canelos Quichua culture by off-balancing the ubiquitous *yuyayuj* and *ricsij* conceptual statuses. The threshold of change is a moving one, wed to frontier dynamics which are in turn made up of the great contemporary antinomy of Amazonian cultural ecology, on Nayapi Llacta's side, and national developmentalism, on that of Nueva Esperanza.

CONCEPTUALIZING POWER IN AMAZONIAN ECUADOR
Socioeconomic History of Ethnic Asymmetry

Puyo began to form into a nexus for frontier Amazonian-sierran trade toward the end of the Amazonian rubber boom during the 1880s. Its growth was stimulated by external, international events such as the rubber boom, oil exploration, World War II, plantation development, more oil exploration, mission activity, and finally by nationally sponsored, sustained large-scale development. From the mid-nineteenth century to the present the Dominican order has sought to maintain hegemony over native peoples of what is now Pastaza Province. What has emerged among the Canelos Quichua and many of the Achuar there is a duality of ethnic patterning (Sacha Runa/Alli Runa symbolic opposition vis-à-vis civil-religious national symbolic integration—see N. Whitten 1976; D. Whitten 1981). Carleton Coon might tell us that in the area of Puyo, the land of Jivaroan disorder, dissidence, and insolence became conjoined systemically with the land of Christian order and social domestication. And Lévi-Strauss might regard the searching quest of the Canelos shaman and the vivid Amazonian ceramic creations of his wife and sisters as masking the harsh reality of a fractured world groping for its lost egalitarian locus within a system of rigid hierarchical control. Such academic stereotyping is seductive in its avoidance of issues of power, and it resonates with nationalist perception in modern Ecuador. Today Puyo's population of 10,000-12,000 people contains the children and grandchildren of the original Andean tradesmen with an overlay of more recent colonists. But as Puyo swells and puffs up in its urbanity, so too does indigenous culture on its rim expand and permeate the urban locus of its antithesis.

This rim is made up of three indigenous corporate formations which are part of the national system governed by the "law of communes": Comuna San Jacinto del Pindo, wherein Nayapi Llacta/Nueva Esperanza exists, Comuna Canelos, and Comuna San Ramón. There are also indigenous settlements analogous to Nayapi Llacta/Nueva Esperanza interspersed between the three *comunas*, and there are mixed indigenous-nonindigenous *colonias* sprinkled about as well.

In the Puyo area, which includes Puyo itself and the arc of indigenous cultures with their varied corporate bases, overt conflicts between recent Andean colonists and the native peoples of the area clearly define an idiom of complete, antagonistic, asymmetric separation. As just one highly salient example, the people of the Comuna San Jacinto del Pindo occupied by force of arms a segment of land ceded to them over thirty years ago and drove over 100 entrenched colonists from it in the fall of 1980. Countering this idiom of continuous ethnic struggle, however, is a praxis of continuous, inter-ethnic transaction wherein the idiom of separation of "Indians" from "colonists" is transformed into pragmatic sets of collaborative activity between the descendants of "old colonists," some newer in-migrating *serranos* and *costeños*, and the Puyo Runa (as all indigenous peoples living near Puyo call themselves). As another highly salient example, in the winter and spring of 1982, the Runa of the *isla* of the San Jacinto *comuna* allied with a national development agency *against* the rest of the *comuna* (*tierra negra*), and those of *tierra negra* allied with the provincial government against the counter-alliance.

On the southern fringe of Puyo, in the 17,000-hectare territory, live descendants of the original (indigenous) inhabitants of Puyo and of Canelos. Most of the Puyo Runa people living on the *comuna* have ritual-kin ties with the children of the initial sierran settlers of Puyo, some of whom are now ensconced in national and regional banking, governmental, or developmental bureaucracies.

Today Puyo is dependent on other parts of the country for supplies, trucked in from the Sierra and the Coast; in turn, it is the purveyor of goods to the small colonist towns that have grown up on its periphery. Although the Runa from areas around Puyo maintain autonomy in subsistence horticulture, continuing to control their sylvan-riparian-swidden environment, they are dependent for most of their manufactured goods upon Puyo trade, and are engaged in a sustained way with commercial relationships ramifying out of Puyo. Puyo Runa participation in the modern world is manifest in their options to assume national style in speech, clothing, sports, music and dance, without relinquishing their ceremonial life and without relinquishing the iconic and arbitrary symbolism bound up in the female tradition of fine ceramic manufacture (D. Whitten 1981), or in the male shamanic tradition (Harner 1972; N. Whitten 1976, 1979).

From the founding of the Comuna San Jacinto del Pindo in 1947, pressures emanating from Puyo have been to nucleate indigenous groupings, to produce something of cash (capital) value, and to validate indigenous existence by reference to ownership of land. By the late 1970s these pressures took the form of inducements to raise cash crops—especially the *naranjilla* (*Solanum quitoense*, a fruit of the nightshade family)—and cattle. As the former rapidly succumbed to known (to the Runa) fungal and insect pests when taken from swidden horticulture, greater financial inducements of cash loans for cattle were made directly to men and women of the Comuna San Jacinto, as in other areas of Amazonian Ecuador (see T. Macdonald 1981). As de-

Urban, white, civilized, Christian developmental Puyo (*above*), where Runa, *cholos*, *mestizos*, and *blancos* mingle (*below*).

Puyo's market continues along the streets of town (*above*) as Puyo Runa pose for a photo at the construction site of a new, national, centralized, concrete-and-cement marketplace (*below*).

As the hilly forest looms behind Puyo's urban bustle (*above*), it is cut by the Puyo Runa to make a clearing for a new road (*below*).

Cattle and pigs take over sections of cleared and fallow *chagra*s as the "development" ties the Runa to the modern capitalist economy in Nayapi Llacta.

velopmental disasters emanating from capital-amassing strategies of Puyo's and Quito's developers increased, validation of *llacta* status itself upon the Comuna San Jacinto came to depend increasingly on hamlet vigor in acquiring capital and spending it in such a manner as to attract more capital. Since such capital expenditure seems to create more and more of a wasteland, however, subsistence activities of swidden horticulture in Nayapi Llacta have also expanded and intensified.

Today, just as Puyo represents the thrust of national bureaucracy into Amazonian Ecuador, so too does the Puyo Runa grouping of Canelos Quichua culture represent a prominent spearhead of indigenous culture into the modern republic. By 1980, after a century of transacted (or negotiated) national-indigenous political-economic asymmetry in the Puyo area, two new forces had entered the picture. The first is the force of pan-Amazonian (Ecuadorian) indigenous surgency, on one side, and the second is the new policy of ethnic mobilization initiated by the late President Roldós, on the other (see N. Whitten 1981b; *Anuario Indigenista* 1982). The confrontational social, economic, and political contexts where the surgency is manifest is in Puyo itself and on the Comuna San Jacinto (where the native people supposedly have been "tamed," "civilized," and "capitalized"). Politically, ethnic surgency in central Amazonian Ecuador is manifest, on the indigenous side, by the formation of various organizations, the most prominent of which I shall here call the indigenous organization of Pastaza Province (since its name has changed a few times), and on the national side by the new governmental policy to promote the growth of such organizations as part of a program of ethnic mobilization and the transcendence of "marginality" (see N. Whitten 1981b). The situation that now exists is that the three *comunas* ringing Puyo overtly *oppose* the indigenous organization of Pastaza Province and challenge its pan-indigenous ideology, while some governmental representatives, some political parties or party segments, and the Dominicans *support* the indigenous organization. Moreover, some of the organization's leaders/ officers are themselves children of mixed nonindigenous and Runa parentage.

As a result of the ongoing bipolar (*native* Runa [including Achuar in some contexts]/*national* [*oriental/blanco*]) indigenous debate, the concept of *mestizaje* in all of its multifaceted dimensions (ranging from processes of *blanqueamiento* to those of *choloficación*) is becoming crystallized at a very salient level of public discourse by those previously dichotomized as *blanco* versus *indio* (in Spanish), *Runa* versus *mashca pupu, ahua llacta,* or *ahualta* (in Quichua) or *Achuar* versus *apachi* (in Achuar or Shuar) (see Fig. 1 in Chap. 2). As the bipolar processes unfold in Puyo, they draw sustenance from nationalist rhetoric through the contradictory idioms of ethnic mobilization and *indomestizaje* (N. Whitten 1981b), which emanate from the public ideology of the central government, and find voice through all media.

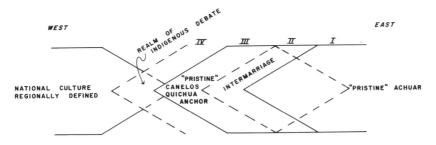

Power

The key—or at least one key—to understanding consistency in the hubbub of verbal play within "charged fields" (V. Turner 1974), where competing paradigms receive special attention, is found in the careful analysis of power. Who controls what, under what circumstances, with what consequences for other parties are fundamental questions to be asked. They constitute the first half of Richard Adams's definition in his exhaustive work *Energy and Structure: A Theory of Social Power* (1975). But if power is only control, then we don't need a special concept for it (as Adams carefully points out). Moreover, we run the risk of reducing the problem of understanding the capacity to respond to a discussion of resource competition and the construction of ethnic boundaries. Power, as the ability to carry out one's will despite resistance—as the personal sense of energized ability to transcend boundaries and to move thresholds that Challua felt in Scene 2 of Nayapi Llacta—must also be studied in its symbolic dimensions. Adams (see also Fogelson and Adams 1977) continuously asserts the premise that, although power rests upon control of energy, it must be understood in symbolic terms. In fact, Adams introduces the notion of *symbol control* into his discussion, suggesting that we may define power, in part at least, as the systemization of symbol control by one party in contention with another party over something of mutual value in a known environment (Adams 1977: 24-26, 41-52). Symbol control mediates two systems: (1) the system of technological control over resources and (2) the cognitive system of "equivalence structuring" (Wallace 1961; Adams 1975, 1977), wherein differentiation of control between contending parties is acknowledged publicly.

Following Sicuanga's journey with Huanduj supai, everyone in Nayapi Llacta—even Sicuanga's major opponents—felt that the conscious
recognition of teacher control over mental and social resources (María's
daughters) restored Runa control over the totality of these resources,
if not over the specificity of the immediate situation. Late into the night
and for weeks thereafter, various Runa spoke of María's *causai* with
the pistol on her hip that Sicuanga "saw" confronting the *zamba* thief.
As they talked they asserted that their children were indeed changing,
learning to read, write, and speak "correct Spanish" so as to interact
in Puyo as Puyo residents. They were becoming another sort of *yuyayuj*
runa and *ricsij runa*. But as they spoke, using the story of the journey
with Huanduj supai as a rhetorical reference point—a triggering base
signal to complex ramifying sign imagery—men and women talked of
an expanded Runa world that could contain and manage the threshold
of change. The educational system should, they said, be used to their
own, Runa, advantage. After all, that is why they had lugged those
heavy cement blocks and steel girders over the old corduroy trail, and
why they had repeatedly requested the construction of a road to Nueva
Esperanza. In other words, one story of one private, fantastic journey
led to considerable public reflexivity over the very nature of mundane
social process.

Once we understand something of the nature of bureaucratic control
over capital resources (as Challua so poignantly did in Scene 1 of
Nueva Esperanza), we can turn to the question of how sociopolitical
asymmetry between goal-oriented actors becomes "negotiated," and
where, how, and under what circumstances the threshold between
acquiescence and subversion (or protest, or transcendence) develops.

By dealing with the construction of a mutually recognized, publicly
expressed symbolic threshold between acquiesence and subversion, of
acquiesence and protest, as this threshold expresses both superordinate-
subordinate relationships and their potential reversal, understanding
of ritual enactment (e.g. T. Turner 1977; V. Turner 1982) corresponds
with the study of political action.

The extremely simplified diagram below, condensed from the portrayal of Richard Adams, sketches this process. Here A has power over
B inasmuch as A and B recognize X as that which objectifies the value
inherent in something, and inasmuch as both A and B recognize A's
superordinate position and B's subordinate position with respect to
control over energy (or resources), the conversion of which results in
an objectification of a desirable commodity and access to that commodity (or access to the means to acquire it).

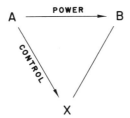

B, then, in any given context, perceives the structure of his environment in terms of the relative invariants of the A-X relationship. The means for revealing or ritually enacting that relationship is expressed through the dynamics of correspondence structuring. Correspondence structuring occurs when people draw on experience in one domain to think or act "knowingly" in another domain. When drawing from the domain of national political economy Challua knew he had to pay back money and thereby lose capital; he felt his powerlessness. But when he drew from the domain of cultural ecology he felt forceful, knew his resources, and re-entered Nueva Esperanza communicating a sense of felt power.

Analysis of these relations, when taken as a continuous process of asymmetrical negotiation in an oppositional process, gives us a model by which to discuss the *duality of power patterning* illustrated in Figure 3. It is by understanding the unending ramifications of the duality of power patterning in all of its syncretic dimensions that the contradictory consistencies of frontier-centralized dynamics may be grasped.

A in Figure 3 is an agent of a government bureaucracy, let us say a banker charged with developing cattle-raising on indigenous territory. In a given context (context A) he clearly controls land, which the agent and the corporate office that he represents perceive and symbolize as "soil" and its potential for providing grazing grass for cattle. B is a Generation II Canelos Quichua shaman whose power is manifest socially by a stem kindred in control of a particular segment (*llacta*) of Runa territory. The shaman's strength derives from his ability to tap cosmic power through the merged spirit forces of rain forest, undersoil, and hydrosphere. His kindred ramifies from his nodal position, and his sons and sons-in-law (who constitute Generation III and IV men for at least some portion of their lives) serve as power brokers and cultural brokers vis-à-vis external agencies.

In the Puyo area, shamans can and do transact their actual landholdings vis-à-vis bureaucratic agents, usually by the brokerage of their sons and sons-in-law. As Generation II son-in-law of powerful shaman Lluhui, and with two Generation IV sons to help him, Challua was in

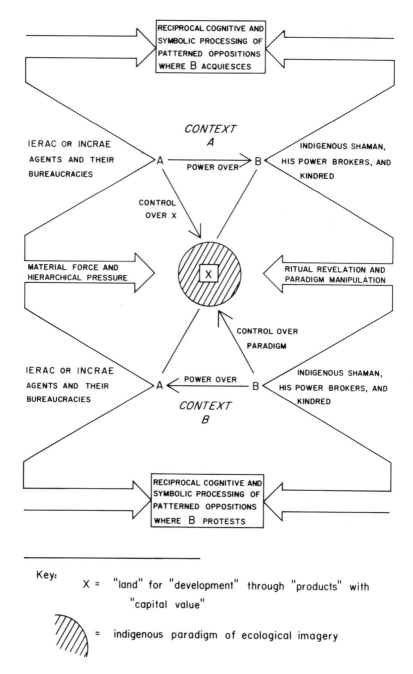

Key: X = "land" for "development" through "products" with
               "capital value"

          = indigenous paradigm of ecological imagery

Figure 3. The Duality of Power Patterning

a perfect position for an intercultural political-economic transaction. But by forming an enduring tie with bank officials, he wound up having to choose between options that reflected his loss of control of his life-sustaining resource. He was forced to return capital he didn't have or actually lose his own jungle territory. In this context of the control of Challua (B) by the agent (A), not only "land" (X) in the legal-bureau-cratic-developmental sense is transacted, but also, from B's standpoint, a known sylvan-riparian-swidden territory suitable for pragmatic activities of horticulture backed up by fishing, gathering, and some hunting. This territory exists, as we have seen, as a symbolic formation in indigenous culture of Nayapi Llacta, just as "land" exists as a symbolic construct in a nationalist, capitalist world-view now permeating Nueva Esperanza. Both dimensions of conceptualization of territory contribute to the duality of power patterning. Both are ideological systems which are contradictory on the same level of conceptualization but potentially complementary on different orders or levels of existence.

In Scene 1 of Nueva Esperanza Challua emerged from his dream threshold to pass out of the portal of ecosystem knowledge signaling negotiated power and into the newer system of control of the flow of hard cash. But in Scene 2 of Nayapi Llacta he sorted his perceptions differently and moved out from under the oppressive, dominating strength of the devouring, development-oriented bank to situate himself within a different plane of existence. On this plane he drew upon ecological imagery as a shaman would to heal a patient, and the projection of the *yachaj*-controlled warrior imagery led to protest as effective strategy vis-à-vis loss of Upper Amazonian resources (territory-land). Challua, in Scene 2 of Nayapi Llacta, felt a sustained surge of confidence born of condensation of symbolic processing of complex information drawn from a known territory. Just as his mother's father, Nayapi, had done before him, he alluded to the conquering of Jurijuri (owl monkey, in this case), the foreign spirit master of other lands.

Within a couple of weeks a clear communication, borne by the *comuna* president, came out of Nayapi Llacta to the bank officials, and it surprised them. "Before we cede our territory to you, we will die fighting you." But as this collective response came forth, Challua's sons and sons-in-law privately went to bank officials and pledged return of the borrowed money. In turn, the officials agreed to accept the return on extended payment terms, without interest.

Nayapi Llacta territory exists cognitively and symbolically in metaphoric-metonymic bundles of concepts signaled by the manipulable and communicable master-imagery paradigm of Amasanga, Nunghui, and Sungui (N. Whitten 1978). The ability to draw this paradigm together and manipulate it during shamanic performances and during ceremonial enactment signals control over the paradigm itself, and brings us back to Adam's concept of "symbol control" and Victor Turner's of "competing paradigms" or even to "root paradigms" in some cases where the concept of sacrifice (i.e. resistance to death) is introduced.

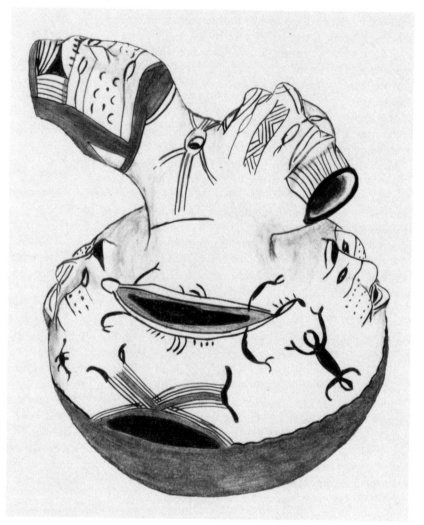

A festival pot showing with striking clarity the duality of patterning. Alicia Canelos, *llacta* Sarayaquillu, Sarayacu.

Let us focus more attention on the concept of duality of patterning. In the analysis of language, of course, the concept refers to the uniquely human phenomenon whereby *the same signals combine and recombine to form different messages*. Returning to Figure 3, we see that context A—where A and B recognize the superordination of A due to mutual recognition of A's differential control over energetic X—may be cognitively constructed by actors as a set of given signals expressing the differential power of A over B. The construction of context B contrasts with that of context A. With this criterion of contrast we not only come up with contextual opposites implicitly manifest in every encounter characterized by, or evoked by, confrontational processes, we also have a recurring *set* of contrasts that order great human clashes or inequities—A over B/B over A, acquiescence of B/protest by B, exploitation of land/ecological imagery, material force/ritual revelation, order/disorder, among many others—as symbolic grist for concrete social dynamics (see, e.g., Cunningham et al. 1981 and Dougherty et al. 1982).

By taking only the basic structural elements of binary contrast, hierarchy, and classification drawn from cognitive anthropology, and the human capacity for correspondence processing drawn from symbolic anthropology, we should be able to understand the sheer force of systems of political-economic control and the shifting patterns of its recognition in relation to flows of power. By understanding material control, its negotiated recognition, its felt force, and the flow of power embodied in symbolic formations, we come to understand more completely the ways by which lifeways riddled with surging antinomy flourish in today's nation-states.

To conclude this section, then, let us summarize what is meant by power. Capacity to respond so as to place one's self or one's gouping "in a situation to carry out [one's] own will despite resistance . . ." (Weber 1964: 152) is the fundamental notion; it is the base of the definition. Such capacity, of course, depends upon available options. These, in turn, depend both upon the system of control within which a person or party exists, the recognition of that system, and the ability to conceive of, seize upon, and effectively act upon such options. In Chapter 2 I sketched two models that should help us overcome simplistic infrastructure-superstructure dichotomies without subverting either of two fundamental realities: (1) the sheer fact of oscillating nation-state expansion to and across its frontiers; (2) the flexible capacity of cultures to respond creatively to such expansion. Juxtaposing the two models gives us an emanating system of political-economic control from above and a pulsating, generative flow of power from below:

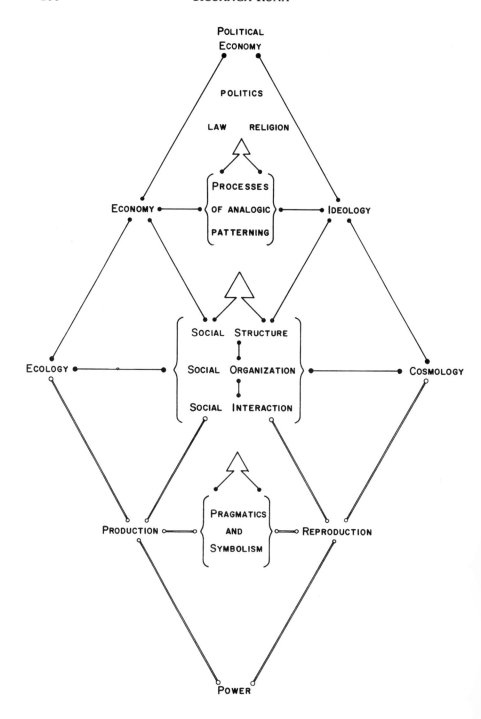

Both Carleton Coon and Claude Lévi-Strauss, in their journeys across the Middle East and South America respectively, touched upon this phenomenon but turned from it when confronted with the sheer, crushing force of national political economy. Without in any way minimizing the latter, we can explore still further the dimension of response capacity in Nueva Esperanza/Nayapi Llacta.

CEREMONIAL ENACTMENT: RELEASE AND CONTROL OF POWER

The social-structural antinomy of Nueva Esperanza/Nayapi Llacta is based upon the polarity of national developmentalism on one side and Upper Amazonian cultural ecology on the other. The spatial opposition, symbolized at its antipodes by the forest of indigenous dissidence and the urbanized locus of bureaucratic control, has a temporal analog. On one side of the antinomy is the annual festival celebrating the triumph of the Christian, nation-state, urban civilization over sylvan savagery. Dorothea Whitten (1981: 767-68) poignantly describes a typical crescendoing ending to day-long activities built upon five months of preparation:

> The military establishment at Shell, 9 klms due west of Puyo, including the band, and the entire Batallón de la Selva conclude the parade to a tune that always sounds to me like "Yankee Doodle Dollar." All available jeeps and trucks roll through town while military planes buzz the central plaza where participants and spectators have assembled. There, from the balcony of the Dominican School building, the crowd is addressed by the president of the republic who, through 9 August 1979, is also head of the armed forces. The president is flanked by the Dominican bishop of Puyo and the diocese of Canelos, the bishop's top aides, the provincial governor, and the top-ranking town officials. The annual review of the parade and address to the people by the president and his allies symbolically and dramatically reassert that Puyo has become a civilized city in a nationalist state, and that the fate of the citizens is in the joined hands of the Catholic church and the state.

On the other, temporal side, about half a year distant, is the *ayllu* ceremony of the Canelos Quichua, enacted in the various *caseríos* where a Christian church or chapel exists, or where Christian ceremonies are regularly held. The crescendoing end to this profoundly indigenous ceremony is called *dominario*, control, from the Spanish *dominar*, to dominate. Late in the afternoon, on Sunday, after days of exhausting, emotionally charged, and symbolically laden stylized activity, when people are tired, cross, and frustrated, an outsider, down-river, powerful shaman gently plays a combination of flute and drum associated with Andean masked ceremonies. The melody itself is a skillful blend of his private Amazonian *taquina* and a public Andean ceremonial melodic motif. As he does this four men known as *lanceros* come forth bearing a bamboo pole with four copal fires burning within it. They move first though arches of flowers previously constructed to venerate Catholic Christianity and then begin to lurch around, to become destructive; finally, they crash right into and through the church, slamming, falling, rising again, running, frightening, going out of control. Rains come, the plaza becomes a sea of mud, the river swells and swells, men and women may cry, and tales of destruction are told.

The bamboo pole represents Sungui as the great devouring force of the anaconda brought from the river; those bearing him/her are different jungle cats—Amasanga representatives—growling back and forth to one another "like a congress" before going off to kill. Women dance and dance with their hair flying to and fro, to and fro, their sideways motion being the analog of the two-tone hum of shamanic chanting that evokes the imagery of encompassing *unai*, mythic time-space. Other drummers, at least some prominently bedecked with toucan-feather headdresses, drum and drum; Amasanga's thunder rumbles, is unleashed; Sungui goes out of control; the pulse-tremolo of snares indiscriminately summons all souls and spirits; chaos reigns, the church is destroyed, and the Runa say they fear *tucurina*, ending everything, in one great transformation of the world of forest and *chagra* and earth and mire into an encompassing, rushing, surging sea.

The Runa enact the contrast between the two festivals within each of them. During Doce de Mayo a small group of indigenous celebrants, brought to Puyo as a tourist attraction and to provide the basic "savage" contrast to a civilized parade, perform a bit of pre-*dominario* drumming and dancing in front of the bandstand just before the terminal blitzing and buzzing of the military. Other Runa, marching with their respective school groups, and a few in the military parade, know that their world of symbol control is still intact. The *ayllu* ceremony itself expresses enduring counter-dominance of the nation-church control system, and as such it is inextricably linked to that control system. Furthermore, the greatest contrast to occur within the *ayllu* festival, that between the Catholic mass and the indigenous *dominario*, is usually expressed by negative information. That is to say, in describing an "ideal" *ayllu* festival, the mass is usually not mentioned. It is never mentioned as an interval propelling ritual activities from one level to another to the final *dominario*. Furthermore, the *dominario* itself, climax of the festival,

Above: color guard of the Brigada de la Selva on parade during the 12 de Mayo celebration, Puyo, 1982; *below:* Canelos Quichua-Achuar group from Río Corrientes in the same parade.

is usually not performed. In fact, one is more likely to see a tinge of pre-*dominario* activity in urban Puyo during 12 de Mayo than at any Puyo Runa hamlet.

The *ayllu* ceremony has been described, as actually observed (including the *dominario*), elsewhere (N. Whitten 1976: 165-202), and subsequent observations by Mary-Elizabeth Reeve and the Whittens substantiate the general flow of events. The 12 de Mayo celebration has also been described elsewhere (D. Whitten 1981: 749-75). It is not the fascinating things that people do during these highly evocative polar events that interest us here, but rather the symbolic patterning of the duality of power within indigenous culture vis-à-vis other environing cultures. To begin with, let me present a common, idealized version of the ceremonial performance by intervals. Any Runa of almost any age can describe these intervals in about this way. As such, they and their sequence mark the movement of concepts through space and time. The ubiquity of this sequencing in Runa role expression condenses knowledge—bundles it, so to speak—such that a tremendous amount of communication about "us" and "them" and clashing systems of control can be continuously processed. A good deal of the *ayllu* festival's preparations and enactments involve *reversals* in the normal way of doing things; the flow is from male *ayllu* transmission to female *ayllu* transmission.

The Runa of Nayapi Llacta/Nueva Esperanza blend and contrast dimensions of the two festivals as they "play with" (*pugllanchi, pugllangahua*) the temporal dimensions of the duality of power patterning.

Ayllu Festival

This festival stresses inside men going out, outside men coming in, and the reversal of ethnic and juro-political asymmetry. Simultaneously, it stresses the *ayllu* continuity through women while maleness remains outside, and the expansive containment of universal and cultural forces by women. Male predation is a focal feature in contrast to female domestication.

Briefly, and ideally, two male *priostes* are chosen at the end of the *ayllu* festival by a visiting Catholic priest, friar, or even bishop, meeting with the assembled (mostly drunk) Runa men and women. These *priostes* are ranked: (1) male, or moon, festival cargo bearer as above or higher, and (2) female, or potoo-bird, festival cargo bearer as below or earthbound. In Quichua these men are known as ritual *chayuj* (conveners), and the noun derives from the Andean Quichua verb *chayana*, which does not exist in Canelos Quichua. Each cargo bearer builds a

large new house, the male-Quilla to the west, the female-Jilucu to the
east. These *priostes/chayuj* gain prestige that rivals the authority of the
church-appointed *varayuj*, the staff-carrying indigenous authority system, analogous to the newer *cabildos* of the *comunas*. In other words,
the ritual system/political system from colonial times to the present
involves off-setting prestige/power systems bound to the domination
of external juro-authority. For a year the wives of the *priostes* labor to
produce an excessive amount of manioc.

As the exact month and day of the *ayllu* festival approaches, male-
sponsored stylized activities break with increasing frequency into the
quotidian flow of human activities. Such breaks are felt, discussed, and
participated in throughout Nayapi Llacta territory, even though no *ayllu*
festival is held in it. The first has no name; it consists simply of one
or the other of the *priostes* asking the priest in Puyo to set the exact
time for the Sunday terminus to the festival. This done, festival activity
is marked off by almost exclusively male activities, as follows:

1. *Yandachina allu cusana*—amassing firewood on the *chagra*—a
male activity—to roast unpeeled manioc. In the roasting process neu-
rospora and other fungi develop on the manioc and firewood. All the
yellow and orange fungi are then put on the manioc and it grows
there, covered by balsa leaves, for days. Men are as prominently involved in production of such *allu* as are women.

2. *Allu mucuna*—masticating the roasted manioc-cum-fungi. This,
too, is done on the *chagra*, and the men may assist. Only in such
circumstances may men make chicha.

3. *Sachama rina*—to go to the forest. Here men "invade" various
areas governed by Jurijuri supai to take excess amounts of meat from
forest and river. The hunting parties are divided so as to have novel
combinations of up-river and down-river people present.

4. *Shamuna sachamanda pactamuna*—to come back from the forest,
to arrive (hunters' return). If the priest has set the festival day for a
Sunday, such return would normally be Wednesday or Thursday, but
not later than Friday.

5. *Upina shamunguichi*—you come to drink. Each *chayuj* sits like a
bump on a log in his respective house near the front doorway, with a
giant *mucahua* (*chayuj marcana*) of heady *vinillu*, "wine" made from
the drippings of the fungus chicha. Assistants drum the thunder of
Amasanga while circling within the house, and the women of the house,
together with the men, force tremendous amounts of strong brew down
the gullets of everyone present. Periodically, those drumming in one
house go en masse to the alter house; this pattern of moving back and
forth, each drummer bedecked in the skins, furs, and plumage of

the hunt—among which the favorite is the *sicuanga* headdress—goes on all night and all the next day. As people leave one house women throw chicha all over them, shouting with glee, "Those who walk and drum like Amasanga must be soaked in rain."

6. *Sisa mandana*—ordering flowers. This is done by strong, often inebriated men, to establish the proper pomp attendant on the arrival of the priest the next day. *Mandana* obviously derives from the Spanish *mandar*, to order, to command. Imagery here is on total acceptance of the coming priest's visit.

7. *Camari*—feast. Two feasts are simultaneously or sequentially enacted as the Runa men and, to a lesser extent, the women, play with the duality of developing force fields. The first is a banquet for the priests and others from rural towns, from Puyo, from Quito, including, at times, unknown foreign tourists. The guests are served at a table, given large amounts of food, and men drum the thunder of Amasanga in front of the table as women dance to Nunghui. Often men and women prestigious in the formal juro-political system of the *comuna* are seated with outside prestige figures. The priest blesses the meal and says a few words in Quichua. While this is taking place, or immediately after it, Runa men and women are seated at a long bench and served rapidly, after being asked for a *jucha* to be paid to the *prioste* or his helpers. The oppositions expressed (see N. Whitten 1976) also fit beautifully into the elaborate system of the *yumbada* of north Quito, described recently by Salomon (1981).

8. *Dominaro*—control. It is with the concept and enactment of *dominario* in the *ayllu* festival that the ritual reversal asserting the power of indigenous people over that of the Catholic Church takes place. But the assertion itself evokes the concept of "ending everything," for the ultimate force of water power is unleashed and the Runa are swept eastward toward the sea. The ancients, it is said, knew how to build great rafts upon which they piled soil and manioc so that they could survive the great flood. Runa, as the flood subsided, returned westward toward their hilly terrain, there finding lost brothers existing as bracket fungi; this is why the Runa men call one another *ala* (fungus), by which is meant "regenerated being."

Let us return for a moment to the basic contrast in this ideal presentation of festive intervals between the Catholic mass—which is not mentioned (and which precedes the *camari*)—and the *dominario*, which is rarely performed. Here we find the triumph of civilized Christianity (the mass) over forest savagery pushed to the salient but silent end of social discourse, and the *dominario*, which calls upon the deep, primal element of the encompassing water system to end everything, lying at the salient, vocal end. The mass always occurs (around 10:00 A.M.), or the priest would not initiate the ceremony; the *dominario* rarely occurs, but is always talked about as imminent as the day wears on and dusk approaches. Stories of the recent past, the time of the grandfathers, Nayapi's time, are quickly but seriously told as the night descends. On the day after the *dominario* (interval 9), it is said, the *lanceros* would hold their own feast, called *lansa*, after which they, as jungle-cat warriors leading other warriors, *sicuanga runa*, would race south from Canelos to attack the Chirapa Jivaroans, returning northward then to hold a head feast that conferred tremendous prestige upon the organizer but led to unending internal warfare.

Interval 10 involves the immediate, post-ceremonial telling of many tales. It creates a bridge back to quotidian routine which itself is punctuated by breaches. In some of the popular stories an analogy is drawn between the accumulation of centralized Quiteño power and the disruption of life in Canelos Quichua territory. For example, legend has it that Canelos Runa and Puyo Runa would trek with ease to the land of the Salasaca Runa. If bad trails or barriers were encountered in their sojourn up the *montaña* they would transform themselves into jaguars and bound and leap over all obstacles. With the Salasaca, the Puyo Runa and their neighbors would travel on to the Quito Runa territory, and thence right into the national palace to make direct petition to the president (or dictator) of the republic. As petitions were granted, local power increased, always in the hands of a *curaga* such as Nayapi of Puyo, or Palate of Canelos.

The same tellers of tales insist that chaos reigned in Canelos due to the activity of the priests there, and the alliance and dissidence vis-à-vis these priests created by the powerful ones (such as Nayapi and Palate) led to endless strife. In such strife the Virgin Mary is said to have climbed out of her picture frame in the Catholic church in Canelos, and to have fled north to hide in the forest near the headwaters of the Villano River. Listening to such tales told by men, women often say, with a sigh, that men seem bent on political moves aimed at the acquisition of power that creates chaos out of the order that power establishes.

Sinchi Muscuj Huarmi–Ñucanchi Sinchi Camhuai

Camai, as discussed in the previous chapter, means "proof." *Camhuai* implies making proof even more tangible to the speaker. "Our strong tangibility" (*ñucanchi sinchi camhuai*) emanates from the ceramic beauty and evocative imagery which is the product of a strong visionary woman (*sinchi muscuj huarmi*). Such a woman reproduces the very stuff of symbolic production. She transforms clay, stone, and water into design and color, using the breath of the fire as mediator. Her knowledge and creativity evoke insight into the very essence of Canelos Quichua culture, as such an essence is linked to changing biosphere and noösphere.

Marta Prepares for a Festival in Nuevo Mundo

Before sunrise on November 12, 1981, Marta sat down on a split-bamboo mat and reached for the cool, damp clay at her side. She had dreamed of water, rapidly but gently flowing around bends in a river, and of her husband, Challua, trekking north with Sicuanga to hunt game. She would rendezvous with her husband two weeks from Friday at Nuevo Mundo, six hours' walk due south, where her brother Sicuanga is *prioste* to the upcoming festival. She had come to the second line of Nayapi Llacta to get away from the *bulla* (escalating noise), as she called it, of the bulldozers and road scrapers now working only a few hundred yards away in an adjacent *llacta*. Pungent smoke from the glowing wood fire penetrated the swirling, chilly pre-dawn mists rising from the surrounding canopied hills. She relaxed as she studied the handsome faces of her children and those of Elena—who had invited her to work in her house since Taruga was off working on a jungle-clearing contract with a local *hacendado*. She looked especially at little Carlos, now healthy after his long bout with various illnesses, and she thought about don Rodrigo's house, which she had never visited, on the hilltop above the Napo River where the entry of the Arajuno River creates a great and treacherous whirlpool. She concentrated on her dream visions, seeking to integrate them with her environmental knowledge. She thought of Papaya Llacta on the upper Conambo River, where her stepmother, Blanca, had once lived. She thought of the great oval houses she had visited there on the edge of the fast-flowing, crystal-clear river filled with rocks and cut by ledges, under which lived abundant armored catfish—so delicious when cooked in a black *uchu manga* with manioc, fiery red peppers, and salt obtained by trade with the Achuar from the lower Río Huasaga.

Segments of mythic episodes came swiftly to mind, as did images of life in jungle, *chagra*, river, *huasi*, and she knew what she would make. As she thought, and studied her surroundings, she decided she would also teach Elena, her son's wife, to make ancient black ware. "*Cachun*," she said, "would you like to make something new?" And without waiting for a response, Marta began to talk rapidly, to laugh, to imbue the entire household with the unleashed enthusiasm of a massive creative effort. Elena joined her in the center of the house; both of the women faced east, their array of clays, paints, water, and little brushes—each crafted from a bit of hair tied with cotton onto a tiny stick to make one size of line only—spread throughout the household. No longer was there a female and a male side; the entire interior of the house was feminine.

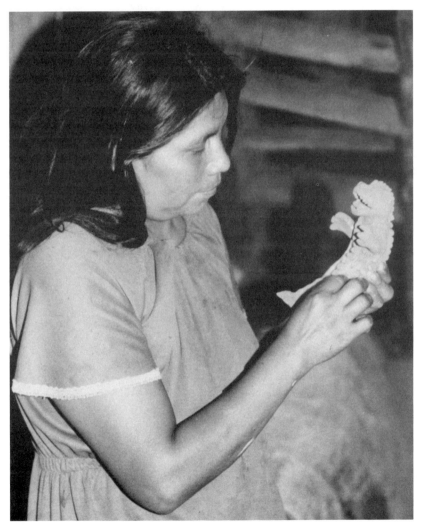

Women at work preparing for a festival, uniting mythic episodes with vivid recent events (*above and two following pages*).

Marta spoke of mythical events, and from them she selected images to guide her pottery-making: mature Quilla, the roguish moon, and Jilucu, moon's sister-lover. Looking at Carlos, whom she dubbed Sicuanga Runa Carlos, Marta said she would make *cagun*, a mythical forest monster with joined tails and two heads that eats people. She would now play with and shape strong cosmic forces in her graphic imagery, just as her father Lluhui—the bright orange-red cock-of-the-rock associated with waterfalls of the Andean slopes—had done in his shamanic trips of magical flight. She would also make an Amasanga figurine and put a little pottery baseball cap on his head as the Jurijuri supai of the North American oil companies who shouted orders that no one could understand. And in addition to drinking bowls especially decorated in imagery that conjoined her special Hualinga *ayllu* with the feminine dimension of Challua's Vargas *ayllu* via her own personal knowledge and reflection, she would make a couple of unusual red *callanas*, as the old Achuar and Zaparoan women she had known in Papaya Llacta used to do. She might take the *callanas* to the festival and serve food out of them at the *camari* or she might just keep them here.

Her special array of ceramics would be completed on the eve of Challua's return, when he would, she told little Sicuanga Runa Carlos, drum the thunder of Amasanga to begin an enactment joining soul substance that she would impart to the ceramics with known and unknown thought systems—"ours" and "theirs." Moreover, she said to Elena, she was going to make three plant pots for don Valverde, the bank official to whom Challua was indebted. She would sell the pots to don Valverde at a low price, "to make friends" but not to bind him to her as a gift does. She would also put very special decorations on these pots reflective of Challua's life situation. *Heeheeheeheeeeee* she laughed-sang, "I'll make that pot first."

Working quickly now, coiling, hand-building, directing Elena, and talking, Marta completed a small pot in the form of a *sicuanga manga*. "Years ago we used to put toucan feathers in pots like this," she said to no one in particular, and she sang a song, "*Urcumanda Yao Sicuanga huarmi mani*" ("I Am Yao Sicuanga Woman from the Hill"):

Urcumanda Yao Sicuanga Woman

I'm Yao sicuanga woman, I'm Yao sicuanga woman, just standing
    on the big hilltop, eating palm nuts there, *tili tili*.
Sitting in the palm tree, eating only nuts, I walk, just walk.
Yao sicuanga woman, eating another nut for her belly, I walk,

looking at the sun's rays.
I walk, singing *wiwiwin* here, *wiwiwin* there.
Sicuanga, Yao sicuanga woman, finishing the palm nuts, just walks,
    singing like that, like that, like that.
She's just saying, remembering, "It seems that they see me."
Distant and alone, this Yao sicuanga woman doesn't kill in eating
    this way.
She's just walking, just singing this way.
Yao sicuanga woman: "Don't eat her flesh," it seems she sings,
    it seems she sings.
By looking, looking at the sun's rays, she will melt, just melt,
    tsiu, tsiu, right there.
Just there she will be so sad; she will sadden your heart.
"Why are you angry with me? You're becoming a sad type—don't
    be angry with me," I said . . . I said.
By returning, she's making your heart silent.
. . . I am going to be standing by . . .
It seems to be your heart.
If your eyes are becoming dark as night, you will walk, just
    walk unable to see.
I sing, just saying that![1]

"This is what don Valverde calls an *olla*," she said to Elena, making
the harsh, voiced *zh* sound for the *ll* used by most *serranos*. "Look
how I'm painting it." Around the rim of the pot she put *quingu*, zigzag,

and Elena knew what Marta was thinking. The zigzag represented, in
this case, bends in a river symbolizing Marta's husband, Challua (the
bocachico fish), as he was going down-river with Sicuanga in a borrowed
canoe somewhere near the headwaters of the Curaray River. Then she
filled in the zigzag, and explained to Elena that the fillers were hills,

urcu, that Challua would traverse—implying the overcoming of obstacles, the conquering of the Jurijuri, and the sheer physical strength
and endurance of her dear one (*cusacu*), trekking and hunting so very
far away and yet symbolically so very near. Underneath the rim Marta

1. Sung by Clara Santi Simbaña, *caserío* Río Chico, Comuna San Jacinto del Pindo,
May, 1982. She is singing to a close relative who is behaving like Shiny Shoes. Transcribed
by Carmen Chuquín, Dorothea S. Whitten, and Norman E. Whitten, Jr., and translated
by Dorothea S. Whitten.

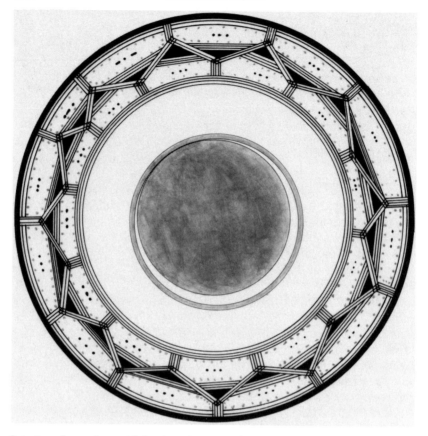

Interior of *mucahua* with basic *quingu* motif, evoking images of water turtle, hills, and/or fishnet. Rosaura Hualinga, Río Llushín.

painted a design that Elena had seen and that she knew different people thought of in multiple ways. She looked at Marta, questioning with her eyes and lips. *"Lica ñahui,"* said Marta knowingly, referring

to the eye of a rectangular fishnet used for catching *challua* when they come down feeder streams of larger rivers. And under the *lica ñahui*, in her mind the net of bureaucratic entanglement within which her husband had psychologically struggled several months ago, and which continued to hem them in from day to day, she painted the triangular pattern of the *amarun*. She looked again at Elena and said, "It is a mud anaconda, the one who comes to eat us."

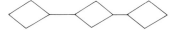

The motif of *challua* the fish caught in the net of a bank loan and now compelled to utilize the most powerful of destructive forces known to the Runa provided a poignant beginning to what would be two weeks of sustained activity within this household, itself symbolizing a contained universe. Marta continued talking: "We used to put toucan feathers in such pots," she repeated, "and when we had enough of them men would make special headdresses and the women would put some of the red and yellow feathers onto white beads and wear the beads as we made pottery. We called this our *tahuasamba huatarina*" ("headdress to get tied into"—symbolizing here the tied-up red woman and black woman and their liberation by the toucan). The men would wear their red and yellow feathers together with noisy bird-bone and seed adornments to visit one another, and carry the headdresses outward to other peoples. Sometimes they would give the feathers to a powerful shaman as payment for curing; sometimes they would trade with storekeepers in Puyo, "for a good deal of money."

The next morning Marta was busily sculpting and painting. That night she had thought about money and decided to forestall her array for the Nuevo Mundo *ayllu* festival and make even more plant pots. "I'd better feature a face of Sacha huarmi," she said to Elena, "and why don't you make a few, too." "The pots with these faces bring the best price now at the Hotel Majestic in Puyo, especially when we tell don Roberto a good story about jungle spirits. The trouble, though, is that he only pays part of what he owes us." As she worked Marta continued to muse over her commercial production. Again she wound the triangular *amarun* motif back from the face (painting that face as she had previously painted her own, with *huiduj*, the evening before) and around the pot, where it failed to join with the triangles coming around the other side. "*Ayllu shina*," she said, looking at the disjuncture, "like an *ayllu*." Then she filled in the triangles at their top corner, saying that the fill was *jista sisa*, festival flowers, referring to the arches that would be set up at Nuevo Mundo for the dancers to weave through. And then she softly whispered, "*Sinchi amarun runa mani*," using the first-person form of the verb *to be* as the powerful anaconda speaking: "I am powerful anaconda person." Then, briefly, she began to cry as she thought simultaneously of her dead daughter, of her brother Jaime who is "oh so modern with his black shiny shoes, and oh so nasty to

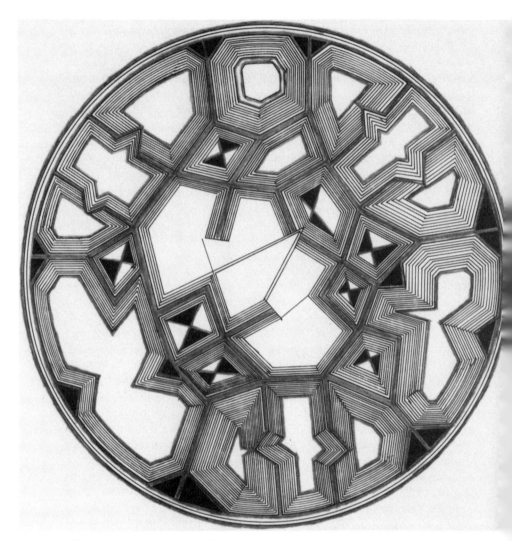

Charapa interior with motif "bent" to produce striking asymmetry. Armadora Aranda, *llacta* Sarayaquillu, Sarayacu.

Charapa with two powerful inserts in its pattern: *amarun* and *jayambi* (iguanid). Alegría Canelos, Curaray.

me when big officials from Puyo come to Nueva Esperanza." She sang a terribly sad song which made Elena cry too. "*Chaiiii*," she said, "my house, my *ayllu*, my dear husband, my sons, my daughters; maybe someday I'll go under the water and die and live like a fish."

The day wore on, the pottery array developed, and as she worked Marta came to be increasingly at peace with herself, with her life situation, and to feel increasingly in touch with the vast resources which she controlled. Meanwhile, Elena sculpted a little canoe with another head in the prow. "*Aaaaiiii*," said Marta when she saw it; "*uraimanda yacu puma!*"

"*Buenas tardes*," someone yelled in Spanish, and the dogs and turkeys set up a ruckus. She and Elena looked up from their tasks and saw that two men and a woman were coming down the hill. She and Elena sat watching until the people had come to the door, the children running first to corral the dogs. "*Buenos días*, don Valverde," she said to the banker, "*venga, descanse*" — "come in, rest." The threesome tromped up the ladder. They were breathing hard and sweating profusely. With don Valverde were two blonds, a young man and a woman, each with a camera. "This couple has come from Germany just to take pictures of pottery-making," said don Valverde, "and the monseñor who is educating your daughter in Puyo sent them to me." Don Valverde also drives a taxi in Puyo and knows a good deal about the Runa and their ways, being the son of one of the town's first settlers.

Reluctantly, because she knew what would probably happen, Marta got up, filled a calabash shell and a large enameled cup with *asua* mash mixed with clean, previously boiled water, and handed the cup to the strange man and the calabash shell to the banker–taxi driver and tourist guide. Sure enough, they all began to discuss her chicha right in front of her, and then the stranger put down the bowl without drinking and started to take pictures of her, his flash popping. After about ten minutes of picture-taking and inane commentary Marta asked don Valverde if he would like to buy some more plant pots. He said he definitely would, and she said "Fifty *sucres* each." Don Roberto at the Majestic paid from 100 to 200 *sucres* for this quality, but he would give only a part of the payment and she'd have to hound him later, or agree to paint more bark cloth that he got from a gift-shop owner in Quito (who in turn got it from missionaries working with the Cayapa in the coastal province of Esmeraldas). This way she could sell to someone to whom she was in debt at a lower price than usual, *and* gain more immediate cash than she could by selling at the higher price. Don Valverde paid her 250 *sucres* for five exquisite little pots, and he and the two *gringos* made their own comments about what the faces must be. At least don Roberto asks, thought Marta, though he doesn't usually remember. Marta quickly took the money, went into the back room, took out a Nescafé coffee jar, and put the money in it, placing the jar back into a wooden suitcase where she kept such valuables. Quietly, since she knew that don Valverde was buying these bowls for the blond couple, she whispered in Quichua, "You are going on a long trip *sacha chagra mamaguna*, to another land, to live in *machin huasis*." Then, into one she quickly put a few toucan feathers.

Don Valverde and the couple then took leave and Marta went back to work. In the distance she could hear the buzz of a chainsaw as Tselctselc cut logs north on the trail to Putuimi. A road was cutting in from that side of the *comuna* too, and big money was soon to be made, everyone agreed. An Atlas Hercules roared overhead, just beginning its descent to Shell. Elena said, "Perhaps Ramón and Rosa are on that flight. They said they'd be visiting about now." Ramón and Rosa are Achuar from the Río Buféo, northeast of Montalvo, who speak Quichua as a second language and are very fluent in Spanish. Marta hoped that they would arrive today or tomorrow, because Rosa was also a master potter from another culture, and her inner universe constituted in Elena's house would thereby continue to expand right up to the *jista*, when the entire Runa world would be situated on Sungui's threshold of *tucurina*, ending everything.

For two weeks Marta and Elena worked on their pottery array. Different clays were mixed for the *tinajas* (large storage jars), *callanas* (eating dishes, both red and black), *jista puruhuas* (festive bowls in the form of animals), *mucahuas* (traditional drinking bowls), and cornets. Over a hundred different designs were integrated, their explicit motifs noted, and the evocation and multiple meanings of their unfolding symbolism discussed as these women made their artistic statement with regard to the known and unknown, their world and other worlds. Over fifty songs were sung, and one night after Rosa and her husband had arrived, Rosa and Marta sang together, one in Achuar, the other in Quichua, intertwining their melodies in an intricate and lovely manner.

The private workshop of symbolic reproduction—Marta's centralization of ceramic production within Elena's house—rapidly became something of a public event. The bishop of the archdiocese of Canelos, together with two young, attractive nuns, visited there about three days before the women were to trek to Nuevo Mundo. The threesome was formally greeted, the room quickly swept clean, and they were served from excellent *mucahuas*. Monseñor Calderón told Marta that her daughter was doing well in her work for the nuns, and progressing

Lumucuchi (peccary), festival drinking bowl. Clara Santi Simbaña, *caserío* Río Chico, Comuna San Jacinto del Pindo.

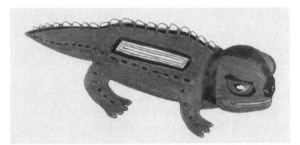

Sacharuna (iguanid). Apacha Vargas, *caserío* Nuevo Mundo, Comuna San Jacinto del Pindo.

Lumucha (paca). Apacha Vargas, *caserío* Nuevo Mundo, Comuna San Jacinto del Pindo.

Pishna uma (otter head) with *amarun* motif. Alicia Canelos, *llacta* Sarayaquillu, Sarayacu.

Catfish. Maker unknown, Curaray.

Cagun. Apacha Vargas, *caserío* Nuevo Mundo, Comuna San Jacinto del Pindo.

reasonably well in her seventh-grade education. "She can be the *catequista* for Nueva Esperanza in another year," said the monseñor. "Sí, *padrecito*," said Marta. "Moreover," said the monseñor, "we are thinking of educating her more fully in Baños so that she can return here in five years as the bilingual schoolteacher of Nueva Esperanza." Marta readily agreed that this would be fine, and quickly asked, "How much money will she make?" The monseñor did not answer her, but the *madrecita* spoke up and said, "We are now negotiating with the director of the Ministry of Education. We have every reason to believe that the True Church, which has been civilizing all of the indigenous people in this zone for centuries, will be in control of all education soon. Then your daughter will be paid well for her work right here in your own community of New Hope." "*Sí, madrecita*," said Marta.

"*Bueno*," announced Monseñor Calderón, "will you please bring fifty *mucahuas*, small ones, to me after the fiesta of Nuevo Mundo. They are payment for your daughter's education. We want you to learn the meaning of money. You can make these in a *minga* with other women; that way you won't forget how." Marta had heard this lecture many times before and pondered once again the exchange system whereby she gave her daughter to the church and gave pottery to the church so that the church could sell the pottery at a very low price (10 *sucres* was what she had seen for one of her bowls worth 100 in Puyo, when she visited the Dominican wholesale outlet store in Baños), and direct her *ushi* to do the church's bidding. But she agreed, because she and her daughter Ermilinda wanted the outside knowledge to be gained only through the formal educational system. She was paying her *jucha*, she thought, just as the old ones from Canelos had to pay the *dominicanos* for their intervention in the killing disputes erupting in this zone. So she quickly countered with "Twenty *mucahuas, padrecito*; I need to sell more in Puyo to help Challua pay off his bank loan."

The monseñor and his youthful escorts departed, each of them helping him up the slightly slippery path heading back to Puyo, each with the gift of a fine *mucahua* from which they had drunk. "Poor woman," said the young blond German nun, "she really doesn't know what money is."

The next day, contained in the still-expanding *huasi* universe patterned by all the elements of spirit force and inside and outside knowledge systems, Marta began to relax, secure in the thought that the life of her cherished ones was proceeding such that all would survive the coming changes. Her brother Jaime—the one with "the black shiny shoes" who had been frightened by spirit frogs long ago—and his wife stopped by to talk, having heard of the monseñor's visit. They were returning from their daughter's *chagra*, which is also on the second line of Nayapi Llacta. Shiny Shoes had had a severe drinking problem a few years before. He overcame it by becoming an *evangélico* and allowing a Runa from Riobamba to baptize him in the Putuimi River. Afterward he stopped drinking *trago* anywhere and cut back on drinking beer in Puyo or at public events. Marta told him forthrightly about the monseñor's plan for Ermilinda and how good it would be to have their own teacher in Nueva Esperanza. Shiny Shoes thought for only a second and then said softly, "No, she will not be our teacher; let her go teach in Baños."

After that statement Marta bore up well, talking to brother Shiny Shoes' wife, her cousin whom she now called *cachun* (sister-in-law), about the pottery she had made. But later, when they had gone, after consuming a good deal of rich, yeasty *asua*, Marta cried again, "*Sinchi chignij*" ("Such strong envy"); "so many bad words." Life would be intolerable for Ermilinda if she tried to return here and take over the role of the *zambu*. Again Marta felt the force of external control, this time applied from the *inside*, from *our cultural knowledge*. And she looked to Elena and explained: "Those from whom we learn outside ways," she said, "must come from the outside." Sighing, Elena replied, "*Así es, comadreiiiiii*," letting her terminal vowel trail off like a phrase of a song.

On November 26 Marta, Elena, and Rosa, accompanied by five children, bundled up all of their ceramics and trekked overland to Nuevo Mundo, arriving just before dark. They had sent fifteen *huangus* of *asua* ahead over a several-day period with in-laws who were coming and going between Nuevo Mundo, Puyo, and Nayapi Llacta, and all of this *asua* was fermenting nicely—really bubbling—in huge, decorated *tinajas* made previously by Marta in Nuevo Mundo, working with her husband's sister there. The women also carried four rum bottles full of *vinillu*, which they had obtained from the drippings of the *allu asua* by placing a screen midway up the shoulder of the *tinajas*.

They began walking purposefully, talking, backs rigid with the weight of sixty-five-pound baskets laden with cargo, including pottery wrapped in clothes, and the bottles of homebrew. Arriving about midday, they immediately hid most of the ceramics about half a mile away from the festival site, taking only a couple of *mucahuas* to the *cari jista huasi*. They would bring forth some of the collection bit by bit, but they intended to sell most of it after the *jista* right there in Nuevo Mundo to the *comerciantes* who would come only for that purpose late Sunday afternoon, before the *dominario*.

Feminine Enactment

Cooking and serving, serving and cooking are the two continuous chores of the *jista mamas*, as the women married to and related to the *priostes* and their aides are called during festival activity. These two activities are punctuated with invitations to dance, *bailana*, whereupon women let their hair fly to and fro, to and fro, as men drum the thunder of Amasanga and a few play songs on transverse flutes. But within the escalating work load of festival maintenance women play with a continuous construction of meaning. Into the festival houses, alternating first one, then the other, then back again, enters the cumulated contained universe of each of the women engaged as Marta has been over the last two weeks. But only a little, albeit highly significant, of each woman's symbolic production is brought forth—much more is left to the active imagination.

Marta thoroughly enjoyed the ongoing performance. Challua and Sicuanga and the rest had arrived in good spirits, literally, for someone in Puyo had given them a bottle of *trago* and they were happily inebriated as they arrived, shouting in falsetto, rending the air with their alcohol-infested breath. Although she had hidden it away to be sold later, Marta brought forth a little armored catfish that first night, filled with *vinillu*, and made everyone drink and drink until their heads reeled. She kept refilling the little fish's mouth from the big festival bowl (on the bottom of which she had painted a large, stylized Datura icon), held by Challua as he sat on his long bench near the opening of the house. Challua, at least, knew that the fish represented the times enjoyed and the knowledge gained from the stay at Papaya Llacta the year before, and was pleased that Marta had come up with such a charming *jista puru*. Later, during the *camari*, while several tourists were looking for ceramics to purchase and the *comerciantes* arriving in pickup trucks were suggesting higher prices due to the presence of the tourists, Marta brought forth the *cagun* that she had sculpted and which had been fired beautifully, teeth intact, with only a few hair cracks. She brought it right to the monseñor eating at the table and made him drink from it—twice—and it was strong *vinillu* that she got into him, too. She suppressed the urge to dump a large *mucahua* full of chicha on him, for this should be done to people whom one really wants to play *with*, like the *jisteros*, and sometimes those whom one wants to mess up a bit while pretending play. The monseñor fit neither class of insiders. But she did force four big *mucahuas* full of rich, sweet, freshly fermented chicha on Shiny Shoes when he arrived, and as other women converged on him with his new, strikingly attractive red jacket,

Two powerful symbols of the release of power juxtaposed during a festival on the road that cuts through the island of the Comuna San Jacinto del Pindo.

she dumped an entire big bowlful of the sticky stuff on his head, making sure that it ran down the front of that expensive jacket.

So many things Marta did during that festival event, and she remembered all of them. Halfway through the night, on Saturday, during a lull when Sicuanga was holding forth about the rivers they had crossed and the hills they had climbed, she came forth with the Amasanga image she had made and made him drink and drink from it; the fact that teeth were painstakingly sculpted and painted as growing out of the back of this Jurijuri's head escaped no one. *"Sicuanga mama camhuai, ñucanchi muscuj huarmi,"* said Shiny Shoes, in genuine, deep appreciation for the work of Marta, his and Sicuanga's sister of Nayapi Llacta, whose daughter's potential role as teacher in Nueva Esperanza he had quietly, but brutally, rejected a week before.

About 11:00 A.M. on Sunday, having drunk the blood of Christ and eaten his body, and having a belly full of meat, plantains, and chicha, the monseñor trudged toward the river, where a canoe awaited him. He had to return to Puyo, he said (for a siesta with two nuns, said Sicuanga quietly). Marta ran after him. *"Padrecito, padrecito"* she called,

and she gave him the Jurijuri drinking bowl with the teeth growing
out of the back of its head that she had labored over just for this
special *jista*. "*Apai, padrecito*," she said—"Take it." She pointed with
care to the three little Christian crosses painted on Amasanga's nose.
Later, she told women in the cooking area that she had made Amasanga
as a Jurijuri supai in the shape of a squash, ancient food of Jilucu. The
bowl also looked like a hill with a magical door at the top where Nayapi
had once entered on a Datura trip to make this his land. All the women
now knew that a master condensed set of symbols was going into the
Catholic church, and they were pleased. The monseñor really had
received a "gift," someone said, a gift of "*ñucanchi ricsiushca runa*"
("our people's perception") bundled into "our tangible proof" by the
profound anchoring device of our own image-making woman.

Male Jurijuri supai in the form of a hill. The motif
around the body is *amarun* blended with *charapa*. The
crosses on the nose juxtapose the power of foreign
people (Jurijuri) with that of the Catholic Church. Apacha Vargas, *caserío* Nuevo Mundo, Comuna San Jacinto
del Pindo.

THE COMMUNICATION OF POWER

The duality of power generated by contradictory, oscillating systems of control is patterned and shaped in many ways. Just as a pulse beat from the national system of bureaucratic control diminishes Canelos Quichua culture into a nearly inaudible jumble, the inevitable counter beat amplifies its structure to unmistakable clarity. The pulsating flow of complex messages that emanate from Puyo Runa festival activity derives its alternating base from male release and female containment. As men move out to the thresholds of change in both Upper Amazonian cultural-ecological and national political-economic systems, women bring those thresholds into the festival houses themselves, into the symbolic enclosure of the expanding and contracting universe. And as men move the thresholds themselves ever outward, women give tangible pattern to the altered imagery through ceramics and audible imagery through song.

Culture and communication cannot flow without alternation or oscillation. Macro-contrasts such as those to be drawn between nation-state political economies and native ecological management systems are no less salient in the understanding of communication than are vital contrasts that guide us unconsciously when we make a very slight distinction, in English, between voicing and not voicing our b's and our p's. Athabascans, most introductory textbooks in anthropology tell us, can't hear the difference between *bin* and *pin*. In a similar way, most Westerners cannot hear the messages emanating from Upper Amazonia. The messages, nonetheless, are there. Some who do listen hear only part of the message and thereby warp it in retransmission. Carlos Castaneda, for example, hears the call of the shaman and the shamanic warrior; he would rejoice in the fantasy of Sicuanga's trip with Huanduj supai. Marvin Harris, a severe critic of Carlos Castaneda's deep, mysterious, inner anthropology from his empiricist, positivist, "scientific" perspective, hears with tremendous clarity the resounding message of ecological degradation attendant upon economic exploitation. But he does not seem to think much of the coincident native power in its own terms. In contrast to both Castaneda and Harris, analysts of ritual activity, led by Victor Turner, delight in the demonstration of how humans can be "betwixt and between" positions in the social structure, at the limen of alternative, co-occurring formations. The latter scholars are getting closer to cultural reality, but again receive too much of the liminal and not enough of the structure. The trouble with all *analytical* polarities is that they miss the fundamental point of human communication itself—simply put, messages are forever relayed to those capable of reading them by "debundling" the symbolic text (see, e.g., Fernandez 1983).

When Shiny Shoes tells Marta that her daughter will not become the teacher in Nueva Esperanza, this is not just a nasty, invidious comment; it is also a highly charged, allusive, allegorical trope. To go so far "outside" as to become a teacher in the national school system is to reverse the anchoring, female role in cultural containment. There is nothing wrong with the reversal, if it itself is contained; but for the latter control system to operate Marta's daughter must go elsewhere, as national outsider, to an analogous small community. The very movement of such a woman in the national educational system of exchanging personnel literally "communicates" the system that separates national education from the mass of native peoples.

When Marta dumps chicha on Shiny Shoes' nice new jacket purchased recently in Puyo, she is not just messing him up a little (though she is certainly doing that). She is also, in this gesture, revalidating her urban brother as a strong festival person, Amasanga-like man of knowledge, compatriot in the world of Nayapi Llacta. Eventually, after the Nuevo Mundo festival, although Marta and her brother were not speaking to one another by then, each was able to articulate the message received in these brief, enacted figures of speech. Thousands of such bundled messages are enacted ritually, and they are brought up into consciousness, reprocessed, and recommunicated at various levels of social discourse. Some of these systems of communication are directed at the national political economy as a coherent system of protest. Protest itself becomes a pulsating system of the communication of power, not only as it emanates from and is received by the Puyo Runa but also as it is received, reinterpreted, and directed back at the Puyo Runa, and through them to other peoples, by developers of the Ecuadorian nation-state.

6

Protest and
the Structure of Antinomy

"Ecuador has assumed a cultural, social, and national personality that permits it to absorb and favorably resolve its own cultural problems . . . [it is] a nation ripe in its *mestizaje.*"—Public statement attributed to the Ministry of Government, *El Comercio*, June 15, 1982, p. 15.

"The ends of the organization of indigenous people of Pastaza (OPIP) [are to] . . . defend and represent the rights and interests of the native peoples, participating in joint actions in the development of the nation collectivity of which [the native indigenous people of Pastaza Province] form a part." Chapter 1, Article 2A, Organization of Indigenous Peoples of Pastaza (OPIP), October, 1981.

"[The] reproduction of the whole of nature constitutes an objectification of the whole of culture. By the systematic arrangement of meaningful differences assigned the concrete, the cultural order is realized also as an order of goods. The goods stand as an object code for the signification and valuation of persons and occasions, functions and situations. Operating on a specific logic of correspondence between material and social contrasts, production is thus the reproduction of culture in a system of objects."—Marshall Sahlins, *Culture and Practical Reason* (1976), p. 178.

Ama Shua! Ama Quilla! Ama Llulla!

"*Shua manamanichu, quilla manamanichu, llulla manamanichu,*" thought Sicuanga to himself—"I'm not a thief, I'm not lazy, I'm not a liar"—as a one-time evangelist, now self-appointed spokesman for native rights, greeted him on a street in Puyo. But out loud he answered the young José Borja gently, politely, "*Buenos días, sobrino.*" "*Huauqui,*" said José, "we shouldn't greet one another in this Spanish language; it is the language of capitalist domination; we should say 'DON'T STEAL! DON'T BE LAZY! DON'T LIE!' as our Inca forebears led by Atahualpa and Tupac Amaru did before they were manipulated by foreigners." "Say that to the *mascha pupus*, then," said Sicuanga, speaking in Spanish, "not to *me*; I'm one of *you.*" "*Mana intindiguichu*"—"But you don't understand," said José, mixing Quichua and Spanish; "to be united against the manipulators who come from the outside we can't be divided as we are now; we must use the same greeting and speak only our Quichua language." Then, in Spanish, he said, "We are more than super-underdeveloped [*más que supersubdesarrollado*] and supermargined [*supermarginado*] because we lack organization. We must get organized like true Ecuadorians in order to preserve our culture, which we are forgetting." "*Cierto es, tupanacunshunchu,*" said Sicuanga—"That's right, our paths will cross again."

This conversation took place on May 12, 1981, at 10:00 A.M., in front of a big oval festival house that Challua and his Achuar–Canelos Quichua Generation IV son-in-law had constructed in a prominent part of urban Puyo. The *municipio* of Puyo had commissioned the house and paid Sicuanga and Eduardo to put it there as a tourist attraction symbolizing the displaced primitives of Upper Amazonia, thereby heightening the developmentalism of civilized, urbanizing Puyo. At the time of the conversation a loudspeaker manned by an evangelist from one of the two local radio stations was blaring out the music from the record *Soul Vine Shaman* (made from the recording of the shamanic session of don Rodrigo), interspersed with messages in Quichua and Spanish about the enduring importance of threatened indigenous lifeways in Amazonian Ecuador, and how the Federation of Indigenous Centers of Pastaza Province now represented all native peoples of this juro-political division: Shuar, Achuar, Quichua, Waorani, Záparo. The parade was about to begin, but the president of the republic would not be there. Instead, he had sent the undersecretary of the Ministry of Government to let organized indigenous leaders know privately that a major event in the cause of native liberation would occur in a week. President Roldós would shortly sign the expulsion document to rid the nation of the North American missionary-developers, the Summer Institute of Linguistics–Wycliffe Bible translators, thereby reclaiming the native peoples of Amazonian Ecuador for all of Ecuador. In the reclamation pro-indigenous and pro-*mestizaje* rhetoric would coincide. Nationalist militarism also reigned in Puyo that day, for a brief war had been fought with Peru near the site of Paquisha,

Sicuanga Runa with *amarun* motif. The toucan is a symbol of protest in Canelos Quichua culture. Alicia Canelos, *llacta* Sarayaquillu, Sarayacu.

in southern Amazonian territory, only four months before, just as preparations for the 12 de Mayo celebration were getting under way.

Inside the oval house, members of the new Federation of Indigenous
Centers of Pastaza Province, FECIP (which later that year became the
Organización de Pueblos Indígenas de Pastaza, OPIP), had set up an
exhibition and sale of ceramics and other native artifacts. The purpose,
to *valorar* (appraise, value, price) the legitimate, authorized culture of
Upper Amazonia, was strikingly manifest in the pricing of artifacts for
sale to tourists. Pots made by relatives of federation officials were priced
the highest (some small bowls bringing $16-20 each, a carved wooden

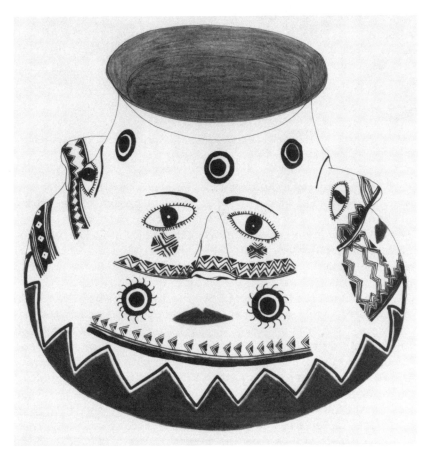

The three faces made to represent the three commands that form the core
symbol of organized protest by native Quichua-speaking peoples in much of
the modern Andes and Upper Amazonia. Rebeca Hualinga de Viteri, Puyo.

The program of literacy for all of Ecuador's people is linked to President Roldós only two weeks before his death.

head $120), next came the pricing of the handicrafts of cultural con-geners of federation officials, and at the very bottom of the pricing spectrum were the black pots for carrying curare dart poison—rarely seen outside of museums—of the Waorani, priced at nickel-and-dime rates. The federation also had a little animal exhibition in the back of the house, featuring a couple of wooly monkeys, a toucan, and two parrots.

Many national tourists visiting Puyo for the 12 de Mayo celebration were present at this *sacha huasi* in urban Puyo. The parade had not yet begun, there was no soccer yet on TV, and the FECIP exhibition was the only attraction in this part of town, other than eating and drinking, or buying a Mickey Mouse balloon with a wooden whistle. As three motorcycles roared by and a balloon salesmen loudly hawked his wares in competition with the chanting shaman from the Napo coming over the loudspeaker, a poor man from Baños, dressed in black wool pants, jacket, hat, and *cabuya* sandals, peered through the split-palm-wood slats to better see the monkeys inside. He overheard me ask Sicuanga who the youth was who was busily tying the toucan to a pole with *chambira* fiber. "That's the son of Atahualpa," said Sicuanga; "don't you remember him?" Quickly the *serrano* turned to us, and

Doce de Mayo, 1981. The sign reads: "Exposición Típica de Valores Culturales 'FECIP.' "

amidst the general hubbub—made more raucous by a passing blue-and-white Volkswagen police car with siren screeching and red and yellow lights flashing—said quite seriously, "No, I don't think so, he's too young." Then he added, equally seriously, "Maybe he's the grandson." Sicuanga laughed and laughed at the ignorance of the man; this *sibulla sicucta* (onion ass) had heard so many Atahualpa stories on the Ambato radio that he thought perhaps not much time had passed since Inca Atahualpa had ruled Ecuador, ancient kingdom of Quito. Lluhui had explained to Sicuanga that long ago, before times of destruction, when President Eloy Alfaro walked the Andean and Upper Amazonian Runa world and the coastal black world during times of revolutionary upheaval, Atahualpa had governed these lands in peace, as indigenous *curaga* of what is now the entire Ecuadorian nation. Lluhui always insisted that all Runa are the "sons of Atahualpa," and Sicuanga had also heard this many times on programs coming from Radio Pastaza, situated just up the street from where he was now standing. Lluhui had affirmed that long ago, before *Alfaro tiempo rucuguna*, those times of destruction that occurred a hundred years back—when Yu (or Yumáa) was in Canelos with Nayapi, and when a *curaga* there, Palate, punched a priest for molesting Runa women, creating tensions that ramified all the way to Quito—Atahualpa had indeed sired the Runa: Quito Runa, Cotopaxi Runa [who call themselves Inga], Salasaca Runa, Canelos Runa—*tucui runaguna*, all the different people. This Lluhui had learned from the Quito Runa. But that was long, long ago, *callari tiempo rucuguna*, and Sicuanga was here and right now, *cunalla*, with a *gringo*, with a *mascha pupu* from Baños, with his own Achuar son-in-law dressed in the urban uniform—gray trousers and dark blue shirt—of the Puyo night scholars, and with many, many others.

A taxi driver pulled up in his yellow Mazda and spied his buddy walking toward us. "*¡Chorongo!*" ("Wooly monkey!") he exclaimed in cordial, enthusiastic, slightly tipsy greeting. "*Hola runa*" ("Hi, Indian"), answered the friend, the ignitable fumes of near-200-proof *trago* coming off his breath. Seven black *esmeraldeños* stopped to listen to the music, then shook their heads and walked off, making comments about how uncivilized it was. "*Cushillu runa*" ("Wooly monkey people"), muttered Sicuanga to himself. The *esmeraldeños* were to play *currulao* music (Afro-American music featuring a marimba and complex drumming) later in the colliseum as a major, "typical," "ethnic" tourist attraction. In the hinterland of Esmeraldas Province, their music is regarded as primitive, black, and cultist; but in urban Puyo it is "folkloric," billed as a genuinely Ecuadorian breath of the sea breeze brought to Amazonian Ecuador to represent a prominent facet of the nation's unified diversity at this celebration of the arrival of civilization to the forest trade site. The *currulao* would be played right before the performance of a dance group from Otavalo, north of Quito in Imbabura Province, long known as both "typically indigenous" and "genuinely national" in style.

Up to Sicuanga came a retired *blanco* military sergeant, resident of Palora, who had been stationed many years in Canelos and had sired children there. Seeing my tape recorder, he hollered "*Yo soy indio,*" and he held forth in near-perfect Canelos Quichua for ten minutes before, laughing and shouting "*¡Viva el Ecuador! ¡Viva el país Amazónico!*" he lurched down the street for another shot of mid-morning *trago*. Then a black man stopped and spoke courteously to Sicuanga in perfect Canelos Quichua, flavored only slightly by the sibilants of Pacific lowlands Spanish. He hailed from Pacayacu on the Bobonaza River, and his half-brother was from Curaray, where the Villano empties into the Curaray. These *ñaupa rucu yana runa* (early-time black people) had come to Amazonian Ecuador with their father, or fathers, from somewhere in Esmeraldas, Ecuador, or Nariño, Colombia. There old Quiñones had come to control the trade on most of the upper and middle Bobonaza, complementing such control with a Peruvian *regatón* (also now resident of Puyo) who worked the lower Bobonaza and Copataza rivers. *"Tucui naciones shamunchi,"* said Sicuanga—"All nations come here."

Then Sicuanga saw an official emerging from the bank across the street. He had his arms linked with two members of an IERAC commission, and he was speaking earnestly with a national representative of INCRAE. Quickly Sicuanga left us and walked over, arm outstretched, to break into this group of Puyo's elite and shake hands. *"Buenos días,* señor Chiriboga," he said loudly, looking quizzically at the group. *"Buen día, buen día,"* mumbled Chiriboga, not introducing Sicuanga to the others. So Sicuanga introduced himself to each man, saying in a loud voice that he was from Nueva Esperanza, founded by his father, Lluhui, who was from Canelos, who was "Shuar," and who once was a powerful *capitán* of the Dominican-dominated town. *"Bién, bién,"* said the group, and as they began to move on, Sicuanga again stretched out his hand to each in turn, saying in Spanish "See you later."

THE NATIONAL PARADIGM OF EL PUYO

Puyu means fog or cloud in Quichua—ubiquitous evidence of the Amazonian water world as it permeates earth and every living thing. It is with fog and rain that the domains of Amasanga and Sungui merge, and it is through fog and by clouds that songs are communicated to their recipients. Fog and cloud are cosmic prisms. *Indi,* the sun, who has a strong mythical association with the toucan, shines through fog or mist to create the spectrum symbolizing ultimate power of previously unleashed water called *amarun* (anaconda), itself considered to be the toucan's primary colors and the domain of shamanic manipulation.

The Puyo Runa are of Puyo, in all of its urban dimensions, just as they are of their greater riparian-swidden-forest environment. Puyo is a familiar place, a resource base representing the national pole of indigenous/national antinomy. As a national city, capital of the province of Pastaza, Puyo ideology and practices replicate in microcosm a significantly regional national structure. Over the past decade Puyo has accelerated into genuine, full-scale urbanization; concomitantly, its dimensions of urban*ism*, the culture of cities, developed (see N. Whitten 1976; D. Whitten 1981; Middleton 1981). Puyo is itself a social prism of the Ecuadorian ethnic spectrum discussed in Chapter 2. It is the site where the Puyo Runa are able to break down the messages, debundle the images being received, and read the texts, so to speak, of nationalist, urban life. One prominent, *urban*, condensed template of the pan-national ethnic, cultural, and class mosaic shines through Puyo's activities as a consistent set of asymmetric contrasts implying a polarity of human capabilities. This template, upon which consistent and contradictory messages may be made up into paradigms, is cast simply, as follows:

Public, National Oppositions

national	indigenous
developmental	resistant
progressive	backward
white	Indian (or black)
urban	jungle[1]
Christian	heathen
hierarchical	egalitarian
decent	common
controlled	free
civilized	savage
educated and adultlike	ignorant and childlike
bureaucratic	segmental
dependent on development	independent of development
light	dark

This set of oppositions must be understood in terms of pyramidal social structure with its cognitive ordering of tripartite antitheses for

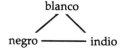

the Ecuadorian nation (see Chap. 2) and for Nueva Esperanza (see Chap. 3). One variant or another of the pernicious, pluralist paradigm is, if not universal in today's world, perilously close to being so. In Puyo—a nexus of civilized, developmentalist, urban, nation-state domination, and of the pulsating system of indigenous insolence/acquiescence in Ecuador's growing system of confluent antinomies—the pairing of public, national oppositions permeates all contexts of communication. Asymmetrical pairing of these concepts of course works to the cognitive, but not necessarily psychological, disadvantage of the Puyo Runa—including in this designation all native people within Puyo's sphere of influence as well as people who identify Puyo as their ancient habitat. Puyo itself as a political culture is self-consciously liberal both in its tolerance of strategic diversity in political-economic affairs and in its own conceptualization of *mestizaje*, the ideology of ethnic intermingling.

---

1. Not "rural" in Ecuador: to be rural is to be oriented toward the urban. Jungle is the antithesis of urban; to be oriented toward the forest is to be oriented away from the urban.

For the Puyo Runa, Puyo is the prime site for testing the waters of nonpernicious pluralism, for reversing the asymmetry in the pejorative template, for understanding the duality of their ethnic heritage, and for strengthening the duality of power patterning.

Political-Economic Antinomy: Power and Protest among the Puyo Runa

In 1978 one antithesis of urban Puyo, the heartland of Canelos Quichua culture — Sarayacu — became a political wellspring of ethnic surgency. Sarayacu lies midway between Puyo and Peru on an east-west axis; less than a century ago it lay between Zaparoan territory to the north and Achuar Jivaroan to the south. Today Sarayacu hunting, fishing, and *chagra* territory ranges northward from the Bobonaza. People living, say, on the Río Rutunu at any given time are *Sarayacu-manda*, from Sarayacu. Although many men from Sarayacu hunt and fish southward, to near the Capahuari River, they do not proceed further to the Copataza, for that is clearly *Achuar partimanda*; people there (and around the Capahuari) are "pristine Achuar." In Sarayacu we find the heartland of Canelos Quichua culture to be characterized by strikingly beautiful ceramics, rich material culture, powerful shamanic activity, strong lore of being Quichua as opposed to Achuar or Zaparoan, and multiple ties of marriage and kinship to both Achuar and Zaparoan peoples. Indeed, one small sector of Sarayacu is known from Puyo to Iquitos, Peru, as being a site where one can trade with relatives in Achuar and Maina Jivaroan, and in Andoa or Záparo Zaparoan. We also find in Sarayacu a strong Catholic and Protestant evangelical presence, a national school, and a health clinic. Sarayacu, we could say, is Nayapi Llacta writ large, and cast both traditional and modern.

The upper Bobonaza River trade has long been dominated by a black family who came originally from the Pacific lowlands of either Ecuador or Colombia, and who apparently intermarried somewhat with Brazilian and Peruvian blacks during or subsequent to the politically torrid times of the Amazonian rubber boom. Members of this family settled in Pacayacu, Curaray, and Puyo, and fanned out northward, eastward, and westward. To the south trade was controlled by various *regatones* from Peru, one of whom eventually settled in Puyo, where his commercial world continues to bind Achuar of the lower Copataza through various broker linkages with Generation II and III Canelos Quichua peoples of the upper Copataza and Canelos and with Puyo merchants.

The children of the traders are scattered through Canelos Quichua and Achuar territory, and they have various relationships with one

Ama Shua! Ama Quilla! Ama Llulla! Federation officials on parade, 1982: treasurer, vice-president, president, and secretary. The president, from the Napo area, wears the traditional toucan headdress of the Achuar. The vice-president, to his right, carries the national flag of Ecuador.

Various portrayals of indigenous persistence and demand for national service, in the 12 de Mayo celebrations, 1982 (*below and facing page*).

another that create a lattice gently superimposed upon the other patterns described. In other words, Canelos Quichua territory is salted with people who are of Canelos Quichua culture by flesh and by custom, and *not* of it if any aspect of the *mestizo-zambo-indio* paradigm is invoked. The existence of this lattice was somewhat disguised by the double phenomenon of being *runa* in all settings of Canelos Quichua or Achuar Jivaroan residence and of being *ecuatoriano* in Puyo or elsewhere in the republic. Progeny of the traders (who were and are fluent in Quichua and Achuar) were placed automatically in the category of Generation IV Canelos Quichua, if they chose to act the part required by such categorization.

The lattice of traders' children who intermarried with Canelos Quichua is further disguised by the tripartite ethnic polarities described in Chapters 2 and 3. One can all too easily talk of "Indian" versus "white" identity systems in Amazonian Ecuador, and then seriously, if foolishly, raise the question about who the blacks speaking Quichua are, who the sons and sons-in-law of "white" Puyo residents are who speak Quichua fluently, and now wear their hair in the style presumed by nonindigenous peoples to be that of the Shuar of yesteryear. To so talk is to broadcast the myth of a biethnic, polar system best reproduced by the list of pejorative, asymmetric, false opposites listed above.

When ethnic bloc awareness surged in Puyo in 1978, being generated out of meetings in Sarayacu that included, at various times, foreign representatives from the Inter-American Foundation of Washington, D.C., OXFAM-England, the Dominican order and the Protestant evangelical movement, it was borne by militant Runa (including Achuar) already known to the Puyo residents as the children of non-Runa. In other words, the antinomy of forest-oriented Sarayacu native and urban-oriented Puyo townsmen fused or condensed into a powerful, evocative, multi-vocalic, ethnic symbol of political potential. The antinomy borne by the conjoining of opposites was expressed by the indigenous request and demand—made in writing and over the airwaves, publicly as well as in many, many private meetings with native peoples and national spokesmen for rival political parties and rival economic development plans—that all territory inhabited now or in the past by indigenous peoples be returned to indigenous peoples. Moreover, the organization of indigenous peoples within Pastaza Province was not to be by ethnic-cultural determination, as in the prototype case of the Shuar Federation to the south; rather, using the northern prototype of the Federation of Indigenous Organizations of Napo Province (FOIN), the new native alliance ramifying out of Puyo (and surging out of Sarayacu and a bit later out of Arajuno) was to be on a provincial basis. The first and most pervasive split to occur within those affiliating with organized protest was between those who regarded themselves as *cristianos* and those who regarded themselves as secular. The former called the latter *comunistas*, and those so labeled reciprocated with such terms as *capitalistas* and *gringuistas*.

Autofinancing, an idea and strategy developed at the Central University of Ecuador in Quito, as understood and interpreted by a major leader of the new Federation of Indigenous Centers of Pastaza Province (FECIP), was the initial means by which the federation was to give value to the underlying concept of *runapuralla* (people among ourselves). But to begin the process of self-determination within the national political economy, political and financial help was sought from the government of Ecuador and from foreign institutions. The protest movement of central Amazonian Ecuador, as initiated by its Canelos Quichua and Achuar spokesmen and women, sought to simultaneously mobilize political-economic systems of control of resources from above and to retain and expand capacity to respond by indigenous peoples in their varied habitats from below. The rhetoric syncretized the paradigm manipulations from above and below to resonate with contradictory nationalist rhetoric as manifest, for example, in 1981 by President Jaime Roldós Aguilera and Vice-President Osvaldo Hurtado. The nationalist rhetoric, which ushered in the new era of parliamentary democracy, featured Roldós's vision of a genuine cultural pluralism in Ecuador devoid of a unifying center on one side, and Hurtado's insistence on a unifying *indomestizaje* on the other (Hurtado 1981; N. Whitten 1981b: 777-94). This facet of ideology, contradictory though it was, swept Amazonian Ecuador like a strange mingling of coastal sea breezes and Andean drafts after nine long years of escalating military domination. Rhetorical political antinomy of the indigenous protest movement generated even greater cultural antinomy by drawing upon and manipulating ideas and concepts in many novel ways.

At the same time, strategic, pragmatic concerns were at work. To obtain hard cash from organizations oriented to "helping Indians survive as Indians" one must be of the indigenous culture as this culture is perceived in the eyes of representatives of the funding agencies. Simultaneously, to receive funds for national development one must be perceived as "developing" or being receptive to "development" by the money-givers. To obtain money in order to give value to a movement is to place the movement between capital formations such that outside needs are fulfilled by the inside, ideological stance. As this process of *valorización* of culture goes on, those Runa receiving funds from the outside are perceived by the Runa in settings such as Nueva Esperanza as falling increasingly outside indigenous culture. But these very people are seen from the nationalist stance as "pristine" representatives of native culture. Simultaneously, as the urban Runa representing the forest of indigenous dissidence to outsiders become more wealthy, townsmen view them as increasingly of the republic. Let's pause a moment and introduce two concepts.

Epochalism and Essentialism

I draw these terms from Clifford Geertz (1973) but deploy them somewhat differently. Epochalism refers to the international validation of a nation's statehood. Essentialism is the affirmation of a common style, quality, and culture—the oneness of a people—that revitalizes a sense of historical depth at each crucial moment of epochal emergence and consolidation. Stated simply by Anya Royce (1982: 84), "Nations frequently borrow the imagery and rhetoric of ethnicity." I am sure that she would agree to the converse of this, that in epochal emergence of ethnic blocs the essentialist imagery and rhetoric of nationalism are often borrowed.

The epochalism of ethnic surgency ostensibly radiating out of such jungle sites as Sarayacu and Arajuno became manifest in urban Puyo, and Puyo itself became, by 1981, a crucible of indigenous debate over its essential character. There, in a section of town where many outsiders, including oil company bosses, Peace Corps volunteers, evangelists, and others, reside from time to time, and where some of the oldest non-indigenous families of Puyo also live, the federation set up an office on the third floor of the most modern high-rise built to that date. By 1982 the new organization, OPIP, representing all indigenous peoples of the province, was dominated by a young president from Arajuno, a black man from Pacayacu, a Generation IV Canelos Quichua (who is also Generation II Achuar), and the son of the Peruvian *regatón* long controlling the Copataza trade routes. In Shell, the newest area of urban growth, the rival Christian Organization of Independent Indigenous Pastaza Peoples took root. For both the Christian and secular organizations, to be "indigenous" was to be "national," and to be "national" meant to be so only on indigenous terms.

As the two primary organizations became increasingly epochal in their simultaneous emergence as the "legitimate" voice of genuine, bona fide native peoples vis-à-vis national politicians, developers, and ideologues, some spokesmen even discussed the inner, essentialist qualities of being *indio* in Spanish. Being *indio*, some said, reflected a genuine inner *national* essence, or soul, of a people long excluded by traditional nationalist standards.

To the people of Nayapi Llacta such spokesmen for "being Indian" appeared increasingly similar to those nonindigenous peoples from other parts of the Republic of Ecuador against whom they had long been struggling. But at the same time there was a certain pride that these Runa, their relatives, their known compatriots, appeared *more* indigenous to outsiders, as their fluency in Spanish and sophistication with political rhetoric increased vis-à-vis representatives of the "civilized," white, Christian, urban, "Ecuadorian" political-economic control groups.

In 1982 several OPIP leaders were formally expelled from the Comuna San Jacinto, and all such leaders were ordered to refrain from entering *comuna* territory. Simultaneously, alliances between OPIP leaders and *comuna* members took place. As the tensions between OPIP and the *comuna* grew, the leaders of the former organization accused Nueva Esperanza members, such as Sicuanga and Challua, of being bumpkins, of not understanding the nature of politics and economy either in the modern republic or in the rebellious movement to bring ethnic cultures into the modern republic on their own terms. And they simultaneously accused other members of Nueva Esperanza, such as Shiny Shoes, of only wanting more money to become national, at the expense of genuine, essential, indigenous being. Those from Nueva Esperanza collectively countered with an accusation that OPIP was seeking to control the resources traditionally held by indigenous people (e.g. *comuna* lands), and to deny to the Puyo Runa their access to native power formations such as those found in shamanic and ceremonial activity.

By 1982 every single native hamlet, *llacta*, and territory surrounding Puyo (Comunas San Jacinto, Canelos, San Ramón, and other sites as well) were formally, publicly opposed to OPIP (now often called *upi* in Quichua), as this organization developed out of FECIP and became a microcosm for national developmentalism cast in the mold of indigenous protest. Simultaneously, 1982 found the Runa in all of these areas actively expelling all nonindigenous peoples from their territories and actively requesting national and regional support for their continued development through schools, roads, and marketable products. Every hamlet wanted to develop on its own, while retaining its environmental-management support within its *llacta* system. In addition, every hamlet rejected the idea of an inside, bilingual schoolteacher and requested an outside, non-Runa or *chaupi* Runa, national teacher.

The other side of political-economic development, Sicuanga Runa's side, has both epochalist and essentialist dimensions borne on the twin vehicles of nationalist and ethnic rhetoric and reproduced continuously

as the driving antinomy in such microcosms as Nueva Esperanza/
Nayapi Llacta.

Doce de Mayo

The Twelfth of May celebration of the founding of Puyo is an object
lesson in the staging of power and expressing it through ritual paraphernalia. The polarity of indigenous savagery and nationalist civilization could not be more strongly expressed. And transcending the
expanding antinomy is the proclamation of a new regional division of
Ecuador—*nosotros, los orientales* (we, the eastern bloc) or, more recently,
los amazónicos civilizados. Mestizaje during 12 de Mayo takes on the
characterization of heightened national culture regionally defined.
Schoolchildren dress in the costumes of stereotypic indigenous and
black people from the Sierra and Coast, while older children march to
a very repetitive drum cadence. Not only does one hear the legend of
the founding of Puyo blaring over radios and loudspeakers to stress
the civilizing force of church and state united, but also of the development of a genuine, third regional culture contrasting with Sierra and
Coast. The Queen's float is usually designed as a great *mucahua* with
the prominent zigzag encircling it. And on its sides are the large carved
caymans, toucans, and other recent ethnic crafts of the Puyo Runa
men and women. Above all, the civilizing thrust of national education
reigns, as wave after wave of schoolchildren pass by the reviewing
stand, followed by demonstrations of the effects of bilingual education,
nationally delivered, in creating a new indigenous countenance, a "developing" one.

   Let us look again at the oppositions being heightened by their very
transcendence as presented on page 224. The features in each column
co-adhere internally, as a linear chain of association, identifying urban
dwellers. Such people *deny* that the forest itself exists except as a distant,
alien, and savage place beyond the limen of civilization. The concepts
contained in the left and right columns, in other words, occur next to
each other; they are contiguous in Ecuadorian thought. With but minor
changes, most industrializing nations in the modern world contain
similar highly condensed, if usually implicit, strings of pernicious association. "Progress," whether by nationalist force or indigenous protest, is seen as the transformation of right-column attributes into left-
column ones. For only one of dozens of prominent examples, consider
the adult-education program. Sicuanga's Generation II Achuar son-in-
law, Eduardo (who is also Generation IV Canelos Quichua), together
with Sicuanga's Generation III Canelos Quichua son, are currently

involved in this program of bilingual education, and Sicuanga is constantly exposed to the imagery that it invokes, fed back to him by close family members. "The National Plan for Adult Education and Literacy Training of 1977," as published in *El Comercio* on August 10 (the day of national militarist heroism when Quiteños triumphed over colonial rule in the Battle of Pichincha), contrasts the "marginalized person or group" with "the new type of Ecuadorian" as follows (from Stutzman 1981: 71):

The New Type of Ecuadorian	The Marginalized Person or Group
1. He is a *trabajador*, industrial or technical worker, or anyone who is "working" for national development.	1. He is a *campesino*, rural laborer, including the unskilled, unlettered migrant to the urban center.
2. He is confident of his capacities and potentialities.	2. He has been deprived of his human dignity.
3. His consciousness is reflective and critical. Everyday realities and problems are seen clearly so they can be dealt with.	3. His consciousness is magical in character; he sees his situation in terms of euphemisms and sophistries. He is prejudiced, superstitious, and taboo-ridden.
4. He thinks as an Ecuadorian, as master of his own destiny, acting with determination to better the environment where he was born and grew up.	4. Waiting for others to do his thinking and acting for him, he has difficulty taking decisive action to resolve his own problems.
5. Labor integrated with education becomes a human blessing, liberator from misery, illness, and ignorance.	5. Forced to sell his labor for pennies, the uneducated sees his work as a curse of God.
6. The literate individual finds better work opportunities, thus lending his positive support to the development of the country.	6. His illiteracy signifies unemployment, underemployment, backwardness on all levels, conformity, and poverty.
7. The new Ecuadorian is integrated into the free world. He exercises his rights and fulfills his obligations. He is disposed to produce and consume more.	7. Long accustomed to the semifeudal hacienda system, the illiterate supplies his own basic needs. He neither produces nor consumes.

The 12 de Mayo celebration swells with observers from throughout the nation.

At night, after the parade, a new bilingual teacher, wearing a toucan headdress, dances with his wife.

Two modes of participation in 12 de Mayo: as Sicuanga Runa with toucan headdress (*above left*); as *yuyayuj runa* with cassette recorder (*above right*).

Sons and sons-in-law of powerful ones participate variously in 12 de Mayo (*below*).

Runa from Sarayacu are "prepared" by a priest to represent the burden of savagery that the Dominican order bears.

The Dominican mission at Puyo, where state and regional officials view the pageantry of Christian, civilized triumph over sylvan savagery.

Enactment of *dominario* in front of the Catholic church. *Above:* a shaman from down-river plays an Andean melody; *below:* the *lanceros* go to the brink of "ending everything."

The difficulty with such a mental set, of course, is that the left-column chain of associations—called syntagmatic, or linked by contiguity, in technical literature on the analysis of tropes—forever rests on paired contrasts that are *asymmetrical*. Control over the contrast sets, learned by the new Runa high school students (*yuyayuj runa*), does not overcome the barrier of being indigenous. For such "being" implies in the contrast sets a "becoming" of *blanco* and hence a denial of being Runa. It places one "betwixt and between," to use Victor Turner's phrase, the social order of ethnic- and class-stratified national political economy and the segmentary, egalitarian system of native cultures. Moreover, the perceived contiguity of the right column depends upon the contiguity of the left column. All of the right-side associations are simply derivative of the left side—an unfortunate, pejorative, and unnecessary projection of powerful, false, ascribed, stereotypic attributes upon a nation's peoples. This simple pairing of powerful concepts confronts the Runa with an enduring ideological structure of domination revealed in the town of El Puyo. This is perhaps most apparent in the concept of *indomestizaje*, the blending of the two contrastive columns to create an ideology of nationalist transcendence based on a recast polarity.

This recasting comes about when it is asserted that today's Indians are not those of yesteryear. They are the unfortunate, margined, deprived, ignorant, common, semi-civilized, half-Christian remnants of centuries of colonial, republican, and modern domination. It is the task, as this argument goes (a task discussed from the rarefied wings of Quiteño academia to the school in Nueva Esperanza, in Puyo saloons or in the more sanctified Catholic church, in a banker's office or on an agricultural experimental plot paid for by the Episcopal church of Erie, Pennsylvania—such a plot exists near Tarqui, on the edge of the Comuna San Jacinto del Pindo), to teach native people their genuine heritage and to teach them to be Ecuadorian citizens. The bilingual scholars of high school, whether day school or night school, become the purveyors of this quasi-"enlightened" continuance of neocolonial mentality, which emphasizes that their parents and grandparents are imbued with right-column attributes and that they themselves must prove that they are capable of moving into the left-column string of associations, without denying their roots on the right side.

Within this enduring, symbolic structure of ethnic and cultural domination, the 12 de Mayo celebration concretizes both the ethnic-cultural polarity and its nationalist transcendence. Some Runa march in school uniforms with their Puyo day schools or night schools. A couple of others watch over the town's tranquility and festivity as genuine uniformed police. A dozen or so march with the military, and hundreds upon hundreds dress as urban citizens and simply wander, watch, eat and drink, dance, chat, and, perhaps above all else, reflect upon that which the Puyo prism reveals about urban lifeways. A few Runa agree to "play" native, and provide right-column contrast sets for the parade. They dress in national stereotypic costumes of "typical," nonexistent, one-time savage people, complete with grass skirts, spears, and feathered headdresses. They punctuate the parade with native dances and skits, to the delight of near-hysterical radio announcers.

Sicuanga himself once carried a writhing eight-foot boa constrictor in the parade. This he would never do within his own culture. But he stood on a new threshold during the parade and was actually playing the part of a Colombian medicine salesman who comes to Puyo to sell his wares once every three months, often buying genuine *amarun shungu* from Sicuanga. Usually one or another Runa group manages to dance for five to ten minutes before the bandstand, often enacting the buildup to the *dominario* there, right in front of the Dominican mission cathedral and school, upon whose balcony sit the president of the republic (or his appointed representative), the archbishop of Canelos, the governor of the province, a military general, and a prominent emissary of the Ministry of Education.

The Puyo Runa can, from many, many vantage points, "see" the discrete national categories through Puyo's colorful social prism. They are as familiar with the ins and outs of Puyo and their varied, creative options there as they are with the large-scale *ayllu* festivals and their quotidian activities. They are more familiar, although in a different way, with aspects of Puyo's urbanization than they are with those of Nueva Esperanza, and they say so. In fact, after a rift has occurred in Nueva Esperanza, there is greater chance of resolution in Puyo than in Nueva Esperanza.

Playing (pugllana) is the principal means by which the ideological structure of domination is debundled and recast in urban Puyo by the Puyo Runa. To be *ricsij*, one who sees, or *yuyayuj*, one who learns, is important here, for debundling occurs constantly. When Sicuanga sees, for example, reluctance to shake his hand and reluctance to give a cordial goodbye to him by bank officials, he knows that sheer accumulation of money cannot place him in a higher position in the eyes of the bank officials and their development- and self-help-oriented IERAC and INCRAE friends. And when he hears the taxi driver and his friend greet one another he can see their equation of monkey and Indian as contrasted with Christian and white. And when he hears a black *esmeraldeño* make a crack about savagery he can readily perceive that he and they are as far apart as can be imagined, while at the same time they are quite similar. Perceiving in this way is no more difficult than understanding that the discrete colors of the rainbow are a complex result of Indi's eye looking through clear water, mist, or fog. And the perception of the national categories in all of their pejorative and oppressive dimensions is no more (and no less) frightening than the image of the mighty, devouring anaconda.

In Sicuanga's mental play great leaps are sometimes taken that provide the insight necessary for him to perceive the mundane order of the social realm by reference to myth and legend. Stated another way, the political economy bearing down on him may be perceived in terms of revelatory power. For example, he knows, figuratively, and he believes, publicly and privately, that the Runa penis is anaconda; that it comes out of the watery domain to devour humans (who then kill it and make substances [e.g. *amarun shungu*] increasing their response capacity); that the origin of the segmented *ayllu* system lies in the highly predatory act of the giant river otter, who, in *unai*, chops off Cauchullu's penis and salts it throughout Amazonia. He thinks sometimes in a bundle of images that are difficult to sort but are no less clear. For example, working from the last to the first of the above mythical event-segments, he knows that some outsiders to Amazonia have placed their seeds in the *huarmiguna*; the predatory trade system has seeded the growth of capital throughout Runa territories, and such outsiders (who are now insiders as well) could figuratively devour the Runa. He also thinks, indeed knows, that the Runa themselves can use the substance of this devouring system to gain strength. When Sicuanga thinks in this way he violates the syntagmatic chains of association previously presented, restructuring them on various mythical templates with a number of paradigmatic processes such as metaphor, irony, and synecdoche.

Sicuanga likes to play mentally with the forces revealed to him in urban Puyo. He is no more afraid of the contradictions there than he is of the mighty forces that permeate the familiar riparian-swidden-rain forest environment. Sitting at a table in a Puyo saloon with three friends, he listens intently to a group of men from Nuevo Mundo and Rosario Yacu talking to a mixed group including two North Americans, a Catholic priest from Cayambe, and two Achuar from the Copataza (his nephews) at another table, while watching people pass by on the street. His cracked beer glass is decorated with yellow zigzags and flowers, and he is amused by the resemblance between these designs and those painted by María on her new *tinaja*. The group at the other table does not invite him over, for they are speaking in earnest, rapid Spanish about polarities in nationalist development (regionalism versus national identity, ethnic diversity versus national unity, a society of classes versus a dual society) and switching rapidly from time to time to indigenous oppositions (Shuar culture versus Quichua culture, *caserío* Nueva Esperanza versus *caserío* Nuevo Mundo). He listens and thinks, but eventually the play tires him, as it does Challua, Marta, María, and most of the rest. It is as fatiguing to jump back and forth between the polarities contained on either side of Puyo's symbolic template as it is to trek back and forth between Puyo and Canelos. So before the day ends, Sicuanga almost always winds up talking to someone who is *caru llactamanda*, from a distant territory. This is more relaxing, and it is as easy to find such congenial company in urban Puyo as elsewhere.

Puyo is the primary residence of only a few Runa; most of the native peoples ringing Puyo live in the alternating *caserío-llacta* pattern described in Chapter 3, articulating to the urban ambience in ways also discussed there. To understand the other side of development we cannot remain too long in the regional center of political-economic developmentalism. Regardless of Sicuanga's capacity to respond to crushing political-economic forces, he does not now have the strength to stay there. Nor does he wish to remain in a world of cement, dust, grime, garbage, and foul water, even though he enjoys its fried fish, rice, baked bread, and broiled chicken, its beer and *trago*, its hubbub, movement, marketing activity, movies, television, radios, and jukeboxes. The food and drink tastes no better to him, though, than fish and meat prepared by María, cooked with hot peppers and salt, and served with steaming plantains and manioc, and the beer is no better than *asua*, still warm and with a wide range of tastes and sensations. He enjoys listening to music on a little Sony radio he has, but he also loves to hear the song of *jilucu*, the whisper of bat wings, the slight, ubiquitous, and familiar sounds of the forest and its fringes at the juncture with *chagra* and hamlet. To be in Puyo on a full-time basis is as dangerous as to be in *unai*. It would be to move into another world, to die as a questing Runa. So Sicuanga thinks.

The crucible of continuity and change exists within the structure of antinomy of the *caserío/llacta* for Sicuanga Runa, just as it does in analogous settings for the majority of Ecuador's peoples. The developer's bugaboo is that these settings in the Ecuadorian forest (or Andean slopes, or deep valleys, or monsoon plains, or *páramo*) are as vivid, dynamic, and vibrant places as are the bustling urban centers, swelling as they are with migrants from their antitheses.

NAYAPI LLACTA/NUEVA ESPERANZA, May 22, 1982

At noon on Saturday, May 22, Sicuanga and María bathed in the stream by their small house on the *chagra*. They then walked the forty-five-minute distance to Río Chico to visit Tselctselc and Faviola, by way of the high ridge where Challua had walked some months before. When they were within five minutes of Tselctselc's house, entering by a *runa ñambi*, they put on their best clothes, usually reserved for visits to Puyo on Sunday. As they dressed they looked at each other; never had they heard such a racket here on the *comuna*. There was so much engine noise in the distance that it reminded them of the waist-deep mud near Mera where the Ambato-Puyo road was eventually to be paved.

Entering the house, Sicuanga sat on the west side, on a long bench, while Tselctselc sat near the center on a log recently cut with his son-in-law's chain saw (made in Homewood, Illinois, and purchased in Puyo). Both looked east down to the river, which was quite low and deep brown, and out across the jungle toward the Sigüín range, where thunderclouds were rapidly gathering. Soon it would rain hard, the forest behind Tselctselc's house would reverberate, and the Chingosimi River would rush, swelling as it emptied into the Puyo River just up from Rosario Yacu. The wonderful moist coolness, often borne by the strong breath of the Cacalurcu Hills to the south, was about to envelop Nayapi Llacta. "All the fish have died," said Tselctselc; "the mud from the tractors is more potent than our poison." "Others should return from downstream, though," said Sicuanga, "when the water clears." Then Sicuanga's son, Taruga, together with Elena, arrived to pass the time away before trekking on to the second line. Sicuanga and María planned to spend the night with Tselctselc and Faviola, to be prepared for the great Sunday event—the inauguration of the new bridge across the Chingosimi River—when Río Chico would replicate in microcosm far more features of urban Puyo than ever before.

"I know a secret," said Taruga, "a hidden transformation of Amasanga." "How do you see this," asked Sicuanga, interested in hearing the new story, although he'd already heard it three times. "You go to Santo Domingo de los Colorados," said Taruga, "on the way to Quevedo, where the *enganche* [system of labor contracting] exists for work in Manabí with Sr. Jon of the oil company. You don't drink *ayahuasca* or *huanduj*. Instead, you take a couple of gallons of *trago* and go off into the jungle. You climb and climb and get up on top of a great hill, with the forest all around." He paused, and took a long pull of chicha as María refilled his *mucahua* and the *mucahuas* of everyone else present. The story was about to change from the general to the specific. Taruga had decided to tell of an actual event rather than to relate a tale.

Arriving.

"I did this," he said softly, "this is my knowledge," and again he began to talk. "I was with Aníbal Grefa and Wilson Hualinga, who I met in the hotel in Santo Domingo where Sr. Jon put us up for the night. Right below our window was a lot of *bulla*, so we went down and there was a big wheel that went around." Here Taruga diverged from his tale to describe the little traveling carnival with its ferris wheel and merry-go-round, which he had enjoyed riding for a couple of hours. Then he returned to his theme. "We bought *trago* and got a taxi driver with a pickup truck to drive us eight kilometers out of town. There we trekked from the road, across two streams and up a hill. We were looking for a large cave in the hill; we wanted to find the *allpa pungu* [earth door] that opens at 11:00 P.M. every night. There should also be a special plant there with a flower that blooms only once every two years. The door we were looking for looks like a bamboo door in the earth. We got there by 9:00 P.M. and drank and drank *trago*; we were laughing and talking and we passed out. We awoke with a tremendous wind blowing; the jungle was swaying and the trees were shaking. Everything was alive. The door appeared near to where we were sitting and we looked in; strange lights glowed. There were little devils in there, dimly visible. Satan appeared. He was a great *supai*. He was so big that the other devils only came up to his waist. Satan [*satanás* in his pronunciation] had long hair on his arms; the hair was four inches long." ("Like Jurijuri," thought Sicuanga and Tselctselc.) "What do you seek," asked Satan. "We have come to learn," said the three youths, almost in unison, speaking Spanish. "Come in if you dare," said Satan in Spanish. They entered, just a little way, very drunk on *trago*. "Quickly we learned to play the guitar, something we all wanted to do," Taruga explained. "We played like an orchestra—music filled the cave, like in a saloon in Puyo on Sunday. Satan had a book of magic but we wanted to learn just a little [*por medias*] and so we left. We got to the doorway, it was dirt, it was small, too small to get out, and we were very drunk and the doorway was getting smaller and smaller, and Satan with his book and lights and all the devils were back behind us in the cave. But we were strong, we had the capacity to get out, and we thrust ourselves out through that earth door. We will go back, re-enter the cave through the earthen door of bamboo, and spend enough time in there to really learn to play the guitar."

The hubbub and noise level swelled and all watched the spectacle of *maquinaria* before them—just about a hundred meters away: a large Komatsu bulldozer was working away right on the plaza as a road scraper graded the road where once a large oval house had stood. Seven dump trucks were working, one behind the other, first coming up a hill, then turning and backing to the area in front of Jaime's house before dumping their loads of heavy stones taken from the Pastaza and Pindo rivers. There was also a heavy roller there making everything flat, squeezing the water out of the plaza and making a giant Andean-type *cancha* that was already becoming sun-parched even as the rain approached, so certainly there would soon be a lagoon right in front of the modern, rural school in Río Chico.

"*Tianguichu gumba*," called Marta. "I'm here," said Sicuanga as Marta and Challua entered. "*Ashca bulla shamunchi*" ("Lots of noise coming"), Marta said, referring to the sound of bulldozers, scraper, roller, and trucks that had continued and intensified work that Saturday afternoon in preparation for an inspection group from the Ministry of Public Works due the next morning; Río Chico must look sufficiently developed to be inaugurated. "Lots of hubbub," everyone acknowledged. "As your father Lluhui told *ichilla gobernador* [little governor]," said Tselc-tselc to Sicuanga, referring to Lluhui's interpretation of the frogs that had so frightened Jaime back in 1968. Jaime had become a prominent *comuna* official for the second time, and several people now referred to him as the "little governor" in response to a recent propensity to order people around and issue proclamations about who was, and who was not, a genuine, legitimate, *comunero*. Two children were making *maquinaria* noises, *room, vrrrooom, aaarrrggggh*, and as a bull bellowed, little Carlos answered in perfect imitation. "*Huagra shimi*," laughed Sicuanga, embarrassing the little tyke—"He speaks cattle-talk."

Marta looked quickly at my stereo recorder. "You have your recorder, *gumba*," she said. Then softly added, "*Cantangaruni*" ("I am going to sing"). And she sang, for an hour and a half, sad songs, sending out, creating an emotional mood of unquenchable longing (*llaquichina*) to restore rifts in social fabrics. The listeners became pleasantly nostalgic, and a longing to continue to be close to one another (*llaquirina*) was shared. Everything described in this book, and much, much more, was condensed into ninety minutes of song lyrics, texts, and evocative imagery and reprocessed in Marta's reflecting self, embodied as it was within the collective, emotional entanglement of Nayapi Llacta, which was now utterly tied up in urban, bureaucratic ensnarlments of Nueva Esperanza—the great divided town house that it had developed into.

Whheeeeeeeeeeyuh came the falsetto through the air, just as the rain hit. "*Whay*," said Tselctselc instantly, as Marta laughed midway through her tears. "*Yaicui*" ("Come in"), Tselctselc said to Antonio, who was carrying a full flour sack on his back and a 100-dollar radio over his left shoulder. Antonio, a youth of twenty-four years, was en route to Shell, but he had decided to drop by this growing household, escape

the rain, and ask about all the preparations for the festival unfolding
amidst the hubbub of terminal, heavy construction. He went around
the room in a circle, shaking hands with each man and woman. "What's
in the bag," asked Sicuanga. "*Cambaj tucayu*" ("Your namesake"), said
Antonio. He opened his bundle and pulled out one of twenty-five balsa
toucans with their beaks pointing straight up. He and his two brothers
had spent a week making them. First they cut the balsa, then one man
blocked them out while another did the finer work and the third
polished them with a small knife and sandpaper. Friday night they
had burned them with wires heated in the cook fires. Sold strictly by
length to either the indigenous buyer for the Christian federation in
Shell or to a *comerciante* there, these brand-new *sicuanga*s would bring
300 *sucres* each, for a total of 7,500 *sucres* or $300. "*Chuta!*" said
Sicuanga, "they're worth as much as a cow, and almost as much as
my 800-cane *finca* when the cane matures."

"*Ashca valorishca*," agreed Antonio, accepting a bowlful of chicha
from Faviola, drinking, and accepting a refill. "Everybody is buying
these birds," Antonio said, "but my *sicuanga*s are better than most. I'm
going to sell twenty in Puyo and Shell at half their worth and take
five to Quito to sell for more than they're worth. Then I'm going to
find out where the paint comes from in Quito, buy some, and bring
it back, so that my father, brothers, and I can paint the birds and make
ashca culqui [lots of money] as the Machin Runa in Quito do." Dolorisa,
Antonio's young wife, spoke up: "All he does is talk about money,"
she said; "he's even got me helping to sand, cut, and burn. I haven't
made any pottery for a month and we spend as much time hunting
for balsa as we do gardening." Tselctselc spoke too, as the group
warmed to the theme of the meaning of money: "Don Ramón in Tarqui
says that I should plant much more sugarcane," he said. "I got these
sections from 100-cane stalks that he gave me after I sold him my pig
for 1,800 *sucres*." "But the pig was worth 4,000," said young Antonio,
"and the stalks he gave you were worth only about 700 *sucres* roadside
last month." Faviola spoke up then: "The pigs ate everything in the
garden and I had to feed them all the time." Tselctselc added, in Spanish,
"The *machins* of Tarqui now respect me because I have money." "They'd
respect you more if you knew its worth," said Antonio. "Careful, *churi*,"
Sicuanga said in Quichua, "you don't know as much as you think you
do about money and the way the *mashca pupus* use it to bind you to
them."

As Antonio and Dolorisa took their leave, splashing toward Puyo
on the new road as the rain subsided, Sicuanga began to talk, his voice
rising: "I no longer want to live without money," he said forcefully,

"but I also don't want to live in the midst of constant upheaval. Nueva Esperanza is just like your *caserío*, and we are all of this land. Tomorrow hundreds of outsiders will come here, and they will know you, and they will soon know us, in the same way. We're strong, our *llacta* is great, and one day it will be a city like Puyo, a city just like those inside the hills ruled over by the Jurijuri supai. We become as we have been, *sinchi runa, yachaj sami runa*, and I will not lose my strength to the traps of the federation or to the snares of the Machin Runa. I'll carve toucan birds to sell in Puyo, Shell, and Quito, but I'll carve what I want to carve, when I want to, and when I need money." "And," said Marta (now speaking simultaneously with Sicuanga), "I'll not stop working with my clay and fire and breath and water; I'll make what I know and what I see and I'll not make what anyone tells me to make." But then she said softly, "I'm going to make hundreds of *mucahuas* and sell them. They're worth more than balsa birds." Sicuanga laughed and said to Challua, "She'll have lots of money *compadre*, and then maybe she'll go to Quito and the United States to visit, as the Salasaca Runa do."

Marta laughed and then again became pensive, and her melancholy increased. "*Ishcai mundo tian, gumba*" ("There are two worlds, *compadre*"), she said, "and we live in both of them, right here and now in our hamlet and *llacta*. We breed like ants and live in our territory, and we become too many for it. But we don't grow wings to fly away and colonize." "Our ancestors did," Sicuanga said. "They came from the forest and they trekked and spread out and made this land ours." "Those were times of war and destruction," said Marta. "So are these," said Sicuanga.

And they talked away the afternoon and the night, analyzing, commenting, and reflecting on their side of development: Challua, still caught in the entanglements of a bank loan; Sicuanga, who worried about the bonds themselves and how to cut and unravel them; Tselctselc, who sought to maintain informal ties across lines of conflict within a system of capital expansion and bureaucratic control; Marta, the image creator, who longed for increased power to be realized in a sense of ordered beauty; and all the rest. The talk went on and goes on in hundreds upon hundreds of similar settings, and word spreads to those who will listen—to that extent there is a communication of power that buttresses a capacity to respond.

Conversations that reach the urban, increasingly bureaucratized Runa are now reinterpreted, and as the messages of capacity go outward to those in control of national political economy they again become reinterpreted, and as they return, as the voice of protest, they often sound

Río Chico, May 23-24, 1982: Civilization arrives.

like a rewording of age-old, crushing political-economic oppression. As this occurs, the power system of the Runa of Nayapi Llacta becomes turned against the protest *rhetoric* of the urban Runa (but not necessarily against the Runa themselves), at the very moment that this rhetoric is incorporated into the structure of antinomy of Nueva Esperanza.

In the early morning of May 23, 1982, the bulldozers, road scraper, trucks, and roller completed their job and the great celebration began. Almost everyone from Nayapi Llacta had arrived by 10:00 A.M., where they enjoyed visiting with other guests from Nuevo Mundo, Unión Base, Nueva Vida, Rayu Urcu, Rosario Yacu, Amazonas, Putuimi, San Ramón, and Canelos. Everyone from Tarqui and many from Puyo and Shell arrived as well. No one from Madre Tierra came, for everyone in that frontier community was still bitter about their relatives and friends having been expelled by force of Runa arms a year and a half ago. Two soccer games were played; a ribbon-cutting ceremony was performed; an Indigenous Queen from Río Chico and a Parish Queen from Tarqui were there to provide essential and epochal beauty. Beer and *trago* flowed freely, and in addition to the chicken and rice for the national visitors, there was superabundant meat from forest and river for all the native visitors, complemented by mounds of steaming manioc and plantains.

By nightfall there were twenty vehicles parked in front of the school, and pickup trucks and a few motorcycles were roaring back and forth. As the party continued, many of the visitors from Nayapi Llacta hived off into separate households, there to visit in their own festive ambience, with as many as fifty people to a house, and to watch the Puyo-like festival from a little distance. Visitors from Tarqui and other such frontier towns had a wonderful time, and all agreed that the festival was much more fun than those held in their own small communities — more like a big blast in Puyo itself, many said.

"When the road from Putuimi reaches our second line next year we'll be like this," mused Jaime, his eyes glittering from *trago*. "*Ciertomanchin*" ("We sure will"), said Sicuanga, refilling Jaime's plastic drinking cup from the bottle he had purchased in Tarqui earlier that afternoon, "we sure will." And then he said in a strong voice, "We must put our children everywhere in the republic and beyond, protect our turf, and let all nations come here, but only to visit."

"*Buenas noches*," called José Rodríguez. "*Buenas noches*," answered a dozen Runa men. "Come in, *maestro*—have a drink." Maestro Rodríguez, formerly a schoolteacher in Río Chico, had returned just for this event. After downing a couple of shots of bracing white cane liquor he turned back, spit, and asked a big question: "I hear you're fighting here?" he queried. "We sure are," said Jaime, laughing. "It's like *Gran Bretaña* and *las Islas Malvinas.*" And he continued, as everyone laughed while riveting deadly serious eyes upon him: "The *Malvinas* are over there, the *federaciones* of the *isla* of the *comuna*, and we're here on our black earth getting ready to bomb them." "*Carai,*" said Maestro Rodríguez, "you just won that land back a year or so ago and now you're fighting among yourselves." "Maybe we're civilized," said Sicuanga. "Maybe so," agreed the *maestro*.

"We're united but we're fighting among ourselves," spoke up Challua. "But don't worry about it; among ourselves we're working on a solution." "I hope so," said the *maestro*. Turning to me he said, and all the Runa listened, "I think they had a right to take over the island to defend their rights, just as Ecuador had a right to defend its rights over Peru at Paquisha. Peru is always the aggressor and always tries to dominate and enslave Ecuador, and Ecuadorians are always trying to, to, to . . ." and he drifted off and started again. "Runa are Ecuadorians," he said, "and they must live in the republic; we are all *mestizos* here, but this territory is [pointing to the Runa] *their* territory and they have a *right* to defend it; they should, though, do it through national agencies like IERAC and INCRAE, because their territory is Ecuadorian territory and when they throw Ecuadorians off Ecuadorian territory people think they're savages."

"*Claaaaaaro,*" said the *ichilla gobernador*, raising his upper lip in a mock smile (*enseñando los dientes*), doing his best parody of Ecuadorian meaningless agreement within the limen of assent and non-assent. Looking at him, Sicuanga said to me, under his breath, "*Cuti machin huasi, gumba*" ("Another foreigner's house, *compadre*"). And he looked at Marta, who had painted her face with genipa the night before, to give the outsiders a view of genuine indigenous life, but also to reflect more deeply on her own external mythic persona. He sighed as three more residents of Tarqui clomped in, and, seemingly out of context, he began telling of the exploits of Nayapi, jumping almost instantly to the story of Jilucu and Quilla and then right into the story of how the ancient ones held festivals so powerful that the mountains quaked, the rain came down, lightning was everywhere, the rivers swelled and swelled, and the Runa were swept away eastward toward the sea. Maestro José Rodríguez—now an official within the National Ministry of Education with considerable leverage by which to alter courses of unfolding national policy, regionally defined—had heard all this before, in other contexts on the Bobonaza River and right here in Río Chico. He had glimmers of what Sicuanga's message meant, and he knew that there was something profound there if only he could grasp it.

"Upinguichu, upi, maestro," said Tselctselc—"Won't you have another drink? drink!" *"Pagrachu ala,"* said the *maestro, "salud." "Sírvase,"* all answered.

And night wore on and the story goes on: great transformations occur at the national level, and no less are those in Puyo and Nueva Esperanza. Vast changes rack Amazonia and they are no less in Nayapi Llacta. Conversations taking place as the world is wrenched to and fro have ramifications both great and small. People such as those presented in this book discuss the events in which they participate, those they watch, those they hear about, and those they imagine, just as do those who sit in board rooms and on planning councils to devise new schemes for "development."

Nueva Esperanza is a small community in a lovely setting becoming incorporated into the Republic of Ecuador on its own terms, as constrained by shifting options, as negotiated constantly with national developers and with the people whom they regard as "of our way; of our speech; of our culture, of us." They live in a known world characterized by two apparently reasonable principles or laws: that they are *of* urban Ecuador, and that they are *of* Amazonia. They seek to tap the political-economic control systems of the republic while retaining the indigenous power base of their known and cherished habitat. Their lives are racked by the ensuing antinomy and consequent contradictions, and the messages generated by the oscillations within a system of duality of power patterning are there to enrich the analytical capacity of anyone who cares to listen and tries to "see" whatever it is that is going on.

Epilogue, 1983

Nueva Esperanza fissioned in 1983 as Sicuanga and Jaime squared off in a series of rifts involving access to forest territory, access to urban resources, manipulation of strategic indigenous and nonindigenous social relations, and interpretation of who is and who is not from indigenous culture and national culture regionally defined. The hamlet became permanently divided and the cultural ecology of Nayapi Llacta became the scene of local, regional, and national confrontation. Sicuanga continued to live in his house near Nueva Esperanza and to maintain his *chagra* adjacent to that of Shiny Shoes in Nayapi Llacta. But at the same time he and his sons and sons-in-law moved their hamlet affiliation to an ancient hunting site on a brand-new road near where Taruga had dreamed of a mighty war-horse coming toward him from Palora. Challua and Marta remained affiliated with Nueva Esperanza for awhile, but tensions grew to intolerable levels and they had to decide whether to join Shiny Shoes and his Nueva Esperanza compatriots, or Sicuanga and his.

While on the threshold of change with regard to local identification, Challua and Marta affiliated regionally with OPIP, as Sicuanga had done several months before. As affiliates they marched with a Nueva Esperanza banner in a major indigenous protest in Puyo in July. After that Shiny Shoes and his brothers would have no more of Challua and his family. They called them communists and bumpkins, revolutionaries and backward savages. So, soon after they paid off the bank loan, Challua and Marta joined Sicuanga and María in hiving off from Nueva Esperanza and began to attend the Friday *mingas* in Punto Verde, the new national focal point in the full-canopied forest site that had now become Sicuanga Llacta.

The Nueva Esperanza/Punto Verde division was but a microcosm of hostility, because by the spring of 1983 the entire Comuna San Jacinto del Pindo had fissioned. There were two presidents, one of whom was Shiny Shoes, the "little governor"; the other was a former

253

officer of OPIP. Each president had his contingent of elected *cabildo* members, each communicated the *comuna*'s needs and aspirations directly to officials in Puyo and Quito. Moreover, since the Ley de Comunas was changing through confusing national legislation and institutional interpretation, there were two or more access channels to various provincial and national officials open to each president and *cabildo* (or *directiva*) at any given time. One faction—that of Shiny Shoes—became the active opposition to OPIP; the other faction, led by Alejo Vargas, became affiliated, either formally or informally, with OPIP.

OPIP itself, upon the request of Sicuanga as made through Alejo Vargas, drew on increasingly international, national, regional, and local support to provide Punto Verde with a plaza, bulldozed off in two days, and a school with a new teacher and comunal house (*casa comunal*) as well. Nueva Esperanza, after the split, became a bastion of indigenous resistance to indigenous protest. It became an intensified site of regional culture nationally defined. It became decidedly rural, oriented toward urban existence. Every Saturday night its own *casa comunal* reeled and rocked as men and women from Tarqui came there in pickup trucks, taxis, and motorcycles to pay 15 *sucres*' admission and 28 *sucres* a beer to dance and drink away the night to the raucous sounds of coastal and Andean music secure in an 80- to 120-decibel range thanks to the new electric plant installed just across the road. Shiny Shoes himself carried his vendetta with Sicuanga to the military at Shell, to the national and rural police, and to the governor of Pastaza Province. He claimed that Sicuanga and his group at Punto Verde were the recipients of Cuban arms brought in by OPIP from secret caches near Santo Domingo de los Colorados. He also said that those of Punto Verde were allied with the Organization of Indigenous Peoples of Pastaza Province and with the Shuar Federation to overrun the rural towns surrounding Puyo (Veracrúz, Tarqui, and Madre Tierra) and, later, to attack Puyo itself. Shiny Shoes said awful things about Sicuanga and his struggling group; and people from Puyo to Quito and on to the United States listened. With active guerrilla war and its attendant pro-indigenous rhetoric in Peru, led by the Maoist Sendero Luminoso movement to the south, and with the M-19 movement to the north, in Colombia, already allegedly allied with some contingents of black people and indigenous groups in Esmeraldas Province, Ecuadorians were ready to listen to and believe incredible lies about any dissident forest people beyond the pale of urban order.

One of Sicuanga's sons began referring to Shiny Shoes as the *mudo campeche*, and the name stuck. *Campeche*, in Spanish slang in some parts of Ecuador, refers to one who goes out into the field to reconnoiter the movements of people in order to locate "the enemy" prior to military action. To be *mudo* is literally to be mute—not able to speak; figuratively it means to be stupid. The military did indeed reconnoiter the entire area of Sicuanga Llacta and beyond, taking depositions by cassette recording from everyone there for analysis in Shell and later in Quito. Jaime himself, together with several other native peoples from Nueva Esperanza and two other *caseríos*, accompanied by many residents of Tarqui, went to Quito to meet directly with the minister of government and, thereby, to appear on national television, where they claimed that "foreign and strange elements" had entered the peaceful life of Nueva Esperanza and that national armed forces should be deployed to remove them. They were referring especially to members of OPIP, who had come from areas beyond the Comuna San Jacinto, and also to their own relatives, whom they no longer understood.

OPIP, now closely associated with the Confederation of Indigenous Peoples of Amazonian Ecuador, asked the president of that organization to represent their position to national power wielders, and he did so—before the congress of the republic. In making his presentation that alleged military torture of indigenous peoples and military occupation of indigenous communities, he was joined by a spokesman for black and indigenous protest in Esmeraldas Province over allegedly similar activities by police and military there. This protest by the indigenous and black spokesmen for Amazonian and coastal human rights of ethnic minorities and "popular cultures" was also aired on national television.

Punto Verde became increasingly viewed by a segment of Puyo as subversive but genuinely indigenous, and Nueva Esperanza became increasingly viewed by a counter-segment of Puyo as just plain crazy but genuinely regional-becoming-national. Those power wielders of Puyo who came to view the Runa of Punto Verde with sympathy argued strongly for rapid development of this new hamlet, while those who viewed Nueva Esperanza as having crossed the threshold into national culture argued for a developmental slowdown. As Ecuador itself polarized into seemingly doctrinaire left-wing/right-wing rhetoric in preparation for the January 1984 elections, left/right polarities came to characterize the inter-indigenous schism with Punto Verde on the political left and Nueva Esperanza on the political right. Both hamlets entered national ideology as polar indigenous postures vis-à-vis one another; one had to win and one had to lose the coming nationalist struggle. So was each seen by nationalist developers and political rhetoricians, and so was each viewed by the male members of each indigenous hamlet. Each in its own way claimed intensive alliance as native people with other Ecuadorians. Each denounced the other in pejorative rhetoric drawn from ethnic schisms and national-international political-economic schisms.

Intra-indigenous conflicts moved to the brink of armed clashes, as did indigenous-nonindigenous standoffs in 1983. In one case Puyo Runa from a Comuna San Jacinto hamlet blocked a new road and threatened a truckload of Puyo Runa from another hamlet with bodily harm. This was done when a rumor swept through the greater Puyo area that the people of Punto Verde were accepting Cuban arms brought back by an indigenous missionary recently returned from a trip to visit native peoples of Canada and the United States. In another case an *hacendado* on the Vía Napo endeavored to drive native people from his land by importing a sierran group of machete wielders and rock throwers, only to find a hundred Runa there with their own sticks and stones.

Events such as these were reported to officials as indigenous violence, indigenous potential for violence, indigenous instability, indigenous resurgence or potential resurgence, and especially indigenous receptivity to foreign and internal subversion. Punto Verde today is the nationalist focal point of Sicuanga Llacta, some of the territory of which is carved out of a segment of Nayapi Llacta. At one and the same time Punto Verde is entering rapid developmental progress funded by national and international programs, while Sicuanga Llacta remains dependent upon intensified resource utilization of Upper Amazonian-montane cultural ecology. The materials discussed in the body of this book, in other words, are being reproduced at an accelerated rate and have been incorporated into a rhetoric of pending national violence that may, or may not, erupt.

Orthography

Ecuadorian Quichua is now an official written language standardized by the Ministry of Education. For consistency with *Sacha Runa* I continue to follow Orr and Wrisley (1965), with an orthography based on Spanish. Exceptions to Orr and Wrisley, and one conventional inconsistency, are noted below.[1]

Vowels

a   Spanish *a*
i   Ranges from Spanish *i* to Spanish *e*
u   Ranges from Spanish *u* to Spanish *o*

Consonants

b   English *b*
c   Unaspirated *k*
ch Unaspirated *ch*, voiced after nasals to give French *je* sound[2]
d   English *d*
g   English *g*, written *gu* before *i*
hu English *w*[3]
j   English *h*, a fricativized *k* (voiceless velar fricative) sound when terminal
l   Spanish *l*
ll Spanish *ll*
m   English *m*
n   English *n*
ñ   Spanish *ñ*
p   Spanish *p*
qu Unaspirated k before *i*[4]
r   Spanish *r*
s   English *s*
sh English *sh*
t   Spanish *t*
ts Similar to English *ts* as in ha*ts*, but aspirated and sometimes voiced
y   English *y*

1. Deviations from this orthography occur when Spanish, Achuar, or Shuar terms have not undergone significant phonological change. For example, the Spanish *tiempo* is rendered *tiempu* rather than *timpu* because most speakers still retain the Spanish dipthong in the Puyo area.

2. I've grouped the allophones of the /zh/ phoneme under the /ch/ graph. So *puncha* (day) is pronounced *punzha* (like *punja* in English orthography).

3. Here *huasi* (house) is pronounced *wasi* and Nunghui (spirit master of garden soil and pottery clay) is pronounced Nungwi. A notable exception here is with *asua* (a yeasty brew), which is pronounced *aswa*. This exception follows both standard Ecuadorian renditions and the Orr and Wrisley spelling.

4. Here again, English readers must think of the k sound so that *Quichua* is pronounced *keéchua*.

Glossary

Achuar. An indigenous language and culture of Amazonian Ecuador and Peru. See also *Jivaroan.*

Ahua (Jahua). High; Andean, highland.

Ahua llacta. Highlander, outsider; anyone from the Andes; the Sierra of Ecuador. Nonpejorative.

Ahualta. Contraction of *ahua llacta;* highlander.

Aicha. Body, flesh, meat.

Ala. Mushroom (generic); shelf or bracket fungus with reference to mythic brother.

Alli (also Ali). Good.

Alli Runa. Native person of the hamlet, of civilization, of Christianity.

Alli upina huanduj. Lit. good drinking datura; datura that humans use.

Allpa. Clay, soil, "turf."

Allu. Fungus, mold; edible sac fungi (*Ascomycetes* sp.).

Allu asua. Fungus chicha.

Alma. Soul.

Ama llulla! Don't lie!

Ama quilla! Don't be lazy!

Amarun. Anaconda, boa constrictor. See also *Sungui.*

Amarun shungu. Preparation made from heart, lungs, and stomach of boa constrictor.

Amarun yaji. Banisteriopsis species. See *yaji.*

Amasanga. Spirit master of the rain forest.

Amasanga huarmi. Spirit master of the rain forest in feminine form.

Ama shua! Don't steal!

Ando⁻ See *Shimigae.*

Apaci... Non-Jivaroan, in Jivaroan languages.

Asamblea general. General assembly.

Ashanga. Basket.

Ashca. Much, too much.

Asua. Chicha; fermented manioc mash mixed with water.

Asua mama. Chicha maker, chicha server; during festival the wife of a male participant.

Atahualpa. Incaic ruler of Quito, sixteenth century.

Auca. Mildly pejorative or nonpejorative Canelos Quichua word for Jivaroans, Zaparoans, and Waorani. Used in Ecuadorian Spanish and Andean Quichua to mean "heathen" or "savage."

Aya. Soul, soul substance.

Ayahuasca. Soul vine; Banisteriopsis species; hallucinogens of the Malphighiacea family.

Ayllu. Kinship section, unit, or group.

Bancu. Seat of power; stool, bench.

Biruti. Dart.

Blanco. White.

Blanqueamiento. "Whitening," "lightening"; acquisition of *mestizo* culture and civilization.

Bulla. Noise, racket.

Cabildo. Council.

Cachun. Sister-in-law.

Callana. Black or red bowl for eating cooked food.

Callari. Ancient time.

Callari tiempo rucuguna. Ancient times; beginning time old ones (people); original or first people.

Callpachina. "To make run"; frighten.

Camai. Proof.

Camari. Feast.

Camhuai. "Tangible proof."

Campesino. Peasant.

Cancha. Clearing.

Candoan. An indigenous language of Amazonian Peru; includes Shapra and Murato (Candoshi).

Canelos. Cinnamon.

Canelos Quichua. An indigenous culture and language of Amazonian Ecuador.

Cari. Male; husband.

Caru. Distant.

Caru llactamanda. From a distant place.

Carunzi. Chachalaca (*Otalis columbiana*).

Caserío. Hamlet.

Catequista. Catechist.

Cauchu. Rubber.

Cauchullu. Rubber penis.

Caudillo. Leader.

Causai. Life; life force.

Causana. To live.

Chagra. Swidden garden.

Chagra mama. Master spirit of swidden life (garden soil). See also *Nunghui.*

Challua. Suckermouth (*bocachico*) fish.

Chambira. Palm fiber.

Chaquichina. To dry.

Chaquichisca panga. Lit. dried-up leaf; "leaf litter"; leaf mat of rain forest.

Charapa. Amazonian water turtle.

Chaupi runa. "Half human."

Chayana. To arrive.

Chayuj. Convener.

Chignij. Envious, hateful; one who envies.

Chirapa Jivaroans. Shuar speakers once inhabiting the area south of Palora.

Chola. Some marketing women.

Cholo. Polysemic construct connoting various dimensions of *mestizaje.*

Choloficación. Becoming *cholo.*

Chonta. Palm.

Chorongo. Wooly monkey.

Chu. Suffix, interogative. See *Mana* for negative.

Churi. Son.

Colonia. Colonist settlement or hamlet.

Colono. Colonist.

Comadre. Female ritual coparent.

Comerciante. Profit-oriented trader. See also *regatón.*

Compadre. Male ritual coparent.

Comuna. Communal territory. A legal land grant to indigenous people who choose to incorporate within Ecuador in a manner other than in the canton-parish system; usually includes many hamlets and subterritorial divisions.

Comuna Canelos. The land grant ramifying out of Canelos.

Comuna San Jacinto del Pindo. The land grant to indigenous peoples south of Puyo.

Comuna San Ramon. The land grant to indigenous peoples living north of 10 de Agosto, along the Arajuno River.

Comunero, -a. Member of a *comuna.*

Costeño, -a. One from the coast.

Cuento. Tale, story.

Culqui. Money.

Cunalla. Present time, right now.

Cunan. Present time, today.
Curaga. Chief, head, leader.
Currulao. Afro-American music featuring a marimba and complex drumming.
Cusa. Husband.
Cusacu. Dear husband.
Cusca. Straight up.
Cushillu. Wooly monkey.
Cushillu runa. Wooly monkey people.
Cushillushina. "Like a wooly monkey."
Cushiyachina. To make one happy.
Cushiyarina. To become happy.

Desarrollo. Development.
Directiva. Council, *cabildo*.
Dominar. To dominate.
Dominario. Climax of the *ayllu* ceremony of the Canelos Quichua.

Enganche. System of labor contracting.
Esmeraldeño, -a. One from Esmeraldas Province; slang for black person among Puyo Runa.
Evangélico, -a. Protestant Evangelist.

Gente. Person, people.
Gran Bretaña. Great Britain.
Gringo. North American, European.
Gringuistas. Those who favor ties with foreigners over those with Ecuadorians.
Gumba. Compadre, fictive kinsman.
Guna. Plural suffix.

Huagra. Cattle, tapir.
Huahua. Baby.
Huaira. Wind.
Huanduj. Datura; hallucinogens of the nightshade family.
Huanduj supai. Datura spirit.
Huangu. Package, bundle, bunch.
Huarmi. Woman, wife.
Huarmiguna. Women.
Huasca. Vine.
Huasi. House, household, enclosure, abode.
Huasipungu. Entrance to the house; kitchen garden.
Huauqui. Brother (male speaker).
Huayulumba supai. Black spirit.

Huiduj. Genipa americana.

Huiduj huarmi. Black woman.

Huira. Fat.

Huira tamia. Cool misty drizzle associated with the ripening of certain fruits and nuts in the rain forest canopy.

Ichilla. Small.

Ichilla huasi. Woman's side of the house; woman's pottery shed.

Ila. Great tree with massive flying buttresses.

Ila supai. Amasanga transformation as a great tree.

Inca. Empire radiating out of Cuzco, Peru, that spread the Quechua language northward and southward.

Indi. Sun.

Indígena. Native person.

Indi ñahui. Sun's rays. See also *ñahui.*

Indio. "Indian."

Indi yaicushca. Sun's twilight domain west of the Andes.

Ingaru supai. A spirit demon whose heart is carried outside his body; Amasanga transformation.

Ischai. Two.

Isla. Island.

Islas Malvinas. Falkland Islands.

Iwianch. Demon.

Jacu. Let's go.

Jacu pugllangahua. Let's go play.

Jahua. High, above. See *ahua.*

Jahua llacta. See *Ahua llacta.*

Jahua nunghui. Upper *nunghui;* coral snake living in the leaf mat of the rain forest.

Janaj. Up-river, above.

Janajmanda. From up-river, from above.

Janaj runa. Up-river people.

Jatun. Large, big.

Jauya. Relationship established between parents of spouses, with extensions.

Jayambi. Iguanid.

Jilucu. Common potoo (*Nyctibius griseus*); mythical sister and lover of Quilla, the moon.

Jista. Festival.

Jista puru. Ceramic bowls for festivals.

Jista puruhua. Ceramic festival effigy bowls.

Jívaro. Spanish rendition of Jivaroan peoples; pejorative for Shuar and Achuar in Ecuador.

Jivaroan. Native cultures and languages of Amazonian Peru and Ecuador; major groupings include Shuar, Achuar, Aguaruna, Huambisa.

Jucha. The cost of blame or sin; something given up to Catholic church or mission.

Juing. Dendrobatis sp. (frog).

Junculu. Large, edible frog; daughter of Nunghui.

Jurijuri supai. Dangerous, foreign peoples' spirit master; Amasanga transformation.

Jursa. See *Ursa.*

Lica. Fishnet.

Llacta. Specific, named subterritory containing swidden gardens and rain forest and occupied by intermarried *ayllu* segments.

Llaqui. Love, affection, sadness; "proof" in some contexts.

Llaquichina. To make suffer, to make one long for, to make one love.

Llaquirina. To become sad.

Lluhui. Cock of the rock (*Rupicola peruviana*).

Llujchina. To send out, to cause to go out.

Llullun. Fresh, young, green, newborn.

Llullun huahua. Newborn, naive.

Lulun. Egg.

Lulun huahua llucshin. Birth.

Lumucha. Paca.

Lumucuchi. Peccary.

Lurira. Shield.

Machin. Monkey; Capuchin monkey.

Machin Runa. Monkey people; foreigners.

Malvinas. See *Islas Malvinas.*

Mama. Mother.

Mana. To be.

Mana. Negation when *chu* suffix is added to verb (e.g. *Mana ushangachu,* "He can't do it").

Manchachina. To frighten, to make tremble.

Mancharina. To tremble, become frightened.

Manda. Suffix meaning "from."

Mandana. From Spanish *mandar,* to order, to command.

Manduru. Bixa orellana.

Manduru huarmi. Red woman.

Manga allpa. Pottery clay.

Manga allpa mama. Spirit master of pottery clay; Nunghui.

Maquinaria. Heavy-duty machinery.

Máquinas. Machines.

Mar. Sea.

Marcana. To hold; to name as in a christening service.

Marginado. Margined, in the sense of pushed to the edge of society.

Mashca. Barley flour.

Mashca pupu. Barley flour umbilicus; pejorative term for a *serrano*.

Mestizaje. Ideology of racial and ethnic mingling.

Mestizo. Person of stipulated European and indigenous American descent.

Minga. Goal-oriented collective action group; system of collective or communal labor; system of labor exchange.

Mishu. Mestizo.

Moreno. Dark; polite term for black person.

Mucahua. Ceramic bowl for serving and drinking *asua*.

Mulato. Person of stipulated European and African descent.

Munditi. Hoatzin (*Opisthocomus hoazin*).

Mundo(u). World.

Muntun. Kindred.

Muscui. Image, sense perception, dream.

Muscuj huarmi. Woman who "sees," woman who creates and reproduces imagery. See also *Sinchi muscuj huarmi.*

Muscuna. To dream, to envision, to "see."

Ñahui. Eye, gaze. See also *Indi ñahui.*

Ñambi. Trail.

Naranjilla. Solanum quitoense; a fruit of the nightshade family.

Ñaupa. Space: ahead of, in front of, immediate; time: earlier, preceding.

Ñaupa rucumanda llacta. Territorial sector that comes to us from the early people; territory from the early old ones (people).

Ñaupa rucu yana runa. Early time black people.

Ñaupa shimi rucuguna. Early ancestor's talk (speech).

Nayapi. Swallow-tail kite (*Elanoides forficatus*).

Negro. Black.

Nina. Fire.

Nina samai. Breath of the fire.

Nina tamia. Fire rain.

Ñuca. First-person pronoun (singular).

Ñuca causai. My life force.

Ñucanchi. First-person pronoun (plural).

Ñucanchi pungu. Our entrance.

Ñucanchi ricsiushca runa. Our people's perception.

Nunghui. Spirit master of pottery clay (Manga allpa mama) and of swidden life (Chagra mama); corporeal representative is harmless coral snake.

Oligarquía. Oligarchy.

Paccha supai. Waterfall spirit; Amasanga transformation.
Pactamuni. I am arriving.
Pactana. To come up to; to arrive.
Pahua. Guan (*Mitu salvini*).
Palu. Snake (not boa constrictor); certain sentient poles.
Panga. Leaf.
Partida. Division.
Partimanda. Where one is from in terms of territory, culture, and ethnicity.
Pasu. A tree with Zapote-like fruit.
Pasu supai. Spirit of *pasu* tree.
Paushi. Great curassow (*Crax rubra*).
Pijuano. Six-hole bird-bone flute.
Pilchi. Gourd.
Prioste. Carrier of the sumptuary charge of a festival. See also *chayuj*.
Pucuna. To blow; blowgun.
Pugllana. To play.
Pugllanchi. We play.
Pugllangahua. See *jacu pugllangahua*.
Pungu. Entrance, door, entryway; mouth of a river; opening.
Puñusha muscuna. Sleep-dream.
Pura. Suffix meaning "among."
Puralla. Suffix meaning "just among."
Purina. Trekking; trek.
Puru. Bottle gourd or calabash.
Purungu. Palm-leaf drinking cup.
Puyu. Fog, cloud.

Quechua. Language adopted and spread by the Imperial Inca. See *Quichua*.
Quichua. Many dialects of Quechua, including all of the Ecuadorian ones, are spelled this way; pronounced *keéchua*.
Quindi. Hummingbird.
Quingu. Zigzag, bend.
Quiquin llacta. "Proper" territorial sector.

Rasu. Ice.
Rasu tamia. Hail.

Raza. People.

Reducciones. Centralizations, concentrations, and "reductions" of native peoples.

Regatón. Peruvian trader. See also *comerciante.*

Ricsij. One who observes.

Ricsij runa. Know-all, see-all person; could be *curaga.*

Ricsina. To know, experience, perceive, comprehend.

Rina. To go.

Rucu. Old, old one.

Rumi. Stone.

Runa. Person; indigenous person.

Runa ñambi. Human trail (implies considerable knowledge of rain forest and of territory).

Runapura. Humans among ourselves.

Runapuralla. Humans just among ourselves.

Runa shimi. Human speech; Quichua language.

Runga supai. Water-jaguar spirit.

Sacha. Forest; rain forest systematics and dynamics of Amazonian region, in Canelos Quichua; n. "brush," "scrub," in Andean Quichua; adj. undomesticated, wild, in Andean Quichua.

Sacha allcu. Bush dog.

Sacha chagra mama. Feminine spirit of forest gardens. The gardens are analogs of human swiddens.

Sacha huarmi. Forest (spirit) woman; spirit enchantress.

Sacha mama. See *Sacha chagra mama.*

Sacha Runa. Person of the forest. The concept ranges from forest spirit master Amasanga to knowledgeable people of rain forest ecology and systematics.

Sacha supai huarmi. Forest spirit woman; Amasanga feminine transformation.

Sacha supai runa. Forest spirit person. See *Amasanga.*

Salvaje. Savage.

Samai. Breath.

Samhuai. "Tangible" breath.

Sami. Class, type.

Sapu. Frog or toad.

Saquina. Let alone, let be; allow.

Saquirina. To stay, remain, endure, last.

Saquiringui. "Stay that way."

Satanas. Satan, Devil.

Serrano, -a. One from the Sierra.

Shamui. Come.

Shamuna. To come, to arrive.

Shayana. To stand.

Shayarina. To stand, appear standing; to be ready.

Shimi. Speech.

Shimigae. Zaparoan peoples and language.

Shina. Like (in making comparison), as.

Shingu shingu panga. Shaman's leaf bundle.

Shitana. To blow spirit missiles.

Shitashca. To be hit by a blown spirit missile.

Shuar. A Jivaroan language and culture of Amazonian Ecuador.

Shuj. One, another, other.

Shuj shimi. Another language.

Shuj shimita yachai. Another speech knowledge, another culture.

Shungu. Lit. heart; fig. will; heart-throat-stomach.

Sibulla sicucta. Onion ass.

Sicuanga. Toucan; white-throated toucan (*Ramphastos tucanus*).

Sicuanga manga. Toucan pot; small decorated pot for storing valuables, including toucan feathers.

Sicuanga Runa. Toucan person, feisty person, warrior; person who releases others, liberator.

Sinchi. Strong.

Sinchi chignij. Strong envy, implying a radiating, odious force.

Sinchi curaga. Strong leader.

Sinchi muscuj huarmi. Strong woman who "sees"; image maker; master potter.

Sinchi muscuj runa. Strong one who "sees"; strong image maker.

Sinchi yachaj. Strong shaman; one who can cure and injure.

Siqui. Rear end; "ass."

Subdesarrollado. Underdeveloped.

Sucre. Ecuadorian currency; worth about 27/U.S. dollar until 1983.

Suma. Beauty.

Sungui. Spirit force of the water system encompassing forest and *chagra* spirits; master spirit of hydrosphere; first shaman; ultimate source of power; corporeal representation is anaconda.

Suni. Long, large.

Supai. Spirit.

Supai biruti. Spirit dart or spirit missile.

Supai ñambi. Spirit trail.

Supai pungu. Spirit entrance.

Suuuuuuu. Sound of blowing breath.

Tamia. Rain.

Taquina. Shaman's song.

Taruga. Deer.

Tiana. To be, to exist.

Tiari. Sit down.

Tiarina. To sit down; sitting-being (always on a *bancu*).

Tiaunimi. I am here.

Tinaja. Storage jar for *asua*.

Trago. Raw cane alcohol.

Tsalamanga. Powerful spirit shaman of Andean lakes.

Tsungui. See *Sungui*.

Tu. Familiar second-person pronoun (address).

Tucayu. Namesake.

Tucui. All.

Tucuna. To transform; transformation.

Tucurina. To end everything.

Tula. Digging stick.

Tupac. See *tupaj*.

Tupaj. Return of.

Tupana. To encounter.

Tupanacunshunshu. "Until we meet again."

Tupi. A language and culture of Coastal and Central Amazonas, which spread expansively in precolonial and colonial times to the base of the Andes and beyond.

Uchu. Capsicum.

Ucu. Down; straight down.

Ucui. Within.

Ucui mama. Cutter ant.

Ucui nunghui. Inner *nunghui;* coral snake living under the leaf mat of the rain forest.

Ucui yacu. A strong chicha.

Ullu. Penis.

Unai. Mythic time-space.

Unaimanda. From mythic time-space.

Ungushca. Sick.

Upina. To drink; drink.

Urai. Down-river, below.

Uraimanda. From down-river.

Urai runa. Down-river people.

Urcu. Hill.

Ursa. Force; capability to perform a task; capacity to respond.

Ushana. To be able, to be capable.

Ushi. Daughter.

Usted. Impersonal second-person pronoun (address).

Utipana. To be capable; sometimes "cosmic power."

Uunt. Great man.

Uyarij Runa. Noisy (and brightly and beautifully dressed) person (a spirit).

Uyarina. To be heard.

Valor. Value.

Valorar. To appraise, value, price.

Várzea. Floodplain of the Amazon.

Vinillu. A heady, strong drink made from drippings of fungus chicha.

Waorani. Native people of Amazonian Ecuador.

Yachai. Custom; culture; knowledge.

Yachaj. Knowledgeable; one who knows; shaman.

Yachaj huarmi. Knowledgeable woman (i.e. master ceramicist).

Yachaj sami. Shaman's class.

Yachaj sami rumi. Shaman's class stone.

Yachana. To know, to learn.

Yacu. Water, river, liquid.

Yacu huanduj. Water Datura; not for human consumption.

Yacu mama. Water spirit master in feminine form. See *Sungui.*

Yacu puma. Giant river otter.

Yacu supai runa. Water spirit people.

Yaicui. Enter, come in.

Yaji. Banisteriopsis or psychotria species; leaves are used in preparing soul-vine hallucinogenic brew.

Yami. Common trumpeter (*Psophia crepitans*).

Yana. Black.

Yaya. Father; wife's father.

Yuyana. To think.

Yuyarina. To remember, reflect.

Yuyayuj. Possessor of thought; thinker, philosopher.

Yuyayuj runa. Advanced student.

Zambo, -a. Person of stipulated indigenous and African descent.

Zambu. Quichua pronunciation of *zambo, -a.*

Zaparoan. Indigenous languages and cultures of Amazonian Ecuador and Peru; includes Andoas-Shimigae, Záparo, Iquitos, Arabela.

Bibliographical Essay

Sicuanga Runa is written to communicate to readers at several levels, only the popular and technical of which are discussed here. This brief guide and commentary stresses materials of value to a general reader seeking further information about comparable settings. It also suggests technical sources that could escape the professional social anthropologist not a specialist in Andean or Amazonian literatures. For the development and deployment of the rest of the relevant literature I fall back upon a sequence of publications that are essentially technical: *Class, Kinship, and Power* (1965), *Black Frontiersmen* (1974), *Sacha Runa* (1976), and *Cultural Transformations* (1981). Cultural anthropology is clearly undergoing a multifaceted shift in the paradigms that its practitioners choose for data exposition, illustrated by three special issues of the *American Ethnologist: Symbolism and Cognition* (1979), *Symbolism and Cognition II* (1982), and *Economic and Ecological Processes in Society and Culture* (1982). Editing these volumes has influenced my choice of framework.

Chapter 1

"Forces of Destruction in Amazonia," Stephen Bunker's centerpiece article in the special issue of *Environment* entitled *Ecological Disruption in the Amazon* (1980), is a good starting point for the concerned reader. It could be followed with Bunker's 1984 book, *Underdeveloping the Amazon*. For Ecuadorian sources that tell and retell the legend of the founding of Puyo, one should consult the Dominican magazine *El Oriente Dominicano*, which recently became the *Carta Misionera, Vicariato Apostólico de Puyo*. *El Comercio*, Quito's major newspaper, carries such stories every year around May 12, and intermittently during the year. A couple of good examples include a piece published May 12, 1974, entitled "El Puyo Cumple Hoy Bodas de Diamante de Su Fundación," and Villarroel G.'s August 14, 1981, byline, "La Amazonía Comienza en Puyo." *Sacha Runa* gives more of the history of Puyo, including the history of the Comuna San Jacinto del Pindo. For the history of Canelos consult Marcelo Naranjo's 1977 reconstruction. An account of the "technical reunion" held in Puyo is given in the 1982 *Anuario Indígenista;* note that this summation omits every single indigenous presentation. Such presentations come through clearly, however, in the June, 1983, issue of *Nueva* entitled "Revuélta y Desafío: La Cuestión Indígena en el Ecuador."

Rafael Karsten's *The Headhunters of Western Amazonas* (1935) should be consulted by the serious scholar bent on reconstructing the past fifty to eighty years. Among other things, there are still people living in the Puyo area who offer information similar to that which Karsten collected and who can also identify people and places from photographs in the Karsten volume, which identifications correspond with the observations published by Karsten. It is obvious today (to me at least) that Karsten was working within the same sort of setting as Nayapi Llacta (from his entry via the mouth of the Pindo River and his treks to Canelos and on down the Bobonaza). Unfortunately, he used the term *Jívaro* for the Achuar of Canelos, Indillama, and elsewhere, and then erred by mixing the data on these Achuar with the Shuar of the Sierra de Cutucú (whom he did not visit). With this in mind the serious reader should re-consult Michael Harner's *The Jívaro* (1972) so as not to throw the bilingual Achuar–Canelos Quichua baby out with the Shuar bathwater.

To understand more of the metaphor "development" applied to nation-states, glance through the recent *Encyclopedia of Developing Nations* (Thompson, Anderberg, and Antell 1981).

Chapter 2

For the flora, fauna, ecosystems, and peoples of Amazonia there is a rich and expanding popular literature. The National Geographic publications (Bennet 1982; Schreider and Schreider 1970; White 1983) are all recommended, as is *Exploring the Amazon* (1970), which features a "pristine" Achuar on the dust jacket. Another good popular book with lavish color photographs is Tom Sterling et al., *The Amazon* (1973), a Time-Life publication, although it lacks information on human beings. Fritz Trupp's 1981 book *The Last Indians* has beautiful photographs of many of the people mentioned in this chapter, including the Shuar, Achuar, Canelos, Tucanoans, and Yanomamö; its dust jacket also features an Achuar man with toucan headdress. A good, thorough, and productive review of what anthropologists and geographers have been doing (and speculating upon) in Amazonia is given by Anna Roosevelt (1980), and Emilio Moran's 1982 review of complementary literature in the *Latin American Research Review* discusses symposia and other sources that have recently become available. One could turn to the 1978 special issue of *Interciencia* on *Amazon Basin Ecosystems* and to Carl Jordan's 1982 article "Amazon Rain Forests," following these up with Gillean T. and Anne E. Prance's 1982 book *The Amazon Forest and River*. For an overview of technical cultural ecology in Amazonia see Hames and Vickers (1983).

John Hemming's *Red Gold: The Conquest of the Brazilian Indians* (1978) carefully documents human destruction in Amazonia. For orientations to the New World that include Amazonia and the Andes see Denevan (1976) for a discussion of native population collapse; Curtin (1969) for a demography of the African slave trade; and Crosby (1972) for the incredible exchange in biological materials between the two hemispheres. For more technical material on Central Amazonas see David Graham Sweet's two-volume doctoral dissertation, "A Rich Realm of Nature Destroyed: The Middle Amazon Valley" (1974). Art and iconography and the speculations that can be derived from them are richly illustrated in Lathrap (1977). A technical article on the cayman and its role in ecosystems characterized by nutrient-poor waters is that of Fittkau (1973), and I extrapolate this material and apply it to the anaconda on the cautious advice of several ecologists. The best popular source on the Amazonian rubber boom is Collier (1968), and the best primary source is Casement (1912). For a lucid, interpretive account of terror, death, and the genesis of bizarre cultures during this period of Amazonian holocaust see Taussig (1982).

Books on native peoples living around the Amazonian rim are, for the most part, not easy reading. A partial exception is Napolean Chagnon's *Yanomamö: The Fierce People* (1968), updated in 1977 and 1983 to give us a glimpse of the processes which I describe herein. The book dwells upon violence, as does the more sensational *Yanoáma* (Biocca 1969). Smole's 1976 technical work on the Barafiri grouping of Yanoáma culture offsets the savagery image, as does the Ramos and Taylor 1979 monograph that documents the continuing struggle in Brazil for Yanoáma territorial rights and cultural integrity. A delightful book on the neighboring Makiritare written by Marc de Civrieux, *Watunna: An Orinoco Creation Cycle*, was published in English in 1980. I recommend that one begin with this work to understand more fully and deeply native patterns of thinking in this vast territory. As the author puts it so plainly: "Sacred or profane, the *Watunna* is a living tradition in constant use. It is hard to pass a day among the Makiritare without hearing a tale or at least some isolated fragment of a story as it relates to the circumstances at hand . . . there will always be a *Watunna* tale to a hero or an episode. Perhaps it will be late at night and you'll be lying in your hammock and there'll be time for much more than that. Whatever the situation, there will be a story about something that happened a long time ago." If this book does have appeal, then it is recommended that one go on to read the more technical, though brief, 1973 monograph by Nelly Árvelo Jiménez, which demonstrates the ways by which Makiritare society manifests alternative formations according to its articulation to dominating Venezuelan society and to its varied riverine, forest, and other habitats. Other good, though technical, social anthropological studies are those by Wilbert (e.g. 1970, 1981) on the Warao, Schwerin (1966) on the Kariña, Kaplan (1975) on the Piaroa, Dumont (1976, 1978) on the Panare, and Thomas (1981) on the Pemon. Coming around the arc into Colombia, Goldman's 1963 tour de force on the Cubeo is a superb presentation of culture, social structure, and ecology, and he is presently working on its sequel on religion and cosmology. The extensive writings of Reichel-Dolmatoff (1976a, 1976b, 1981, and especially *Amazonian Cosmos*, 1971) have been pivotal, motivating anthropological forces to restore a sense of meaning to indigenous lifeways, on their own terms, as well as a Freudian resuscitation. The two books recently published by Christine and Stephen Hugh-Jones (1979) continue the theme of richness by reference to the neighboring Pirá-paraná Tucanoans, without Western psychoanalysis but with a surfeit of Leachean structuralism. Jean Jackson (1983) has just published her ethnography of the Bará, who are part of a wide-flung, "open-ended" Tucanoan system involving peoples who speak sixteen different languages. The reader should be warned, however, especially with regard to the latter, that these works are highly technical and aimed at a specialized sector of a professional anthropological audience.

The general reader interested in comparing materials in this book with analogs and congeners in Peru might begin with the short 1976 paper by Lathrap and think about his remarks more fully in reading the brief mongraph entitled *The Forest Indians in the Present Political Situation of Peru* by Stefano Varese (1972). Gerald Weiss's 1975 monograph on the Riverine Campa should be read by the specialist for its rich portrayal of native cosmology, and Peter Roe's *The Cosmic Zygote* (1982) demonstrates a controversial "general cosmography" of Amazonian-Andean thought. Peter Stahl's 1983 doctoral thesis applies Amazonian cosmography to coastal Ecuadorian archaeology. Doctoral theses on the Aguaruna by Brown (1981) and the Llamistas by Scazzocchio (1981) demonstrate convincingly that the Canelos Quichua indeed share a common set of cultural paradigms with Jivaroan-speaking and Quechua-speaking congeners to the south. Wonderful scholarly resources are also now available in Peru, including the journal *Amazonía Peruana* and books such as *"Duik Múun . . . ," Universo Mítico de los Aguaruna* (Chumap et al. 1979), and *Los Nativos Invisibles* (Stocks 1981). No longer must the committed specialist search for bits and pieces of mythology; the rich world available to the scholar who wishes to enter another thought system is at our doorstep.

In the vast area of Brazil, where native societies are often at great distances from one another, the general reader might want to begin with either the classic *Tristes Tropiques* by Claude Lévi-Strauss (1964), or perhaps with Adrian Cowell's *The Tribe that Hides from Man* (1973). Charles Wagley's *Welcome of Tears* (1977) has the same focal intents as does *Sacha Runa*, and the two books, together with that of Stocks (1981), provide evidence from across Amazonia of the continuity and remarkable adaptability of native peoples. Since Wagley's book is oriented more to a general reader, as is the Villa Boas brothers' *Xingú: The Indians, Their Myths* (1970), one might well wish to simply relax and read *Xingú* and de Civrieux's *Watunna* together, to get a north-south axis on mythology. If one does so, however, it should be kept in mind that such lore is extraordinarily adaptable to the chaos which its tellers seek to order symbolically. For the specialist, the most striking work to date on Amazonian mythology has been circulating in manuscript for more than a decade. In "Fire of the Jaguar," Terrence Turner, of the University of Chicago, revises, by reference to Kayapó mythology, the entire perception of the ordering of thought processes. This is done by focusing on Lévi-Strauss's key myth garnered from the Bororo and treating it in a Piaget-like structural fashion, elaborating and macro-scoping its framing qualities. To view the Nambikwara in a revised light see Price (1981), for the Kawahib, Kracke (1979), and for the Mundurucú, Murphy and Murphy (1974). For readers especially interested in psychoanalytic theory, the latter two fit nicely with Reichel-Dolmatoff's work.

Returning to Ecuador, the general reader will find Broennimann's book on the Waorani (1981) to be a spectacularly successful photographic portrayal and a welcome counter to the highly biased reports by Rachel Saint and her evangelical writers (e.g. Wallas 1973), as is Yost's 1981 article in the lavishly illustrated book *Ecuador: In the Shadow of the Volcano*. The fact that Broennimann finds it necessary to state that " 'Auca' is actually a contemptuous Quechua term for jungle barbarians but the name has so firmly taken root that it can hardly be avoided today" bears testimony to the spiritual need of those who think they are civilized to have a living reminder of savagery in the flesh. It also shows how readily concepts from the non-Runa world are projected onto the Runa themselves. To place this book and the rest of the Oriente in perspective, consult N. Whitten (1981a). For a superb treatment of the Waorani and the Wycliffe Bible translators, see Stoll (1982). For the native reader in Spanish or the professional, there is now abundant material on Shuar and Achuar cultures, thanks to the Mundo Shuar series, which has published fifty monographs of varying lengths and quality. Doctoral dissertations have been written based upon fairly recent field research on the Cofán (Robinson 1979), Siona-Secoya (Vickers 1976), Achuar (Kalekna 1981; Descola 1981; Taylor 1981), and on the Quijos or Napo Quichua (depending on the terminology preferred) by T. Macdonald (1979, 1981). The articles in N. Whitten (1981b) include this material, as well as professional ethnography on the Waorani by Yost (1981a). With the work of Harner (1972) on the Shuar of the Cutucú sierra, T. Macdonald (1979) on the Quijos just south of the Napo, Reeve (1984) on the Canelos Quichua of Curaray (on the edge of Waorani territory), the Descola and Taylor materials (1981) on the Achuar, and with histories provided by Conde (1981) and Bottasso (1982), among many other works in manuscript or recently published or circulated, we can easily situate the materials presented in this book within Amazonian Ecuador (see, e.g., N. Whitten 1981b). In 1976 I explored the complementarity of ethnocide and ethnogenesis among the Canelos Quichua. This theme is given hemisphere-wide treatment in the publication *Indianité-Etnocide Indigénisme en Amérique Latine*, introduced by Françoise Morin (GRAI 1982). The importance of technical work like this is that facile acceptance of dominant ideology is curbed by consideration of such arguments.

For national Ecuadorian society itself the general reader should consult Osvaldo Hurtado's *Political Power in Ecuador* (English ed. 1981) and Raymond Bromley's *Development Planning in Ecuador* (1977). The reader of Spanish who wants the flavor of the Roldós years (including the periods right before his presidency and after his death) might enjoy *Ecuador, Hoy* (Drekonja 1978), with essays by Gerhard Drekonja and many other critical appraisers of the republic; the collection of Roldós's speeches entitled *¡Viva la Patria!* (1981), published posthumously almost overnight; or *Política y Sociedad, Ecuador: 1830-1980* (Ayala Mora 1980). The Instituto Otavaleño de Antropología has recently published about twenty-five volumes of a fifty-volume series, giving those who can obtain copies considerable material, some of which was heretofore either unavailable or difficult to come by. It is lamentable, however, that this institute has also suppressed several works of a critical nature which gather dust, "published" but unreleased, in its warehouse. The papers and references included in *Cultural Transformations* should be consulted, as they provide the immediate context for this book.

The "Framework for Anthropological Analysis" draws from specialized literatures not usually associated with Native American studies. One wishing to read more on how to describe and conceptualize the richness of human lifeways within a framework of power shifts and changing sensibilities and alliances in a real world is urged to consult Geertz (1973, 1983) and Sahlins (1981a, 1981b). For a heavy dose of pluralism, M. G. Smith's classic *Plural Society in the British West Indies* (1965) and its follow-up edited by Leo Kuper and Smith, *Pluralism in Africa* (1971), are required reading. For political economy the 1980 article by Pierre-Michel Fontaine published in the *Latin American Research Review* is an excellent beginning, as is *New Directions in Political Economy*, edited by Barbara Léons and Francis Rothstein (1979). Eric Wolf's *Europe and the People without History* (1982) and Richard Adams's *Paradoxical Harvest* (1982) demonstrate how much anthropologists can offer to an understanding of world systems, just as Adams (1975) and Fogelson and Adams (1977) demonstrate that conceptualizing power is no stranger to our discipline. In the area of ideology I recommend Therborn (1980), and for the dynamics that drive correspondence-processing of complex materials see especially Sapir and Crocker (1977). To tie the work on political economy and the structure of domination to correspondence-processing is difficult, and the intellectual apparatus available in anthropology is still partially inchoate. Thrusts in that direction, though, are significant; the introduction to *Symbolic Anthropology* by Dolgin, Kemnitzer, and Schneider (1977) and Michael Taussig's *The Devil and Commodity Fetishism* (1980b) may be singled out as outstanding. Marshall Sahlins's *Culture and Practical Reason* (1976) should also be studied with care, especially with regard to his discourse on the "two Marxisms," and his 1981 monograph *Historical Metaphors and Mythical Realities* is a must for the specialist in social structure, history, and mythology. Whitten and Ohnuki-Tierney (1982) pull some of these materials together by reference to a set of highly diverse articles.

Chapter 3

For more detail on kinship see N. Whitten (1976) and Whitten and Whitten (1984). For systems radiating out of Nayapi Llacta/Nueva Esperanza consult Harner (1972) for the Shuar, T. Macdonald (1979) for the Quijos Quichua, Yost (1981a, 1981b) for the Waorani. With the exception of Harner and Yost, none of these works is for anyone other than a kinship specialist. To compare Andean, Amazonian, and central

Brazilian (Gê-Bororo) systems see Mayer and Bolton (1977, 1980), Kensinger (1984), and Maybury-Lewis (1979).

My warnings about early relations of language and culture in Upper Amazonia are set forth in *Sacha Runa* (1976) and in "Amazonia Today at the Base of the Andes" (1981). Specialists today should certainly consult the articles by Renard-Casevitz, Taylor and Descola, Chaumeil and Fraysse-Chaumeil, Ales, Scazzocchio, Renard-Casevitz, and Saignes, and the excellent maps that accompany them, all published in the *Boletín del Instituto Francés de Estudios Andinos/Bulletin de l'Institut Français d'Études Andines* (1981, 10: 3-4). Since my first tentative cautions published in 1976, the linguist Gary Parker apparently has reconstructed "Proto-Ecuadorian" Quichua and has concluded, according to Ruth Moya (1981), that the existence of a *pre*-Incaic Ecuadorian Quichua (sierran and Upper Amazonian) is consistent with subsequent imperial, Incaic influence. The tree diagram that Moya (1981: 170) attributes to Parker places the three main dialects of Amazonian Quichua (Orr and Wrisley 1965) as coterminous with the Andean ones of Ecuador. With the linguistic and ethnohistoric evidence capable of swinging either way, but still suggesting an early, *eastern* (Upper Amazonian) entry into what is now Ecuador, I again caution the reader to beware of assertions based on dubious scholarship that Quichua speakers today in the rain forest of Ecuador's Oriente are but remnants of a colonial tribe subjected to two successful centuries of Quichuaization by Spanish friars.

The tri-ethnic paradigm has not been explored well for Latin America; most scholars are content with either black/white or Indian/white variants. Magnus Mörner (e.g. 1967) has long warned us against such bipolarization. A notable exception to bipolar myopia for the tropical lowlands is Lee Drummond (1977, 1980) of McGill University, who endeavors to relate ethnic structure to mythology and both of these social-cognitive systems to thought systems in general (including anthropological thinking). But again, his articles are for specialists in South American society and lore. With regard to cosmology it is quite interesting to note that Johannes Wilbert (1981), working with the Warao of the Orinoco delta, and Peter Roe (1982), working on Shipibo materials of Upper Amazonian Peru and on other comparisons throughout Amazonia, come up with a very similar diagrammatic rendition of the cosmos. For rich anaconda mythology see especially ethnographies on the Vaupés of Colombia (e.g., Goldman 1963; Reichel-Dolmatoff 1971; C. Hugh-Jones 1979; S. Hugh-Jones 1979).

Chapter 4

For an overview of shamanism the Western reader is not to be deprived. A superior book entitled *Stones, Bones, and Skin* is available through Artscanada (Brodzky et al. 1977) which features not only spectacular pictures in black and white and in color, but also a bold and useful introduction entitled "The Roots and Continuities of Shamanism" by Peter T. Furst. Also Michael Harner, anthropological theorist and ethnographer of the Shuar, Achuar, and Shipibo-Conibo, has published *The Way of the Shaman* (1980), a serious book on shamanic procedure for those seeking alternatives to contemporary Western religion and modern medicine. A popular work is John Halifax's *Shamanic Voices* (1979), and a standard source is Eliade's *Shamanism* (1964 [1951]), published in paperback in 1972. Works that can be of scholarly value but that can also be read just for the fun of it are Douglass Sharon's *Wizard of the Four Winds* (1978) and Harner's *Hallucinogens and Shamanism* (1973), which provide us with materials from the coast of Peru and from Amazonia and Europe respectively. For more information on hallucinogens and culture see the work by Furst by that title (1976) and his edited book, *Flesh of the Gods* (1972). Technical material on Datura is given in the monograph by Conklin (1976). For strictly professional articles and materials one can peruse the *American Ethnologist* for the past five years or so for some quite extensive literature review (e.g., Ohnuki-Tierney 1980a; Peters and Price-Williams 1980; Peters 1982).

For relationships between Amazonian shamanism and the political economy of the colonial state see Salomon (1983). Lawrence Carpenter (1980) has developed a technical article about the duality of the self in north Andean thought (and Sibby and I have also noted *ñucanchi*, the first-person *plural* pronoun, applied to what we Westerners would call the "first-person self" in the Andean Quichua of Ecuador).

"Taruga's Trip to Visit Rodrigo Andi" is taken from the monograph that I prepared for the record made by Neelon Crawford entitled *Soul Vine Shaman* (1979). In order to make the transcription and subsequent translation for such a rich shamanic performance I worked with Julian Santi Vargas and his wife, María Aguinda Mamallacta, for several days. This rendition is somewhat different from that published with the record but more faithful to the field recording. For excellent material on Quichua songs see Macdonald (Harrison) (1979) and Harrison (1979, 1982).

Chapter 5

Sections of this chapter, although prepared with this book in mind, were published in part elsewhere in somewhat different form. The opening "scenes" and some of the text were delivered in 1982 at the American Ethnological Society plenary session on "The Future of Plural Societies" chaired by David Maybury-Lewis, and, in the same year, at the International Congress of Americanists in the symposium on "Jivaroan Societies" chaired by Michael Brown. A small section of the pottery-making scene is taken from the Whitten and Whitten article "Ceramics of the Canelos Quichua" (1978), published in English in *Natural History* and in Spanish in *Miscelanea Antropológica*. One captivated by the more fantastic side of some of these materials might enjoy reading Carlos Castaneda's *Tales of Power* (1974). If so, the reading should be tempered by heeding the warnings set out by Marvin Harris in the same year and by Richard DeMille et al. in 1976. If the reader then decides to take the magical-versus-scientific as reflective of an idealist-versus-materialist stultifying polarity, the message that *Sicuanga Runa* seeks to convey has not been received.

The references cited in the text and in previous notes cover the materials on political economy to which the general reader is referred. Professionals will recognize my debt to the early work of Edmund Leach, *Political Systems of Highland Burma* (1964). For resources to help understand ceremonial enactment wherever it occurs, readers should consult Victor Turner's *Celebration: Studies in Festivity and Ritual* (1982) and his earlier work *Dramas, Fields, and Metaphors* (1974). Rather than "liminality" as an analytic device, however, I choose to deal with the sorts of pressures that Harris identified as the material bases of exploitation, together with the mechanisms of symbol control (Adams 1975) bound up in the structure of domination (N. Whitten 1974; Genovese 1975) as discussed by Dolgin, Kemnitzer, and Schneider (1977) and by Taussig (1978, 1980a, 1980b). Without denying exploitation, my concern is to document the surging native power potential contained and released through symbolic mechanisms, including protest, rather than to fall back upon "alienation" as a necessary concomitant of domination and exploitation. To understand more about mental dynamics, I recommend George Lakoff and Mark Johnson's *Metaphors We Live By* (1980). For more specialized reading, see Sally Falk Moore and Barbara Myerhoff's edited work, *Secular Ritual* (1977), and Barbara Babcock's edited volume, *The Reversible World* (1978). To put this material into Ecuadorian context see *Cultural Transformations*.

Chapter 6

Michael Taussig's *The Devil and Commodity Fetishism in South America* (1980b) picks up where *Sicuanga Runa* leaves off — with the folklore of the devil in South America reflecting in black and indigenous thought the new element attendant upon what Marx called the "fetishism of commodities," itself a part of the ideological structure of domination. To underscore the vigor of the devil-Christian association, see also Stutzman (1981). References to indigenous protest of special merit include Albornoz P.'s *Las Luchas Indígenas en el Ecuador* (1971), Segundo Moreno's *Sublevaciones Indígenas en la Audiencia de Quito* (1976), and Blanca Muratorio's *Etnicidad, Evangelización, y Protesta en el Ecuador* (1982). The reader wishing to review periodically, or even to monitor, indigenous activities in Ecuador should consult the recent Ecuadorian newsletter *Kipu: El Mundo Indígena en la Prensa Ecuatoriana*. A publication of Abya-Yala, an organization that developed in 1983 from Mundo Shuar publications, *Kipu* provides a clipping service for all news of indigenous peoples published in Ecuadorian newspapers.

Author's Note (August 1984)

A spate of popular and technical articles, monographs, books, and television programs on rain forests in general and Amazonia in particular appeared during 1984 and could not be incorporated into this essay. Two resources, however, must be mentioned. Norman Myers's book *The Primary Source: Tropical Forests and Our Future* (1984), published by W. W. Norton (New York), is both highly informative and most readable. It would be *the* most important follow-up reading for Chapter 2. Jacques Cousteau's television documentary on *The Amazon* (shown in three parts in 1984) is "required viewing" to appreciate the water world that Chapter 2 tries to describe. Among many other striking scenes is the first showing of both the great tidal bore at the mouth of the Amazon and the flooded forest of Central Amazonas. Part 3 focuses special attention upon the Peruvian Achuar of Upper Amazonian Peru and features a visit by a powerful shaman of these people to the president of Peru.

References

Acosta-Solis, Misael, et al.
1981 *Ecuador: In the Shadow of the Volcano*. Quito: Ediciones Libri Mundi.
Adams, Richard Newbold
1975 *Energy and Structure: A Theory of Social Power*. Austin: University of Texas Press.
1977 "Power in Human Societies: A Synthesis." In Raymond D. Fogelson and Richard N. Adams, eds., *The Anthropology of Power*. New York: Academic Press, pp. 387-410.
1982 *Paradoxical Harvest: Energy and Explanation in British History, 1870-1914*. Cambridge: Cambridge University Press.
Albornoz P., Oswaldo
1971 *Las Luchas Indígenas en el Ecuador*. Guayaquil. Editorial claridad.
Ales, Catherine
1981 "Les Tribus Indiennes de l'Ucayali au XVe Siècle." *Bulletin de l'Institut Français d'Études Andines* 10(3-4): 87-97.
Amazonía Peruana
1976-present   Lima: Centro Amazónico de Antropología y Aplicacíon Práctica.
Anuario Indigenista
1982 *Primera Reunión Técnica sobre Problemas de las Poblaciones Indígenas de la Cuenca Amazónica*. Mexico City: Instituto Indigenista Interamericano.
Arvelo Jiménez, Nelly
1973 *The Dynamics of the Ye'cuana ("Maquiritare") Political System: Stability and Crisis*. Copenhagen: International Work Group for Indigenous Affairs, doc. 12.
Ayala Mora, Enrique, comp.
1980 *Política y Sociedad, Ecuador: 1830-1980*. Quito: Corporacíon Editora Nacional.
Babcock, Barbara A., ed.
1978 *The Reversible World: Symbolic Inversion in Art and Society*. Ithaca, N.Y.: Cornell University Press.
Barth, Fredrik
1959 *Political Leadership among Swat Pathans*. London: Athlone Press.
Belzner, William D.
1981 "Music, Modernization, and Westernization among the Macuma

Shuar." In Norman E. Whitten, Jr., ed., *Cultural Transformations and Ethnicity in Modern Ecuador.* Urbana: University of Illinois Press, pp. 731-48.

in preparation   "Armadillos without Mouths: An Ethnography of the Shuar of Amazonian Ecuador." Ph.D. dissertation, University of Illinois, Urbana-Champaign. Ann Arbor, Mich.: University Microfilms.

Bennet, Ross S.
1982   *Lost Empires: Living Tribes.* Washington, D.C.: National Geographic Society.

Bianchi, César
1982   *Artesanías y Técnicas Shuar.* Quito: Mundo Shuar.

Biocca, Ettore
1969   *Yanoáma: The Narrative of a White Girl Kidnapped by Amazonian Indians.* Translated from the Italian by Dennis Rhodes. New York: E. P. Dutton.

Blust, Robert
1981   "Linguistic Evidence for some Early Austronesian Taboos." *American Anthropologist* 83(2): 285-319.

Bohannan, Paul, and Laura Bohannan
1953   *The Tiv of Central Nigeria.* London: International African Institute.

Bottasso B., Juan
1982   *Los Shuar y las Misiones: Entre la Hostilidad y el Diálogo.* Quito: Mundo Shuar.

Brodzky, Anne Trueblood, Rose Deneswich, and Nick Johnson
1977   *Stones, Bones, and Skin: Ritual and Shamanic Art.* Toronto: Artscanada.

Broennimann, Peter
1981   *Auca on the Cononaco: Indians of the Ecuadorian Rainforests.* Basel: Birkhäuser.

Bromley, Raymond
1977   *Development Planning in Ecuador.* Hove, Sussex: Hove Printing Co., for the Latin American Publications Fund.

Brown, Michael
1981   "Magic and Meaning in the World of the Aguaruna Jivaro of Peru." Ph.D. dessertation, University of Michigan, Ann Arbor. Ann Arbor, Mich.: University Microfilms.

Bugliarello, George, and Dean B. Doner, eds.
1979   *The History and Philosophy of Technology.* Urbana: University of Illinois Press.

Bunker, Stephen G.
1980   "Forces of Destruction in Amazonia." *Environment* 22(7): 14-20, 34-40.

1984a   "Modes of Extraction, Unequal Exchange, and the Progressive Underdevelopment of an Extreme Periphery: The Brazilian Amazon, 1600-1980." *American Journal of Sociology* 89(5): 1017-64.

1984b *Underdeveloping the Amazon: Extraction, Unequal Exchange, and the Failure of State Planning.* Urbana: University of Illinois Press.

Carneiro, Robert
1967 "On the Relationship of Population and Complexity of Social Organization." *Southwestern Journal of Anthropology* 23(3): 234-43.

Carpenter, Lawrence K.
1980 "A Quichua Postulate and the Implications for Development." Paper presented at the 79th Annual Meeting of the American Anthropological Association, Washington, D.C.

Carvalho-Neto, Paulo
1964 *Diccionario del Folklore Ecuatoriano.* Quito: Editorial Casa de la Cultura Ecuatoriana.

Casement, Roger
1912 *Correspondence Reflecting the Treatment of the British Colonial Subjects and Native Indians Employed in the Collection of Rubber in the Putumayo District.* Miscellaneous Publication 8 of His Majesty's Stationery House. London: Harrison and Sons.

Castaneda, Carlos
1974 *Tales of Power.* New York: Simon and Schuster.

Caws, Peter
1979 "*Praxis* and *Techne.*" In George Bugliarello and Dean B. Doner, eds., *The History and Philosophy of Technology.* Urbana: University of Illinois Press, pp. 227-37.

Chagnon, Napoleon A.
1968, 1977, 1983 *Yanomamö: The Fierce People.* New York: Holt, Rinehart and Winston.

Chaumeil, J. P., and J. Fraysse-Chaumeil
1981 "La Canela y el Dorado: Les Indigènes du Napo et du Haute-Amazone au XVIe Siècle." *Bulletin de l'Institut Français d'Études Andines* 10(3-4): 55-85.

Chilcote, Ronald H., ed.
1981, 1982 *Dependency and Marxism: Toward the Resolution of the Debate.* Boulder, Colo.: Westview Press.

Chumap Lucía, Aurelio, and Manuel Garcia-Rendueles
1979 "*Duik Múun . . . ,*" *Universo Mítico de los Aguaruna.* Lima: Centro Amazónico de Antropología y Aplicación Práctica. 2 vols.

Civrieux, Marc de
1980 *Watunna: An Orinoco Creation Cycle.* Edited and translated by David M. Guss. San Francisco: North Point Press.

Cockcroft, James D., André Gunder Frank, and Dale L. Johnson, eds.
1972 *Dependence and Underdevelopment: Latin America's Political Economy.* Garden City, N.Y.: Doubleday.

Collier, Richard
1968 *The River That God Forgot: The Story of the Amazon Rubber Boom.* New York: E. P. Dutton.

Conde, P. Tomás
1981   *Los Yaguarzongos: Historia de los Shuar de Zamora.* Quito: Mundo Shuar.
Conklin, Marie E.
1976   "Genetic and Biological Aspects of the Development of *Datura.*"
        Monographs in Developmental Biology, no. 12. Basel and New York:
        S. Karger.
Coon, Carleton S.
1951   *Caravan: The Story of the Middle East.* New York: Henry Holt.
Cordy-Collins, Alana, ed.
1982   *Pre-Columbian Art History.* Palo Alto, Cal.: Peek Publications.
Cowell, Adrian
1973   *The Tribe That Hides from Man.* New York: Stein and Day.
Crawford, Neelon
1979   *Soul Vine Shaman.* L.P. record. New York: Neelon Crawford.
Crosby, Alfred W.
1972   *The Columbian Exchange: Biological and Cultural Consequences of 1492.*
        Westport, Conn.: Greenwood Press.
Cunningham, Clark E., Janet W. D. Dougherty, James W. Fernandez, and
Norman E. Whitten, Jr., eds.
1981   *Symbolism and Cognition.* Special issue of the *American Ethnologist*
        8(3).
Curtin, Philip D.
1969   *The Atlantic Slave Trade.* Madison: University of Wisconsin Press.
DeMille, Richard, ed.
1976   *Castaneda's Journey: The Power and the Allegory.* Santa Barbara, Cal.:
        Capra Press.
Denevan, William M.
1973   "Development and the Imminent Demise of the Amazon Rain Forest."
        Professional Geographer 22(2): 130-37.
————, ed.
1976   *The Native Population of the Americas in 1492.* Madison: University
        of Wisconsin Press.
Descola, Philippe
1981   "From Scattered to Nucleated Settlement: A Process of Socioeconomic
        Change among the Achuar." In Norman E. Whitten, Jr., ed., *Cultural
        Transformations and Ethnicity in Modern Ecuador.* Urbana: University
        of Illinois Press, pp. 614-46.
Dolgin, Janet L., David S. Kemnitzer, and David M. Schneider
1977   "As People Express Their Lives, So They Are. . . ." In Dolgin, Kem-
        nitzer, and Schneider, eds., *Symbolic Anthropology: A Reader in the
        Study of Symbols and Meanings.* New York: Columbia University Press,
        pp. 3-44.
Dougherty, Janet W. D., James W. Fernandez, Emiko Ohnuki-Tierney, and
Norman E. Whitten, Jr., eds.
1982   *Symbolism and Cognition II.* Special issue of the *American Ethnologist*
        9(4).

Drekonja, Gerhard, et al.
1978 *Ecuador, Hoy.* Bogotá: Siglo Veintiuno Editores.

Drummond, Lee
1977 "Structure and Process in the Interpretation of South American Myth: The Arawak Dog Spirit People." *American Anthropologist* 79(4): 842-68.
1980 "The Cultural Continuum: A Theory of Intersystems." *Man* (n.s.) 15(2): 352-74.

Dumont, Jean-Paul
1976 *Under the Rainbow: Nature and Supernature among the Panare Indians.* Austin: University of Texas Press.
1978 *The Headman and I: Ambiguity and Ambivalence in the Fieldworking Experience.* Austin: University of Texas Press.

El Comercio
1974 "El Puyo Cumple Hoy Bodas de Diamante de Su Fundación." May 12, pp. 1, 14-15.
1981 "La Amazoniá Comienza en Puyo." Aug. 14, p. A-8.
1982 "[Claudio] Malo [Gonzalez] Expusó en Comisión Obras en Región Amazónica." June 15, p. 15.

Eliade, Mircea
1964 [1951] *Shamanism: Archaic States of Ecstasy.* Princeton, N.J.: Princeton University Press.

Evans-Pritchard, E. E.
1940 *The Nuer.* Oxford: Oxford University Press.
1949 *The Sanusi of Cyrenaica.* Oxford: Clarendon Press.

Fernandez, James W.
1974 "The Mission of Metaphor in Expressive Culture." *Current Anthropology* 15(2): 119-45.
1977 "The Performance of Ritual Metaphors." In J. David Sapir and J. Christopher Crocker, eds., *The Social Use of Metaphor.* Philadelphia: University of Pennsylvania Press, pp. 100-131.
1982 *Bwiti: An Ethnography of the Religious Imagination in Africa.* Princeton, N.J.: Princeton University Press.

Fine, Kathleen
in preparation "The Social Organization of Ethnic Relations in a Barrio of Quito, Ecuador." Ph.D. dissertation, University of Illinois, Urbana-Champaign. Ann Arbor, Mich.: University Microfilms.

Firth, Raymond T.
1951 *Elements of Social Organization.* London: Watts.

Fittkau, Ernst Josef
1973 "Crocodiles and the Nutrient Metabolism of Amazonian Waters." *Amazoniana* 4(1): 103-33.
———, J. Illies, H. Klinge, G. H. Schwabe, and H. Sioli
1968 *Biogeography and Ecology in South America,* vol. 1. The Hague: Dr. W. Junk N. Y.

Fogelson, Raymond D., and Richard N. Adams, eds.
  1977 *The Anthropology of Power*. New York: Academic Press.
Fontaine, Pierre-Michel
  1980 "Research in the Political Economy of Afro-Latin America." *Latin American Research Review* 15(2): 111-41.
Fried, Morton
  1957 "The Classification of Corporate Unilineal Descent Groups." *Journal of the Royal Anthropological Institute* 87(1): 1-29.
  1967 *The Evolution of Political Society: An Essay in Political Anthropology*. New York: Random House.
  1975 *The Notion of Tribe*. Menlo Park, Cal.: Cummings Publishing Co.
Furst, Peter T.
  1976 *Hallucinogens and Culture*. San Francisco, Cal.: Chandler and Sharp.
  1977 "The Roots and Continuities of Shamanism." In Anne Trueblood Brodzky et al., *Stones, Bones, and Skin: Ritual and Shamanic Art*. Toronto: Artscanada, pp. 1-28.
————, ed.
  1972 *Flesh of the Gods: The Ritual Use of Hallucinogens*. New York: Praeger.
Furtado, Celso
  1970 *Economic Development of Latin America: A Survey from Colonial Times to the Cuban Revolution*. Translated by Suzette Macedo. Cambridge: Cambridge University Press.
Geertz, Clifford
  1973 *The Interpretation of Cultures*. New York: Basic Books.
  1983 *Local Knowledge: Further Essays in Interpretive Anthropology*. New York: Basic Books.
Genovese, Eugene
  1975 "Class, Culture, and Historical Process." *Dialectical Anthropology* 1(1): 71-79.
Germani, Gino, ed.
  1962 *Política y Sociedad en una Época de Transición*. Buenos Aires: Paidos.
Gluckman, Max
  1965 *Law, Politics and Ritual in Tribal Society*. Chicago: Aldine.
————, ed.
  1962 *Essays on the Ritual of Social Relations*. Manchester: Manchester University Press.
Goldman, Irving
  1963, 1979 *The Cubeo: Indians of the Northwest Amazon*. Urbana: University of Illinois Press.
GRAI–Centre Interdisciplinaire d'Études Latino-Américaines Toulouse–Le Mirail
  1982 *Indianité-Ethnocidé Indigenisme en Amérique Latine*. Paris: Editions du Centre National de la Recherche Scientifique.

Gudeman, Stephen, Virginia Kerns, Harold K. Schneider, and Norman E. Whitten, Jr., eds.
1982   *Economic and Ecological Processes in Society and Culture.* Special issue of the *American Ethnologist* 9(2).
Gulick, John
1955   *Social Structure and Culture Change in a Lebanese Village.* Viking Fund Publications in Anthropology, no. 21. New York: Wenner-Gren Foundation for Anthropological Research.
1976   *The Middle East: An Anthropological Perspective.* Pacific Palisades, Cal.: Goodyear Publishing Co.
Halifax, Joan
1979   *Shamanic Voices: A Survey of Visionary Narratives.* New York: E. P. Dutton.
Hames, Raymond B., and William T. Vickers, eds.
1983   *Adaptive Responses of Native Amazonians.* New York: Academic Press.
Harner, Michael J.
1972   *The Jívaro: People of the Sacred Waterfalls.* Garden City, N.Y.: Natural History Press.
1980   *The Way of the Shaman: A Guide to Power and Healing.* New York: Harper & Row.
————, ed.
1973   *Hallucinogens and Shamanism.* New York: Oxford University Press.
Harris, David P.
1972   "Swidden Systems and Settlement." In Peter J. Ecko, Ruth Tringham, and C. W. Dimbleby, eds., *Man, Settlement and Urbanism.* Cambridge, Mass.: Schenkman, pp. 245-62.
Harris, Marvin
1968   *The Rise of Anthropological Theory.* New York: T. Y. Crowell.
1974   *Cows, Pigs, Wars, and Witches: The Riddles of Culture.* New York: Random House.
1979   *Cultural Materialism: The Struggle for a Science of Culture.* New York: Random House.
Harrison (Macdonald), Regina
1979   "Women's Voices on the Wind: Cultural Continuity in Quichua Lyrics." Paper presented at the 78th Annual Meeting of the American Anthropological Association, Cincinnati, Ohio.
1982   "The *Relación de Antigüedades deste Reyna del Pirú*, by Joan de Santacruz Pachacuti Yamqui Salcamaygua." In Rolena Adorno, ed., *Oral to Written Expression: Native Andean Chronicles of the Early and Colonial Periods.* Latin American Series, no. 4. Syracuse, N.Y.: Maxwell School of Citizenship, pp. 65-98.
Hartog, Elsie M., and Mary Mollhagen, comps.
1971   *Del Trabajo y Arte del Selvícola.* Lima: Instituto Lingüístico de Verano.

Hemming, John
1978   Red Gold: The Conquest of the Brazilian Indians, 1500-1760. Cambridge, Mass.: Harvard University Press.
Hugh-Jones, Christine
1979   From the Milk River: Spatial and Temporal Processes in Northwest Amazonia. New York: Cambridge University Press.
Hugh-Jones, Stephen
1979   The Palm and the Pleiades: Initiation and Cosmology in Northwest Amazonia. New York: Cambridge University Press.
Hurtado, Osvaldo
1977   El Poder Político en el Ecuador. Quito: Prensa de la Pontificia Universidad Católica.
1980   Political Power in Ecuador. Albuquerque: University of New Mexico Press.
Interciencia
1978   Amazon Basin Ecosystems 3(4).
Iturralde, Diego A.
1980   Guamote: Campesinos y Comunas. Colección Pendoneros, no. 28. Otavalo: Instituto Otavaleño de Antropología.
Jackson, Bruce
1979   "Inversion in Action." In Barbara A. Babcock, ed., The Reversible World: Symbolic Inversion in Art and Society. Ithaca, N.Y.: Cornell University Press, pp. 258-75.
Jackson, Jean
1983   The Fish People: Linguistic Exogamy and Tucanoan Identity in Northwest Amazonia. New York: Cambridge University Press.
Jordon, Carl F.
1982   "Amazon Rain Forest." American Scientist 70 (July-Aug.): 394-400.
Kalekna, Pita
1981   "Sex Asymmetry in Jivaroan Achuar Society: A Cultural Mechanism Promoting Belligerence." Ph.D. dissertation, Queens College–CUNY, New York. Ann Arbor, Mich.: University Microfilms.
Kaplan, Joanna O.
1975   The Piaroa. Oxford: Clarendon Press.
Karsten, Rafael
1935   The Headhunters of Western Amazonas. The Life and Culture of the Jibaro Indians of Eastern Ecuador and Peru. Helsinki: Societas Scientiarum Fennica, Commentationes Humanarum Litterarum 2(1).
Kensinger, Kenneth M., ed.
1984   Marriage Practices in Lowland South America. Urbana: University of Illinois Press.
Kracke, Waud H.
1979   Force and Persuasion: Leadership in Amazonian Society. Chicago: University of Chicago Press.

Kroeber, Alfred L.
  1963 [1939] *Cultural and Natural Areas of Native North America.* Berkeley:
      University of California Press.
Kuper, Leo, and M. G. Smith, eds.
  1971 *Pluralism in Africa.* Berkeley: University of California Press.
Lakoff, George, and Mark Johnson
  1980 *Metaphors We Live By.* Chicago: University of Chicago Press.
Lathrap, Donald W.
  1976 "Shipibo Tourist Art." In Nelson H. H. Graburn, ed., *Ethnic and Tourist
      Arts: Cultural Expressions from the Fourth World.* Berkeley: University
      of California Press, pp. 197-207.
  1977 [1971] "Gifts of the Cayman: Some Thoughts on the Subsistence Base
      of Chavín." In Alana Cordy-Collins and Jean Stern, eds., *Pre-Colum-
      bian Art History.* Palo Alto, Cal.: Peek Publications, pp. 333-51.
Leach, Edmund R.
  1960 "The Sinhalese of the Dry Zone of Northern Ceylon." In George
      Peter Murdock, ed., *Social Structure in Southeast Asia.* Chicago: Quad-
      rangle Books, pp. 116-26.
  1964 [1954] *Political Systems of Highland Burma: A Study of Kachin Social
      Structure.* New York: Beacon Press.
Leeds, Anthony
  1964 "Brazilian Careers and Social Structure." *American Anthropologist* 66(6):
      1321-47.
Leonard, George B.
  1972 *The Transformation: A Guide to the Inevitable Changes in Humankind.*
      New York: Dell.
Léons, Barbara, and Francis Rothstein
  1979 *New Directions in Political Economy: An Approach from Anthropology.*
      Westport, Conn.: Greenwood Press.
Lévi-Strauss, Claude
  1964 [1955] *Tristes Tropiques.* (New translation 1973.) New York: Athe-
      neum.
  1983 [1979] "Mushrooms in Culture: Apropos of a Book by R. G. Wasson."
      In *Structural Anthropology,* vol. 2. Translated by Monique Layton.
      Chicago: University of Chicago Press, pp. 222-37.
Macdonald (Harrison), Regina
  1979 "Andean Indigenous Expression: A Textual and Cultural Study of
      Hispanic-American and Quichua Poetry in Ecuador." Ph.D. disser-
      tation, University of Illinois, Urbana-Champaign. Ann Arbor, Mich.:
      University Microfilms.
Macdonald, Theodore, Jr.
  1979 "Processes of Change in Amazonian Ecuador: Quijos Quichua Indians
      Become Cattlemen." Ph.D. dissertation, University of Illinois, Urbana-
      Champaign. Ann Arbor, Mich.: University Microfilms.

292 SICUANGA RUNA

1981 "Indigenous Response to an Expanding Frontier: Jungle Quichua Economic Conversion to Cattle Ranching." In Norman E. Whitten, Jr., ed., *Cultural Transformations and Ethnicity in Modern Ecuador*. Urbana: University of Illinois Press, pp. 356-83.

Malloy, James M.
1974-75 *Nación y Estado en América Latina: Nuevas Perspectivas. Estudios Andinos* 4(1).

Marx, Karl
1973 [1939] *Grundrisse: Foundations of the Critique of Political Economy.* Translated with a foreword by Martin Nicolaus. Harmondsworth: Penguin Books.

Mauss, Marcel
1967 [1923] *The Gift: Forms and Functions of Exchange in Archaic Societies.* Translated by Ian Cunnison, with an introduction by E. E. Evans-Pritchard. New York: W. W. Norton.

Maybury-Lewis, David, ed.
1979 *Dialectical Societies: The Gê and Bororo of Central Brazil.* Cambridge, Mass.: Harvard University Press.
1984 *The Prospects for Plural Societies.* Washington, D.C.: 1982 Proceedings of the American Ethnological Society.

Mayer, Enrique, and Ralph Bolton, eds.
1977 *Andean Kinship and Marriage.* Washington, D.C.: American Anthropological Association Special Publication, 7.
1980 *Parentesco y Matrimonio en los Andes.* Lima: Pontificia Universidad Católica del Perú.

Middleton, DeWight R.
1981 "Ecuadorian Transformations: An Urban View." In Norman E. Whitten, Jr., ed., *Cultural Transformations and Ethnicity in Modern Ecuador.* Urbana: University of Illinois Press, pp. 211-32.

Moore, Sally Falk, and Barbara G. Myerhoff, eds.
1977 *Secular Ritual.* Amsterdam: Van Gorcum.

Moran, Emilio
1982 "Ecological, Anthropological, and Agronomic Research in the Amazon Basin." *Latin American Research Review* 17(1): 3-41.

Moreno Yánez, Segundo
1976 *Sublevaciones Indígenas en la Audiencia de Quito desde Comienzas del Siglo XVIII hasta Finales de la Colonia.* Bonn: Bonner Amerikanistische Studien (BAS), no. 5.

Mörner, Magnus
1967 *Race Mixture in the History of Latin America.* New York: Little, Brown.

Moya, Ruth
1981 *Simbolismo y Ritual en el Ecuador/El Quichua en el Español de Quito.* Coleccíon Pendoneros, no. 40. Otavalo: Instituto Otavaleño de Antropología.

Muratorio, Blanca
1982 *Etnicidad, Evangelización y Protesta en el Ecuador: Una Perspectiva*

Antropológica. Quito: Centro de Investigaciones y Estudios Socio-Economicos (CIESE).

Murdock, George Peter
1960 "Cognatic Forms of Social Organization." In George Peter Murdock, ed., *Social Structure in Southeast Asia.* Chicago: Quadrangle Books, pp. 1-14.

Murphy, Yolanda, and Robert F. Murphy
1974 *Women of the Forest.* New York: Columbia University Press.

Naranjo, Marcelo F.
1977 "Zonas de Refugio y Adaptación Étnica en el Oriente." In Marcelo F. Naranjo, José Pereira, and Norman E. Whitten, Jr., eds., *Temas sobre la Continuidad y Adaptación Cultural Ecuatoriana.* Quito: Prensa de la Pontificia Universidad Católica, pp. 105-68.

Nueva
1983 "Revuelta y Desafío: La Cuestíon Indígena en el Ecuador." June.

Ohnuki-Tierney, Emiko
1980a "Ainu Illness and Healing: A Symbolic Interpretation." *American Ethnologist* 7(1): 132-51.
1980b "Shamans and *Imu*: Among Two Ainu Groups." *Ethos* 8(3): 204-28.
1981 *Illness and Healing among the Sakhalin Ainu: A Symbolic Interpretation.* New York: Cambridge University Press.

Orr, Carolyn, and Betsy Wrisley
1965 *Vocabulario Quichua del Oriente del Ecuador.* Serie de Vocabularios Indígenas, no. 11. Quito: Instituto Lingüístico de Verano.

Pellizzaro, Siro
1982 *El Modelo del Hombre Shuar.* Quito: Mundo Shuar.

Peters, Emrys
1963 "Aspects of Rank and Status among Muslims in a Lebanese Village." In Julian Pitt-Rivers, ed., *Mediterranean Countrymen.* Paris: Mouton.
1970 "The Proliferation of Segments in the Lineage of the Bedouin of Cyrenaica." In Louise Sweet, ed., *Peoples and Cultures of the Middle East,* vol. 1. New York: Natural History Press.

Peters, Larry G.
1982 "Trance, Initiation, and Psychotherapy in Tamang Shamanism." *American Ethnologist* 9(1): 21-46.
————, and Douglass Price-Williams
1980 "Towards an Experiential Analysis of Shamanism." *American Ethnologist* 7(3): 397-418.

Phelan, John Leddy
1967 *The Kingdom of Quito in the Seventeenth Century: Bureaucracy and Politics in the Spanish Empire.* Madison: University of Wisconsin Press.

Prance, Gillean T., and Anne E. Prance
1982 *The Amazon Forest and River.* Woodbury, N.Y.: Barron's Educational Series.

Price, David
   1981 "Nambiquara Leadership." *American Ethnologist* 8(4): 686-708.
Ramos, Alcida Rita
   1980 *Hierarquia e Simbiose: Relações Intertribais no Brasil*. São Paulo: Editora Hucitec.
————, and Kenneth I. Taylor
   1979 *The Yanoâma in Brazil*. Cambridge, Mass., and Copenhagen: International Work Group for Indigenous Affairs (with ARC and Survival International-England), doc. 37.
Reeve, Mary-Elizabeth
   1984 "Maintaining Ritual and Social Order among the Canelos Quichua: The Role of Women." Ph.D. dissertation, University of Illinois, Urbana-Champaign. Ann Arbor, Mich.: University Microfilms.
Reichel-Dolmatoff, Gerardo
   1971 *Amazonian Cosmos: The Sexual and Religious Symbolism of the Tukano Indians*. Chicago: University of Chicago Press.
   1976a "Cosmology as Ecological Analysis: A View from the Rain Forest." *Man* (n.s.) 11(3): 307-18.
   1976b "Desana Curing Spells: An Analysis of Some Shamanistic Metaphors." *Journal of Latin American Lore* 2(2): 157-219.
   1981 "Brain and Mind in Desana Shamanism." *Journal of Latin American Lore* 7(1): 73-98.
Renard-Casevitz, France-Marie
   1981a "Las Fronteras de las Conquistas en el Siglo XVI en la Montaña Meridional del Perú." *Bulletin de l'Institut Français d'Études Andines* 10(3-4): 113-40.
   1981b Introduction. *Bulletin de l'Institut Français d'Études Andines* 10(3-4): 1-5.
Ricklefs, Robert E.
   1979 *Ecology*. New York: Chiron Press.
Robinson, Scott Studebaker
   1979 "Toward an Understanding of Kofán Shamanism." Ph.D. dissertation, Cornell University, Ithaca, N.Y. Latin American Studies Program Dissertation Series.
Roe, Peter G.
   1982 *The Cosmic Zygote: Cosmology in the Amazon Basin*. New Brunswick, N.J.: Rutgers University Press.
Roldós Aguilera, Jaime
   1981 "¡Viva la Patria!" Quito: Editorial El Conejo.
Roosevelt, Anna Curtenius
   1980 *Parmana: Prehistoric Maize and Manioc Subsistence along the Amazon and Orinoco*. New York: Academic Press.
Rosaldo, Renato I., Jr.
   1979 "The Rhetoric of Control: Ilongos Viewed as Natural Bandits and Wild Indians." In Barbara A. Babcock, ed., *The Reversible World: Sym-*

bolic Inversion in Art and Society. Ithaca, N.Y.: Cornell University Press, pp. 240-57.

Royce, Anya Peterson
1982   *Ethnic Identity: Strategies and Diversity.* Bloomington: Indiana University Press.

Ryle, Gilbert
1949   *The Concept of Mind.* New York: Barnes and Noble.

Sahlins, Marshall
1976   *Culture and Practical Reason.* Chicago: University of Chicago Press.
1981a *Historical Metaphors and Mythical Realities: Structure in the Early History of the Sandwich Islands Kingdom.* Ann Arbor: University of Michigan Press.
1981b "The Stranger King." *Journal of Polynesian History* 16(3): 107-32.

Saignes, Thierry
1981   "El Piedemonte Amazónico de los Andes Meridionales: Estado de la Cuestión y Problemas Relativas a su Ocupación en los Siglos XVI y XVII." *Bulletin de l'Institut Français d'Études Andines* 10(3-4): 141-76.

Salazar, Ernesto
1981   "The Federación Shuar and the Colonization Frontier." In Norman E. Whitten, Jr., ed., *Cultural Transformations and Ethnicity in Modern Ecuador.* Urbana: University of Illinois Press, pp. 589-613.

Salomon, Frank
1980   *Los Señores Étnicos de Quito en la Época de los Incas.* Colección Pendoneros, no. 10. Otavalo: Instituto Otavaleño de Antropología.
1981   "Killing the Yumbo: A Ritual Drama of Northern Quito." In Norman E. Whitten, Jr., ed., *Cultural Transformations and Ethnicity in Modern Ecuador.* Urbana: University of Illinois Press, pp. 162-208.
1983   "Shamanism and Politics in Late-Colonial Ecuador." *American Ethnologist* 10(3): 413-28.

Sapir, J. David, and J. Christopher Crocker, eds.
1977   *The Social Use of Metaphor: Essays in the Anthropology of Rhetoric.* Philadelphia: University of Pennsylvania Press.

Scazzocchio, Françoise
1981   "La Conquista des Motilones du Huallaga Central aux XVIIe et XVIIIe Siècles." *Bulletin de l'Institut Français d'Études Andines* 10(3-4): 99-111.

Schmidt, Steffan W., Laura Guasti, Carl H. Landé, and James C. Scott, eds.
1977   *Friends, Followers, and Factions: A Reader in Political Clientalism.* Berkeley: University of California Press.

Schmink, Marianne
1982   "Conflicts in Amazonia." *American Ethnologist* 9(2): 341-57.

Schreider, Helen, and Frank Schreider
1970   *Exploring the Amazon.* Washington, D.C.: National Geographic Society.

Schwerin, Karl H.
1966   *Oil and Steel: Processes of Karinya Culture Change in Response to In-*

dustrial Development. Latin American Studies, no. 4. Los Angeles, Cal.: UCLA Latin American Center.

Sharon, Douglass
1978   *Wizard of the Four Winds: A Shaman's Story.* New York: Free Press.

Simson, Alfred
1886   *Travels in the Wilds of Ecuador and the Exploration of the Putumayo River.* London: Sampson, Low, Marston, Searle, and Rivington.

Sioli, Harald
1968   "Zur Ökologie des Amazonas—Gebietes." In E. J. Fittkau et al., eds., *Biogeography and Ecology in South America,* vol. 1. The Hague: Dr. W. Junk N. Y.

Smith, M. G.
1965   *The Plural Society in the British West Indies.* Berkeley: University of California Press.
1984   "The Nature and Variety of Plural Units." In David Maybury-Lewis, ed., *The Prospects for Plural Societies.* Washington, D.C.: 1982 Proceedings of the American Ethnological Society, pp. 146-86.

Smith, Richard Chase
1982   *The Dialectics of Domination in Peru: Native Communities and the Vast Amazonian Emptiness.* Cambridge, Mass.: Cultural Survival Occasional Paper 8.

Smole, William J.
1976   *The Yanoama Indians: A Cultural Geography.* Austin: University of Texas Press.

Sorenson, Arthur
1967   "Multilingualism in the Northwest Amazon." *American Anthropologist* 69(6): 670-84.

Stahl, Peter
1984   "Tropical Forest Cosmology: The Cultural Context of Early Valdivia Occupation at Loma Alta." Ph.D. dissertation, University of Illinois, Urbana-Champaign. Ann Arbor, Mich.: University Microfilms.

Stavenhagen, Rodolfo
1975   *Social Classes in Agrarian Societies.* Garden City, N.Y.: Doubleday.

Sterling, Tom, and the Editors of Time-Life Books
1973   *The Amazon.* Amsterdam: Time-Life International.

Steward, Julian H.
1948   "Tribes of the Ecuadorian and Peruvian Montaña." In Steward, ed., *Handbook of South American Indians, vol. 3: The Tropical Forest Tribes.* Washington, D.C.: Bureau of American Ethnology Bulletin 117.

Stocks, Anthony Wayne
1981   *Los Nativos Invisibles: Notas sobre la Historia y Realidad Actual de los Cocamilla del Río Huallaga, Perú.* Lima: Centro Amazónico de Antropología y Aplicación Práctica (CAAAP).

Stoll, David
1983   *Fishers of Men or Founders of Empire? The Wycliffe Bible Translators in Latin America Today.* Cambridge, Mass.: Cultural Survival.

Stutzman, Ronald
1981 "*El Mestizaje*: An All-Inclusive Ideology of Exclusion." In Norman E. Whitten, Jr., ed., *Cultural Transformations and Ethnicity in Modern Ecuador*. Urbana: University of Illinois Press, pp. 45-94.

Sweet, David Graham
1974 "A Rich Realm of Nature Destroyed: The Middle Amazon Valley, 1640-1750." Ph.D. dissertation, University of Wisconsin, Madison. Ann Arbor, Mich.: University Microfilms.

Taussig, Michael T.
1978 *Destrucción y Resistencia Campesina: El Caso del Litoral Pacífico*. Bogotá: Punta de Lanza.
1980a "Folk Healing and the Structure of Conquest in Southwest Colombia." *Journal of Latin American Lore* 6(2): 217-78.
1980b *The Devil and Commodity Fetishism in South America*. Chapel Hill: University of North Carolina Press.
1982 "Culture of Terror—Space of Death: Roger Casement's Putumayo Report and the Explanation of Torture." Paper presented to the Center for Latin American Studies and the Department of Anthropology, University of Chicago.

Taylor, Anne-Christine
1981 "God-Wealth: The Achuar and the Missions." In Norman E. Whitten, Jr., ed., *Cultural Transformations and Ethnicity in Modern Ecuador*. Urbana: University of Illinois Press, pp. 647-76.

————, and Philippe Descola
1981 "El Conjunto Jívaro en las Comienzas de la Conquista Española del Alto Amazonas." *Bulletin de l'Institut Français d'Études Andines* 10(3-4): 7-54.

Therborn, Göran
1980 *The Ideology of Power and the Power of Ideology*. London: Verso.

Thomas, David John
1981 *Order without Government: The Society of the Pemon Indians of Venezuela*. Urbana: University of Illinois Press.

Thompson, Carol L., Mary M. Anderberg, and Joan B. Antell
1981 *The Current History Encyclopedia of Developing Nations*. New York: McGraw-Hill.

Trupp, Fritz
1981 *The Last Indians: South America's Cultural Heritage*. Wörgl (Austria): Perlinger.

Turner, Terrence
1977 "Transformation, Hierarchy and Transcendence: A Reformulation of Van Gennep's Model of the Structure of Rites de Passage." In Sally Falk Moore and Barbara G. Myerhoff, eds., *Secular Ritual*. Amsterdam: Van Gorcum, pp. 53-70.
n.d. "Fire of the Jaguar." Ms. loaned by author.

Turner, Victor
1974 *Dramas, Fields, and Metaphors: Symbolic Action in Human Society*. Ithaca, N.Y.: Cornell University Press.

1982   Introduction. In Turner, ed., *Celebration: Studies of Festivity and Ritual.* Washington, D.C.: Smithsonian, pp. 11-29.

van den Berghe, Pierre, and George P. Primov (with the assistance of Gladys Becerra Velazque and Narciso Cchuana Ccohuata)
1977   *Inequality in the Peruvian Andes: Class and Ethnicity in Cuzco.* Columbia: University of Missouri Press.

Varese, Stéfano
1972   *The Forest Indians in the Present Political Situation of Peru.* Copenhagen: International Work Group for Indigenous Affairs, doc. 8.

Vickers, William T.
1976   "Cultural Adaptation to Amazonian Habitats. The Siona-Secoya of Eastern Ecuador." Ph.D. dissertation, University of Florida, Gainesville. Ann Arbor, Mich.: University Microfilms.

Villa Boas, Orlando, and Claudio Villa-Boas
1970   *Xingú: The Indians, Their Myths.* Translated from the Portuguese by Kenneth S. Brecher. New York: Farrar, Straus and Giroux.

Wagley, Charles
1977   *Welcome of Tears: The Tapirapé of Central Brazil.* New York: Oxford University Press.

Wallace, Anthony F. C.
1961   *Culture and Personality.* New York: Random House.

Wallas, Ethel Emily
1973   *Aucas Downriver: Dayuma's Story Today.* New York: Harper & Row.

Wasson, R. Gordon
1968   *Soma: Divine Mushroom of Immortality.* New York: Harcourt Brace Jovanovich.

Watters, R. F.
1971   *Shifting Cultivation in Latin America.* Rome: Food and Agriculture Organization of the United Nations, Forestry Development Paper no. 17.

Weber, Max
1964 [1957]   *The Theory of Social and Economic Organization.* Edited with an introduction by Talcott Parsons. New York: Free Press.

Weiss, Gerald
1975   "Campa Cosmology: The World of a Forest Tribe in South America." *Anthropological Papers of the American Museum of Natural History* 52: 219-588.

White, Peter T.
1983   "Nature's Dwindling Treasures: Rain Forests." *National Geographic* 163(1): 3-46.

Whitten, Dorothea S.
1981   "Ancient Tradition in a Contemporary Context: Canelos Quichua Ceramics and Symbolism." In Norman E. Whitten, Jr., ed., *Cultural Transformations and Ethnicity in Modern Ecuador.* Urbana: University of Illinois Press, pp. 749-75.

————, and Norman E. Whitten, Jr.

1978   "Ceramics of the Canelos Quichua." *Natural History* 87(8): 90-99, 152.

Whitten, Norman E., Jr.

1965   *Class, Kinship and Power in an Ecuadorian Town: The Negroes of San Lorenzo.* Stanford, Cal.: Stanford University Press.

1974   *Black Frontiersmen: A South American Case.* New York: Wiley (Halsted).

1976   (with the assistance of Marcelo Naranjo, Marcelo Santi Simbaña, and Dorothea S. Whitten) *Sacha Runa: Ethnicity and Adaptation of Ecuadorian Jungle Quichua.* Urbana: University of Illinois Press.

1978   "Ecological Imagery and Cultural Adaptability: The Canelos Quichua of Eastern Ecuador." *American Anthropologist* 80(4): 836-59.

1979   (with the assistance of Julian Santi Vargas, María Aguinda Mamallacta, and William Belzner) *Soul Vine Shaman: I. Background Notes/ II. Notes on the Recording.* Urbana, Ill.: Sacha Runa Research Foundation Occasional Paper 5.

1981a   "Amazonia Today at the Base of the Andes: An Ethnic Interface in Ecological, Social, and Ideological Perspectives." In Norman E. Whitten, Jr., ed., *Cultural Transformations and Ethnicity in Modern Ecuador.* Urbana: University of Illinois Press, pp. 121-61.

————, ed.

1981b   *Cultural Transformations and Ethnicity in Modern Ecuador.* Urbana: University of Illinois Press.

1982   *Amazonía Ecuatoriana: La Otra Cara del Progreso.* Quito: Mundo Shuar.

————, and Emiko Ohnuki-Tierney

1982   "When Paradigms Collide" (introduction to *Symbolism and Cognition II*). *American Ethnologist* 9(4): 635-43.

————, and Dorothea S. Whitten

1984   "Marriage among the Canelos Quichua of East-Central Ecuador." In Kenneth M. Kensinger, ed., *Marriage Practices in Lowland South America.* Urbana: University of Illinois Press, pp. 194-220.

Wilbert Johannes

1970   *Folk Literature of the Warao Indians: Narrative Material and Motif Content.* Latin American Studies, no. 15. Los Angeles, Cal.: UCLA Latin American Center.

1981   "Warao Cosmology and Yekuana Roundhouse Symbolism." *Journal of Latin American Lore* 7(1): 37-72.

Wissler, Clark

1976   *The Relation of Nature to Man in Aboriginal America.* New York: Oxford University Press.

Wolf, Eric R.

1981   "The Mills of Inequality: A Marxian Approach." In Gerald D. Berreman, ed., *Social Inequality: Comparative and Developmental Approaches.* New York: Academic Press.

1982 *Europe and the People without History.* Berkeley: University of California Press.

Worsley, Peter

1984 "The Three Modes of Nationalism." In David Maybury-Lewis, ed., *The Prospects for Plural Societies.* Washington, D.C.: 1982 Proceedings of the American Ethnological Society, pp. 187-206.

Yost, James

1981a "Twenty Years of Contact: The Mechanisms of Change in Wao ('Auca') Culture." In Norman E. Whitten, Jr., ed., *Cultural Transformations and Ethnicity in Modern Ecuador.* Urbana: University of Illinois Press, pp. 677-704.

1981b "People of the Forest: The Waorani." In Misael Acosta-Solis et al., *Ecuador: In the Shadow of the Volcanos.* Quito: Ediciones Libri Mundi, pp. 97-115.

Young, Crawford

1976 *The Politics of Cultural Pluralism.* Madison: University of Wisconsin Press.

Index

Achuar people, 17, 28, 75, 76, 79, 83, 87, 178, 217, 225; and Canelos Quichua, 78–81, 90–91; cosmology of, 124; as dominant culture, 78, 79; duality of ethnic patterning among, 172; killing vendettas of, 95; kinship systems of, 90–91; marriage among, 16, 78, 90–91, 94; postmarital residence among, 78, 90; "pristine," 225; in protest movement, 229; spirits of, 84; territory of, 80; and Zaparoan, 78

Adams, Richard N., 54, 179, 180, 184

Address words, 239; of classes, 40; among elite, 39, 40; *mestizo* as, 40; in Nueva Esperanza, 93; in Puyo, 222; of Runa, 74, 192; stereotypes reflected in, 82, 83, 84, 86

Agriculture: Amazonian, 31, 32, 59; Andean, 59. *See also Chagra;* Crops

Aguaruna people, 28. *See also* Jivaroan

Ahuano, 145

Akawaio people, 28

Alcohol: at ceremonies and festivals, 191–92, 209, 210; in Nueva Esperanza, 97, 100. *See also Asua;* Chicha; *Trago; Vinillu*

Alfaro, Eloy, 221

Alligator. *See* Cayman

Alli Runa, 75, 172

Allpa supai, 130

Amarun. See Anaconda

Amasanga supai (forest spirit master), 12, 33, 123, 124, 128–34, 137, 167, 183, 198, 210, 223; as androgynous, 60; as antithesis of civilization, 128–29; breath of, 132; and control of nature, 130, 132; and drums, 191, 192; as female, 148; image of on pottery, 211, 212; as jaguar, 130–32, 188; as

Jurijuri, 62; mascot of, 132; in mythic time-space, 62; and Nunghui, 130, 134; as pasu tree spirit, 62; as sign image, 134; soul of, 130; and Sungui, 130, 134; thunder and lightning belong to, 132; transformation of, 60, 62, 129–30, 242; in visions, 141, 142; wood-working aided by, 134

Amazonia, 25–35, 100, 101; agriculture in, 31, 32, 59; blacks in, 83–84; ceramics in, 26, 107; cultural relations with Andes, 18, 19, 26, 78, 122; development in, 28, 34–35, 102–3; ecology of, 17, 18, 27; Ecuador as, 18, 24, 35, 37; European disease in, 26; floodplain and flooded forest in, 26; food processing in, 31–32; leaf mat of, 30, 32, 34; migration from, 27; mining in, 34; peoples of, 26, 28; periphery of, 28, 34; rainfall in, 25, 30–31; rain forest of (*see* Rain forest); rubber in, 27; soil of, 30–31

Amazon River, 25, 26–27, 28

Amhuesha people, 28

Anaconda, 25–26, 223; bench symbol of, 64; black, 4, 137; as design on pottery, 120, 201, 203; destroys world, 125, 188; devours, 68, 70–71, 188, 240; and kinship system, 69; in myth, 67; penis as, 66–68, 69, 70, 125, 240; power of, 68, 70–71; and rainbow, 124; and shaman, 68, 121, 125; as soul, 125; Sungui manifested as, 60, 124, 137, 188; in visions, 137; *yaji* (brew), 136

Analogic patterning. *See* Correspondence structuring

Andes, 57; agriculture in, 59; colonists from in Puyo, 172; culture of, 19, 26, 77, 78, 188; marriage concepts of, 90;

301

strength of, 167; vision of becomes event, 168

Challua (fish), 200, 201

Change: consistency and continuity in, 44–46, 49, 101, 142; and structure of antinomy, 241; threshold of, 170, 171, 180, 213; transformation and, 49. *See also* Antinomy; Consistency; Power

Chango, Alfonso, 139, 141

Chango, Juana Catalina, 63, 133

Chaos: in hamlet, 100, 101, 103; in Nueva Esperanza, 57; vs. order, 56, 103, 193; priests and, 193

Charapa: figurine, 65; motifs, 70, 202, 203, 212. *See also Bancu*

Chicha. *See Asua;* Manioc

Chingosimi River, bridge over, 18, 242, 250

Chiquitano people, 28

Chirapas, 16, 145, 149, 150, 193. *See also* Jivaroan

Cholo, choloficación, 39, 42–43, 84, 178

Christianity, 228. *See also* Catholicism; Civilization; Dominican Order

Christian Organization of Independent Indigenous Pastaza Peoples, 230

Civilization: Amasanga as antithesis, 128–29; arrives in Río Chico, 245–52; concepts of in Ecuador, 41–42, 84; of "Indians" by Church, 9, 174, 187–88

Clay, 109, 112, 205; Nunghui as master spirit of, 33, 123, 124, 125, 128. *See also* Ceramics

Cofán people, 28

Collective action (*minga*), 95–100

Colombia, 28

Colors, 11; of Sicuanga, 124. *See also Huiduj; Manduru*

Communication: ceremony as, 214; power of, 213–14. *See also* Duality of patterning

Community. *See* Hamlet

Comuna Canelos, 172, 231

Comuna San Jacinto del Pindo, 16, 17, 88, 95, 103, 122; capital in, 178; cash crops in, 173; created, 15, 173; development in, 178; fission in, 87, 172–73, 253–54; OPIP expelled from, 231; pressures on, 173

Comuna San Ramón, 172, 231

Confederation, 18, 38, 255

Confederation of Indigenous Peoples of Amazonian Ecuador, 255

Conflict, 92–95, 256

Consistency, 103, 179; cultural, 19, 52, 53; in frontier, 45–46, 181; in radical change, 44–46, 49, 101, 142

Contradiction: defined, 19. *See also* Antinomy; Opposition

Control: in the analysis of power, 179, 180, 181, 184, 185; of Blacks, 87; of boundary by center, 46, 47; in ceramics, 109, 112; ceremony (*dominario*), 187, 188–90, 192, 193, 237, 239; by Church, 172, 208; in dreams, 145; of education, 180, 208; lacking in ceremony, 188; by nation-state, 45–46, 50–51, 54, 163, 166, 168, 180; of nature, 130, 134; of power, 33; resource, 49, 53, 168, 171, 179, 180, 181, 185, 229, 231; separate from concept of power 47, 179; of Sungui, 33, 125; symbol, 179, 184, 188; of territory, 12

Coon, Carleton S., 46, 47, 50, 51, 172, 187

Copataza River, 17, 223, 225

Coral snake, 62, 125

Correspondence structuring, 48–53, 66, 108–34; by ceramicists, 194–213; culture as template of, 47, 163; and duality of patterning, 166–67; and reading of texts, 52. *See also* Duality of patterning; Symbol

Cosmology, 8, 57, 119; Achuar, 124; and anthropological analysis, 48–54, 57; *axis mundi,* 65–66; Canelos Quichua, 123, 124, 128; ceramics as, 119; ecology–social structure, 52; household replicates, 65–66; language and, 78–79; paradigm manipulation, 108–19

Cotopaxi Runa, 222

Cotts Tea Company, 15

Cousin marriage, 74, 89, 90

Crawford, Neelon, 146

Crops: cash, 18, 34, 173; male/female, 58–59; monocultural, 31, 34; polycultural, 31, 32; vegetative reproduction of, 31, 32. *See also* Agriculture; *Chagra*

Cubeo people, 28

Cuenca, 35, 39

Cultural ecology, 17, 18, 27, 47, 48, 49,

A Note on the Author

Norman E. Whitten, Jr., first undertook fieldwork in 1961 with black Ecuadorians of the northwestern rain forest of Esmeraldas. He continued ethnography with black Ecuadorians and black Colombians in various areas through 1968, when, with his wife, Sibby, he first visited various native peoples (Cofán, Siona-Secoya, Napo Quichua, Canelos Quichua, Shuar) of Amazonian Ecuador. He has undertaken field research with the Puyo Runa grouping of Canelos Quichua culture every year since 1970, each project dealing with specialized sectors of this culture area, and spreading into other culture areas in the Andes and Upper Amazonia. He is presently professor and head of the Department of Anthropology at the University of Illinois at Urbana-Champaign, where he has been a member of the faculty since 1970. He is also president and co-founder of the Sacha Runa Research Foundation, Urbana, which works to further indigenous felt needs through judicious application of research findings, and is editor of the *American Ethnologist* through 1984. His previous publications include *Class, Kinship, and Power in an Ecuadorian Town* (1965), *Afro-American Anthropology* (edited with John F. Szwed, 1970), *Black Frontiersman* (1974), *Sacha Runa* (1976), and *Cultural Transformations and Ethnicity in Modern Ecuador* (edited, 1981). His current research is focused on aesthetic resurgence in Amazonian and Andean Ecuador and on power transfers between coastal, Andean, and Amazonian peoples.